raised in the small Alberta city of Wetaskiwin, meaning "hills of peace" in the Blackfoot language. From the time he could walk, Al played "road hockey". At the age of seven tender years, he started playing organized hockey. Ten years later, Barney attended the New York Ranger hockey camp. The following year, he enrolled at the University of Denver. As a "walk-on" player, he earned a four year hockey scholarship and a Bachelor's degree in Business Administration. During that time, the DU Pioneers won two NCCAA hockey championships. Now, at age 70, Barney still plays this silly game ... and enjoys it more than ever."

After earning an MBA and Ph.D. in Business Administration, Al embarked on a career in management; teaching in several U.S. and Canadian universities, then into practice and ultimately as a consultant. He is the author of four management books and a web-site. *Old Pucksters and their Playmates* is his first "creative" book.

For the past 20 years, Al has taught, conducted a variety of management consulting assignments and international development projects in 19 countries ranging from Armenia to Zimbabwe. For his contributions to Canada and his community, he received the Queen's Golden Jubilee Award.

Al is married to Gretchen, an English Literature instructor. He is the proud father of Ann Marie, an I.T. Project Manager with Microsoft and John Alexander, a surgeon who recently worked for Doctors Without Borders in Somalia, Africa.

Old Pucksters and their Playmates

... playing HOCKEY just for FUN

written by al barnhill

july, 2008

AuthorHouse™
1663 Liberty Drive, Suite 200
Bloomington, IN 47403
www.authorhouse.com
Phone: 1-800-839-8640

First published by AuthorHouse 9/4/2008

ISBN: 978-1-4389-0866-3 (sc)

Library of Congress Control Number: 2008907483

Printed in the United States of America
Bloomington, Indiana

This book is printed on acid-free paper.

Dedications

... to the memory of my late father and his endless support

... to the coaches, officials and even the "refs" for making the game possible

... to all the players who have provided the characters and encouragement for this tale of tales

Thank you! Merci beaucoup!

Acknowledgments

Since this epistle has taken more than five years to complete my memory may fail me in recognizing some of the folks who have helped me along the way. But I do remember that my wife Gretchen has been an ongoing, even ardent, source of support. She is sort of the model for Heidi in the book.

Roy MacGregor, a literary genius of great creativity and prodigious output, as well as a young old-timer puckster, merits recognition for his masterful foreword.

Lastly, that man of many accomplishments, both on and off of the ice, Ken Dryden, is acknowledged for urging me to use as much of Home Game as I wanted.

Here's what golfing great, Arnold Palmer says about one of the book's stories entitled "caddying for Arnie".

> *"I certainly enjoyed reading the 'caddy' story ... bringing fond memories to mind of the Mayfair Golf Club in Edmonton. Thank you for all your nice comments about me. Good luck with your book."*

What's this Old Guy Barney Writing About?

Foreword or forward? ... *one of the players who is supposed to score goals and back check!*

by **Roy MacGregor***

Welcome to Joxville. Your town. My town. Al Barnhill's town. Canada's town. And welcome, as well, to the wildest, funniest dressing room in hockey.

Al Barnhill knows his hockey --- a small town boy from the Prairies who was once wooed by three junior hockey teams ... only to have his father refuse to sign the infamous 'C' card ... for fear that his boy might become a "hockey bum". Instead, Al went to the University of Denver and earned a full hockey scholarship, eventually ended up with a Ph.D. in business administration and today has a c.v. that tells the story of a remarkable career that has taken him around the world.

But Al still ended up a "hockey bum". He just waited until he could start playing old-timers hockey in "Joxville". ***Old Pucksters and their Playmates*** *is a love letter to Canada's national game. It is filled with poetry, with memory, with humour, with sadness and with acute observations of a man who has spent a lifetime waiting for the Zambonis to get off the ice so he and his pals could get on.*

You can feel the ice here. You can cheer for the good guys and boo the bad. You can feel yourself growing older and younger at the same time. You can laugh, and often, there are times when you swear you can even smell the equipment as the old bags of gear are zipped open for yet another game --- to be followed, naturally, by a second game, sometimes going into overtime, at Barney's Sports Bar.

There is much to like here --- the stripper and Max's 65th birthday is better than a ticket to the Stanley Cup final – and much to be reminded here of the very good values in a game that, too often focuses on violence, greed and boorish behaviour.

The lads of Joxville play for free. Admission is free. And for those who can't make it some week night at 11, there is gratefully, this book.

** Roy MacGregor, author of Home Team: Fathers, Sons and Hockey, Home Game with Ken Dryden, three dozen other books, including the internationally successful Screech Owl mystery series for young readers and winner of several major literary awards . Mr. MacGregor was named Officer in the Order of Canada in 2005.*

I. from little boys to old geezers

In the beginning ... there was hockey

Believe it or not, for many of the old gaffers who play this silly game, the beginning of life in the sense of really living with some meaning and vitality began when they started to play hockey, of one form or other. To many that may sound incredulous, even ridiculous .... but not to old timer hockey players. Vividly, they still remember playing shinny out on the road, in an alley, on a slough, creek or a neighborhood rink. Candidly they tell about playing under the street lights ... for hours ... on cold sunny days and very cold dark nights .... brrrrr!!! They recall their Moms, sometimes their Dads, whistling or calling for them to come in from the game ... and the reluctance, even sadness, of slowly walking home ... arms, head and body sagging with dismay and growing fatigue ..... dragging their stick along behind them .... listening to the shouts, cheers, groans and other noises of the game fading in the background. They remember the mixed greetings they received from their parents, usually questions about whether they had done their chores or homework, needed a bath and maybe even a cheery query like "Did you have a good time with your friends?" As the lads peeled off their dirty, frozen clothes, "at the back door because I just cleaned the house, darn it", Mom might have a steaming cup of cocoa or hot chocolate, maybe even with a marshmallow on top, waiting for the now chilled, teeth-chattering, shivering little boy standing in the kitchen with just his long johns on.

Playing road hockey was a point of departure for the long twisting and turning, up the hills and down in the valleys journey of life. The games introduced the players to some important lessons of life, like the player and his team didn't always win. Losing was no fun but it happened despite the players' best efforts. Losing, like winning, was part of life and kids learned to live with both results ... at least until the next game was played.

Playing shinny was a youthful exercise in democracy. The leaders, usually the best players, picked the teams. Every kid got to play, more or less, depending on their efforts and skills. Playing shinny was an early form of Darwin's *survival of the fittest* or some other law of natural life. Early on, they learned that teamwork usually beat the "hot shot" individualist. They learned that the game had its joys and its pains, its benefits and its costs. Any old timer could add other lessons of life learned playing street hockey, if they stopped to think about them. It was a vital part of their young lives.

For the "farm kids", hockey began on a frozen piece of dirt in the yard or on the driveway, maybe smoothed over by a tractor with a blade or home made dragging device that took the bumps off and filled in the ruts and low spots. Maybe they were lucky enough to have a slough, pond or creek on or near their family's property where they could skate and play shinny soon after the first few days of freezing. Few accounts capture childhood hockey in the "country" (meaning outside of town, village, hamlet or other community) as well as author and painter Peter Shostak. In a short, beautifully illustrated book, he depicts in words and pictures, the fullness and infinite richness of this silly game of chasing a puck (or facsimile thereof) around a sheet of ice or some other surface during the coldest time of the year. Dwell on his words.

> "Hockey is a game born in a land of young people desperately needing something to do; in a land where ponds, sloughs, streams, rivers and lakes --- millions of them are frozen for five months of the year. Playing hockey made winter almost bearable. Peter Shostak, *Hockey .... under winter skies*,

> Victoria, British Columbia: Yalenka Enterprises, Inc., 2000, p. 8.

Mind you, Mr. Shostak was a boy back before television and family vehicles increased the mobility of the mind and body.... and artificial ice rinks increased the opportunities to play "the game". Let's continue for a few more lines of his wonderful prose about playing hockey as a young boy.

> "We all played hockey. It did not matter if you were big or small, fat or skinny, young or old, had new skates, old skates or no skates. Everyone played hockey
>
> We did not play inside a building where the ice was smooth and always clear of snow. Our ice patch had twigs and grass, ripples and bumps, cracks and gouges. We played on a patch of ice on a nearby pond, or on a flooded area in the school or farm yard**.** *Ibid.*

And many of us played on frozen dirt roads and icy back alleys. And really lucky little guys and gals played with their friends and others on small rinks made by dads who "flooded" the garden with a hose during very cold, dark nights. Thanks, Dad.

Finding some ice or other smooth surface for the game

Sometimes the zealous kids rushed the season. In their youthful enthusiasm they would find out where there was some ice, grab their stick, skates and other gear if they had any, jump on their bikes and ride like crazy to the place where their buddies were playing. They would ignore the impediments to playing --- the twigs, rocks and cracks or the sounds of cracking ice --- so distinctive and sometimes scary, in the clear, cold weather. Once in a while some adventurous lad would sink or break through the ice and then have to scramble like a rodent on his hands and knees to safety ... and a quick run or bike ride home to keep from freezing some of his vital parts. Other times, when the ice was crackling, players would stumble, crawl or skate like hell (very quickly) to more solid ice, even if it meant sacrificing the "puck" ... unless it was the only one they had. Then some brave and incredibly dumb kid would look for it or go after it, even if it had disappeared into the frigid water. They would stand or kneel close to the hole in the ice, look down, mutter some silly words and somehow expect the "puck god" to spit up the little black disk from its watery resting place. Nobody ever drowned or even suffered from that hypothermia that we had never even heard about. But some sure suffered pretty serious frost bite and frozen fingers and toes. But that was "no big deal" for the young lads. Years, even decades, later they would say that they still had their fingers and toes ... even if the blood circulation was not so good.

Meanwhile, back in town, we played our shinny games anywhere we could find a smooth surface and, at night, under the (street) lights, in front of Ronny's, Larry's or Hank's house and, occasionally, in Alf's back alley, especially after he got lights strung across laneway. About the time that Alf's gruff old father snarled "no more flooding the damned alley ... you're wasting water", Hank's dad would decide to make a rink in the family's rather large garden. Hank readily agreed. He thought that was a much better use of the garden than seeding, weeding and hoeing the potatoes, corn, beets, carrots, peas and other vegetables that had to be taken care from some time in May until some time in October. That was a lot of weeks, like an eternity, for the youngster who had to tend the garden (and do other jobs around the house and yard) --- for 10 cents a week. But every now and then, Hank would be reminded rather emphatically, by his mother, that he liked to eat increasingly copious amounts of food. That reminder usually stopped his grumbling, until the next time he had to work in the garden while his buddies were playing ball, football or some other game in the school grounds or the street.

Meanwhile, back to the rink in the garden, (wonder if the old Edmonton Gardens or the Maple Leaf Gardens originated from such a garden rink?) Hank's dad would start levelling the garden after the last vegetables were harvested and the corn stocks were burnt. Hank did not mind helping his dad with that work. Even some of Hank's buddies came around to rake the ground, breaking up clods of dirt and throwing the odd small potato at one another. Since it was a relatively small rink and only about six or eight kids could play, they wanted to be sure they were invited or otherwise allowed to play on "Hank's rink". That small rink bestowed a lot of status on Hank as well as enhanced his ability to play the game, although not to the same extent as Ken Dryden, Wayne Gretzky and other "big leaguers".

By the time really cold weather, like 20, 30 or 40 degrees below 0 on the Fahrenheit scale, set in, the ground was ready for a "flood". No, the "flood" was not some rush of water that resulted from a sudden warming of the weather and melting snow or heavy rain storms. The "flood" was what Hank's dad did to start building up the ice from the black loam to a silvery slick sheet. And that silvery slick sheet did not happen over night. In fact, during many cold, dark nights Hank's dad would be out flooding the ground, cum ice, in the garden. Sometimes, it would be too cold or too late for Hank to help his dad, even if that help was little more than "moral support". The young lad would look out the kitchen window at his dad huddled against the bitterly cold winds, slowly moving the nozzle of the garden hose back and forth in a rhythmic, almost hypnotic motion. Slowly, ever so slowly to the point of virtual imperceptibility, the ice was made thicker and thicker until one morning, usually in late October or early November, Hank's dad would announce that the ice was ready for use, meaning that the young boys could play hockey on it. That day was the official opening of the hockey season on "Hank's rink".

For days prior to the "official opening", maybe even a week or more, Hank and his buddies would play shinny in their boots on the ice without his dad's approval. But his dad knew, especially when one of the boys would break through the ice and leave a boot hole or three that had to be filled in with water, probably during a frigid evening (sure couldn't make ice in non-frigid weather). Hank's dad really did not appreciate such added time out in the freezing nights, making ice for the boys. But Hank's dad was wise, believing that having the boys playing shinny out back in the garden was safer than on the road, slough or creek. He knew that the boys would play shinny some place, come what may. So he figured that they may as well be playing on the garden rink where it was safe and close to home.

Playing "pick-up" games (but not the kind of pick-up games that would be played later in life)

Back in those days and nights, kids usually played road hockey frequently (like several times a day and night) and spontaneously. Some boy carrying a hockey stick or stick-handling a puck, ball, horse turd or other object down the street would soon be joined by other guys and the odd gal --- incredibly like phantoms appearing out of the bushes or shadows of day, the dark of night, or some houses, other buildings or from wherever. The game would start almost instantaneously ... in the street, alleyway, on a rink, wherever. Games were so simple. Teams would be chosen immediately with two players selecting from among those gathered until all were chosen. Goal "posts" would be set out very quickly with pairs of boots, pieces of fire wood or coal, lumps of dirt, stones or bricks, pieces of frozen snow, wood or anything else that would do. In five minutes or less, the game began in all its natural joy -- a starting face-off, running after the "puck", passing, shooting, missing the goal, constant yelling, some cheering when goals were scored, incidental complaining, the odd stoppage in play usually while the players searched for the "puck" in the snow and, quite frequently, scoring. Joy knew no bounds when you scored ... even when playing road hockey.

There were no blue or red lines or off-sides and few, if any, penalties. The game was played on a honor system, a code of conduct that included not intentionally tripping, hitting others with sticks, brooms, shovels or whatever device was being played with. Occasionally, a stick, foot or elbow would inadvertently stray and hit an opposing player, sometimes inflicting pain on him. The game *might* stop momentarily while the injured player recovered sufficiently to play again. The other players would gather around and maybe commiserate briefly with the wounded warrior. Impatience would readily overcome the sympathy for the injured player and the game would continue, with or without the casualty. There were no referees, no regulations and few face-offs. Play was virtually non-stop. After goals were scored, the scoring team retreated to "center ice" and the scored-upon team took possession of the puck and attacked --- so simple, so enjoyable, so beautiful.

Back in the '40s and '50s of the 20th century, playing road hockey became so popular in some towns that the kids formed "leagues", at least temporarily. In Peaceville, Hank's hometown, population 3,000 more or less, four teams of six or seven players played every Saturday morning, starting about ten o'clock and ending around noon, sometimes thereafter which often lead to unpleasant encounters with parents when the players returned home ... for lunch and jobs to do.

The teams were territorial with vague boundaries to determine who was eligible to play for which team(s). In Peaceville, the four teams were simply central, north and south and west. There was no team from the east side of town. That's where most of the bullies lived and the other boys were too afraid to play against them, even if the bullyboys did have a team. (Maybe if they had had a team, several of them would not have gone to jail for beating up a couple of brothers in grade nine. Sports, even road hockey, use up lots of youthful exuberance and energy.)

Putting that issue aside, starting sometime in November or December and ending in March or April, depending on ice, snow pack or other conditions of the dirt roads, the teams would play each other on a rotating basis. No refs, other officials, computer technology, bureaucracy or other impediments to play were needed. The teams kept score, counted wins (forgot the losses) and kept the team standings. There were no awards or trophies; only some bragging rights, usually for short periods of time, like a week or two. This was kids' road hockey at its purest and best.

From those spontaneous "pick up" shinny games in the streets, alleys or the odd backyard rink, the young boys went on to play more organized hockey. For many of them, organized hockey meant being selected for a sponsored team by some association, group of adults or maybe some "coaches". The boys did not care who or how teams were formed. To them, it was a "right of passage" from being a road hockey or shinny player to being a *real* hockey player. The lads keenly wanted to be on a sponsored team, preferably with a good buddy or the best player(s). Basically, even desperately, the young boys wanted a team hockey sweater, socks and all that those prestigious items symbolized, like pride in being one of the relatively few boys in town that was on a team and having the opportunity to play a game they truly loved and would sacrifice almost anything for.

At the start of each season, players were phoned and told to attend a practice. That practice turned out to be the time when the team coaches would watch the players and prepare rosters for the coming season. The coaches put together teams made up of forward lines, pairs of defencemen and hopefully, a half-decent or better goalie. The young boys were given sweaters and socks, introduced to a coach or two and then told what their schedule was going to be for the season .... "subject to change" ... because the ice might melt and several days, if not weeks, would be needed to re-make the ice.

Back in the '40s and '50s of the past century, coaches typically were well-intended men who took the time, often spent their own money and made extraordinary efforts to help young boys play "the game". Most had played some hockey in their younger years. Few, if any, of them had any coaching education or training. They knew little about developing hockey skills or mental preparation. But they did their best for the young boys. They held "practices"; usually starting with a few skating drills for warm up and then let the boys scrimmage for the remainder of the practice time. They arranged for games and transportation, sometimes over night accommodations, and lined up game officials. They made a huge, and relatively unappreciated, effort for the boys and their parents. Bless you, coaches.

Hank's first (real) game of organized hockey

A defining time in the young lives of many old timers comes when they play their first formal, structured game of hockey, complete with a schedule of games, starting times, at designated rinks, coaches, referees, penalties, line changes and a time clock. A youngster's first game of "organized" hockey is sort of similar to a debutante's "coming out", a debut! The young players wear their team's sweater and a pair of matching socks. That's a memorable occasion ... like a debutante's gown, gloves, garters, etc.

After 60 odd years, Hank could still remember his first hockey team sweater: the Inglis Motors Black Hawks, virtual copies of the then-NHL team from Chicago. At that young age, maybe 6, 8 or 10 years of age, the "uniform" was a source of great joy and pride ... a status symbol. That pair of well-used heavy woolen socks, some with holes or darning in them, and a heavy woolen jersey that was often too large or too small, were more important than anything else in the whole wide world.

As long as they had a team uniform, they did not care that what little equipment they had was hand-me-down or well used. So what if the skates had soft toes and boots, the shin pads had broken sticks in them, the shoulder pads were soft, the pants were too large or the gloves had padding missing and splits in the fingers. It was better than nothing and they were playing their game. Who cared about the gear? Those kids sure did not!!!

Hank, one of the Joxville Old Boys who will be introduced somewhere along the way, vividly remembers playing his first game of league hockey. Henry, as he was known back then, was seven years old and in Grade 2. One cold, but sunny, afternoon in the winter of '45, in the 20th century, the whole class went school skating at the "rink", about two blocks away from their Queen Alexandra School. Miss MacMiserable (not her real name and may she rest in peace), a cranky, mean old spinster disciplinarian was his teacher --- the first one to strap him, allegedly for misbehaving. Before the children went to the rink and after "school skating" was finished, Miss MacMisery, the terrible, emphatically told the students several times that they were to go "straight home" (to which the "smart alecs" of the class would mumble sarcastically among themselves: "what about turning the corners?"). Under absolutely no circumstances were they to linger or stay around the arena, if for no other reason than those "ne'er do well" Hanson brothers were managing the arena and, according to rampant rumors, cooking and eating the arena cats that were supposed to catch the mice around the big old building.

Like many other precocious children who misbehaved occasionally but caused no injury to person or property, one Tuesday afternoon after "school skating" Henry disobeyed the teacher and the school system. He hid under the old wooden arena stands until the teacher and all of the other Grade 2 students were gone. Then very slowly, cautiously he came out and stood alongside the fence around the ice surface on the far side of the penalty box so he would not be seen. In fact, he was just tall enough to see over the top of the "boards", as his Dad and other big people referred to the fence around the rink. Henry was really excited and quite nervous about disobeying the teacher and watching the Bantam hockey game between the Inglis Motors Black Hawks and Brody's Bruins. That was the first game that he had watched without his parents being with him.

That January afternoon was dreadfully cold, even for a young boy who was acclimatized to very cold weather, was warmly dressed and very excited to watch his first bantam hockey game. (At that time, bantam hockey was the youngest level of minor hockey in the small town of Peaceville.) Reluctantly and ever so timidly young Henry went into the nearest "dressing room" to get warm by the coal and wood fuelled, pot-bellied stove. He was a scrawny little lad and the deep cold went through him to his bones. When he entered the room, not many players were there. Being a small town, a few of the boys recognized him and started talking among themselves.

Some of the bantam hockey players were five to seven years older than Henry. Players like Mel, Maurice and Roger were his local heroes. He thought they must be almost as good and exciting as the junior team players or the "big leaguers". The mere presence of those "stars" intimidated Henry. He wanted to run out of the room. But he was too cold and did not want to be a "chicken". So he stood beside the stove trying to get warm. After a few minutes, one of the older, bigger boys called to him. Henry was ready to flee when the big boy with a "C" on his hockey shirt asked him if he would like to play in the game. The young boy was close to being dumbfounded but found enough composure to mumble "yes" without screaming in joyous jubilation.

Then reality set in. All he had was a pair of skates --- no other equipment with him. His hockey stick was at home, a distance of several blocks. And, no matter how hard he pleaded, his mother would not let him come back to the arena and play with those big boys. And he owned no other equipment; no gloves, no shin pads, none of the essential gear. As he stood pondering and muttering aloud about his sorry set of circumstances, one boy offered him a beat up old hockey stick to play with. It was quite long for the seven year old boy but he didn't care. And he had some woolen mittens that his mother had knit for him. They would keep his hands warm. Henry never even thought about his hands or other parts of his body getting hurt. He didn't care that the team did not have a sweater or socks for him. He would play in his school clothes. He never gave a thought to his clothes getting wet, soiled or torn. He did not think about his mother worrying about him not coming home from school. Henry was going to play his first league hockey game and that was all he could think about.

So young Henry sat down on the bench and put on his second-hand, well-used skates. He was not a good skater. Despite his best efforts, he skated on his ankles, in part because the skates were too large and the skate boots were very soft and worn from years of use. But the Black Hawks really, even desperately, needed some players or, at least live bodies, to play against the Bruins. By the time Henry tied up his skates, picked up the long stick, fell down, staggered across the floor, opened the heavy door of the dressing room and figured out where he was supposed to go, the other players were on the ice playing the game. He stumbled along the walkway behind the stands and clambered into the players' box and sat quietly watching the game. He was overjoyed just sitting there with the Black Hawks. He was so excited that he felt the call of nature. He had to take a pee ... badly.

Because they were playing during a work day afternoon, the Black Hawks had no coach. A few minutes later, the big boy with the "C" on his shirt yelled at Henry to get on the ice. So the little seven year old boy stumbled onto the ice and ran on the ankles of his skates after the puck ... like a hound after a rabbit. And he came off when someone yelled at him to do so. Between going on and coming off, the young lad never even touched the puck until late in the game.

As luck or the "hockey god" would have it, Henry was going one way while the play was going the other. He was heading toward the other team's goal while all of the other players were going toward or playing around his team's goal. From behind him, the puck slid slowly past him, going the same way he was. He started running on his ankles as fast as he could, pushing the puck ahead of him with the long hockey stick. For what seemed like an eternity, Henry ran and pushed the puck until he was close, maybe two or three feet from the goalie, when he gave the puck one final push. With that big push he fell forward on the ice and slid toward the goal alongside of the puck. To this day, Hank does not know whether or not he "submarined" the goalie before the puck went into the net. And he did not care. *The referee called it a goal*. He played the rest of the season for the Black Hawks and scored at least one or two more goals. Thus beginneth the many years of playing hockey for Hank, one of the good Old Boys of Joxville.

Getting re-started (like "deja vu, all over again" as Yogi Berra says)

Over the years, many of the boys cum men dropped out of hockey. It was too expensive, took too much time, was overly competitive and, by the time they were teenagers, new priorities evolved, like girl friends, jobs, other sports or interests and maybe even becoming serious students. Then they went off to a job or "higher education". A career, family and numerous other obligations followed. Playing hockey was no longer a priority of life or living for most men. Some dads got a lot of vicarious satisfaction and enjoyment from being involved with their boys (and increasingly, their girls) playing hockey. Somewhere in the life cycle of some aging men, playing hockey became a recreational and social priority. They became old timer hockey players.

For others who had never played the greatest game on earth, hockey began as old timers ... at 35, 40 or more years of age ... about the age that Wayne Gretzky and Mark Messier retired from playing in the NHL. Gordie Howe quit when he was 50 something. Can you imagine playing "old timers'" hockey against the Great One, the Mean One or Mr. Hockey?

Getting re-oriented (or overcoming inertia, obesity and doubt)

Playing fun hockey, from kids to old guys' games, is based on amorphous feelings. Hockey playing geezers have a vague yet strongly felt, common set of values and attitudes. In the main (whatever that means), men in their

50s, 60s, 70s, even 80s, play the game because they say it is FUN. They enjoy playing (or, at least, what comes before and after the actual activity on the ice). They enjoy their fellow players, the *joie de vivre* of the game and, best of all, the natural camaraderie of team sports. Without the incalculable sociability, playing old boys' hockey would be just another form of exercise with its inherent stresses, strains, sprains, muscle pulls, bumps, bruises, breaks, dislocations, concussions, cuts, other aches and pains and, for some, that most dreaded attack on their heart ... and wounded egos.

Each season poses a new set of challenges for old timer hockey players. As the years roll by, their aging bodies and metabolisms change. They slow down along with their diminishing energy level. Reflexes are not as sharp. Neither is the mental capacity. Conditioning declines in the underutilized old muscles, ligaments, tendons and all of those stretchy sinews that keep the various body parts together. More aches and pains creep into them and their old bones. The body does not take the shocks of the game or recover as quickly from injuries, even minor ones.

As each season approaches, the self-doubt and ambivalence creep back into the minds of the old guys. "Should I play another season? I'm 58, 65 or 72 years old and there are some new guys out there who are young enough to be my son ... that's scary. Am I taking up a spot on the team that some younger guy would love to have. There's a waiting list of guys who want to play. Can I keep up with the other old timers or am I going to make a fool of myself .... more so than usual? Well, Charley and Mikey ..... and Boom Boom tell me to keep playing ... that I am playing well .... but they are such nice guys ..... they wouldn't have the heart to tell me to bugger off .... or that I wasn't playing worth a "rat's ass", whatever that means. Such ruminations might start at any time during the year but become especially "top of the head" in the weeks leading up to the start of a new season.

A self-doubter's new season poem

Few, if any, expressions convey the annual introduction to old timers' hockey as poignantly as the following poem.

For a lot more years
Than I care to recall,
I've lugged out the hockey bag
Same time every Fall.

More grey in the hair
The old bod' slightly rocky
I think: "Maybe it's time
To quit playing hockey."

But deep down inside
Is that kid from the past
Who had keenness and reflexes
And skated real fast.

Well, the reflexes are slower
The speed's almost reverse
But the keenness is still there
It's the old hockey curse.

So I say, "What the heck
If I don't play this year
I'll sure miss the guys
The game and the beer."

So it's off to the rink,
And I put on my gear
The dressing room chatter's
A treat to my ear.

I pick up my stick
There's a gleam in my eyes
The ol' tummy still churns
With a few butterflies.

Then I'm out on the ice
And into the fray
With each stride I take
The years melt away.

For playing this game
Is still one of my joys
And as someone once said
"Boys will always be boys."[3]

Setting the scene ... for the fun and games

In real down-to-earth, physical terms, Joxville is a jocular metaphor for the typical non-descript small-sized prairie city. It provides the environment, the social, economic and political context for the old guys and others who play hockey and the *common passion* that they have for it. In their classic book, *Home Game,* Hockey Hall of Fame goalie Ken Dryden and renowned sports journalist Roy MacGregor perceptively reveal the very essence, *the common passion,* of hockey and its effects on Canadians.

> Somewhere in our souls is a spiritual Canada. Most probably, its bedrock is of snow and ice, winter and the land. And if we were to penetrate a little deeper, chances are we would find a game. [4]

The *common passion* captures the emotional subtleties of playing hockey; the spirit, the soul, the joys, the sadnesses, the aches, pains, exhilaration and so much more, even for old guys. It expresses the feelings about the game, where it is played and what the "rink" means to people in all walks of life. Hockey rinks or arenas are social institutions, "the backbone of the community."

> In Saskatoon, in Toronto and Antigonish, hockey helps to make a community feel like a community. ... in Radisson (Saskatchewan), the hockey-community connection is literal and absolute. If a new arena doesn't get built, the community may die. 'That's why our recreational facility is so crucial to our town's survival ... . Because there are teachers and policemen who will apply for jobs in small towns if there are adequate recreational facilities. Then we get quality applicants. But if you don't have a focal point in the community – a recreation centre – then we don't have quality applicants and everything starts to deteriorate after that.' 5.

This *common passion* is evident in how much hockey has meant for so many Canadians, especially those scattered across the vast expanses of this large country - with its "bully for winter." In Canada and other northern climes, there is no escaping the realities of the weather. Feel the effects of a prairie blizzard ...

> ... cars and half-tons are crawling so slowly along the highway that ... it is possible to hear the knock-knock that comes from tires that have been squared frozen on one edge as they sat through a day in which the radio warns that "exposed flesh will freeze in less than one minute." Thirteen deaths across the prairies have already been attributed to the storm's cold and snow. A young farmer's truck has quit within

> sight of a farmhouse and yet he has frozen to death before he could walk the short distance. The radio stations have turned over their regular programming to endless lists of cancellations. *No bingo this evening at the Elks club ... no Brownies at All Saints ... Parent-teachers meeting put off 'til next Monday ... curling cancelled until the weekend.* And the radio stations have filled in the spaces with incoming calls from listeners who are trapped in farmhouses and homes from Meadow Lake to Maymont, prairie people who talk about the food and fuel they have on hand as proof that the elements will never beat them, no matter what. *No 4-H tonight ... no darts tournament ... cribbage cancelled ... choir practice off ...*
>
> But out here on the Yellowhead Highway on the northern outskirts of Saskatoon, the road is plugged with idling, blinking cars spewing exhaust as thick as toothpaste. In this unlikely place on this forbidding night, the vehicles' occupants are almost in reach of their evening's destination, Saskatchewan Place. They park in the paved field that surrounds the arena, then hurry through wind and blowing snow and air so cold nostrils lock solid on a single breath. They are going to a hockey game.
>
> ... they will cheer again – proudly – during the third period when the game's attendance is announced: 5,594. 6.

As Ken and Roy plumb the breadths and depths of Canadians' soul and spirituality, they find the game present in its many human dimensions – personal, social, cultural, economic and political. Just like many of us, they found that the game was being re-played and talked about in arenas, on coffee row, in offices, on the streets and most certainly in our homes across the vast expanse that lies mainly above the 49th parallel. To them, hockey brings out the Canadian character, especially the passion and focus on the game. This game of glorified shinny has contributed greatly to a sense of community for people of all ages, races and both genders in towns and cities, east and west, north and south ... from sea to sea to sea. It is an integral part of the Canadian culture, arguably a culture unto itself.

* *

Intermission --- time out for a quiz

As hockey histories and game programs reveal, a disproportionate number of successful hockey players were born, raised or had hometowns that most fans have never heard of and could not find on a map. They were from small towns scattered around the Great White North.

As a brief diversion, like the intermissions between periods in a hockey game, following is a short test of hockey knowledge and memory, often referred to as trivia. The ten great old players listed below came "off the top of the old head". The "greatest", #99, "Magnificent Mario" and many others are too young for this old timers' list.

Dear reader, match the following players (by the numbers) with the place (by the letters) in which they were born. The answers follow, in **bold** type.

Players	Places of birth
1. Apps, Charles Joseph Sylvanus (Syl)	A. Tara, Ontario
2. Broda, Walter ("Turk")	B. Montreal, Quebec
3. Conacher, Lionel (Big Train)	C. Parry Sound, Ontario
4. Howe, Gordon (Gordie)	D. Mitchell, Ontario
5. Hull, Robert Marvin (Bobby)	E. Pointe Anne, Ontario
6. Kennedy, Theodore (Ted, "Teeder")	F. Humberstone, Ontario
7. Morenz, Howarth William (Howie)	G. Floral, Saskatchewan
8. Orr, Robert Gordon (Bobby)	H. Toronto, Ontario
9. Richard, Maurice (Rocket)	I. Brandon, Manitoba
10. Taylor, Frederick Wellington (Cyclone)	K. Paris, Ontario

To save confusion and make it easy to find the answer, follow this simple process. The places of birth are in the reverse order to the list of players' names. For example, Syl Apps was born in Paris, Ontario, Turk Broda in Brandon, Manitoba, etc, etc, etc, only two

of which are large cities, i.e., Toronto and Montreal. Small town boys did and do make good in the National Hockey League.

*

Let the fun times begin!!!

What follows is an eclectic, hopefully coherent series of stories about a few seasons merged or blended into one. With age, memories do have some gaps and get kind of cloudy or fuzzy, maybe from too many blows to the head ... you know, like "prize fighters". Who keeps count of the seasons after you're an old boy? Central to the escapades are some of the old guys who play the game in an association with six teams, an "elected" board of directors and executive, some rules and regulations, a constitution, team selection based on "talent", equity and friendships and a high tech computer-generated schedule that's available on the internet. The tales start sometime in the autumn of the year. That seems appropriate for a bunch of oldsters who are in the autumn of their lives - the supposedly "golden years".

The season could have started in July when some of the Old Boys play in the Charles Schulz (of Peanuts cartoon fame) Snoopy Tournament in Santa Rosa, California. It could have started when the association has its August bar-b-q.

But the shinny season "officially" starts sometime in September when the eager old guys get an email, phone call or some convoluted message on their recorder from their team rep ... somewhat like the following:

"Hank, this is James calling ... just to let you know that you are on team 7.... uh, the referees' team. You play your first game next Tuesday night ... in the Iceplex .... uh, at 8:45 .... at night .... that's so you don't get confused ... uh, what the hell, you're probably not even up at 8:45 in the morning ... you old fart .... where are you? Why don't you ever stay home so I don't have to talk to your damned recording machine?"

Such was the first message (and a practical joke to boot, whatever "to boot" means) that Hank received for the start of another season.

When Hank heard the phone message, he was kind of curious and not very happy and, upon reflection, somewhat dubious about being on team 7 ... in a six team league. "We've never had seven teams", mused Hank half aloud. Since James, the team rep was a serious guy, Hank was inclined to consider the message in the same vein. Hank had been out of town for several weeks and did not know what was going on with the Old Boys. Maybe he had been relegated to a team of leftovers or rejects. "Damn it, I can still play pretty good old timers' hockey", muttered Hank audibly, to himself in a somewhat annoyed tone of voice. "The league only had six teams last year ... must be expanding again ... lots of guys want to play. What's with this team seven jazz," he wondered aloud. "Better phone back and find out what's going on." Hank punched the keys of James' telephone number ... ring ... ring ... ring... "Answer the damned phone, Jimmy," muttered Hank impatiently to himself ... ring ... ring... ring... finally:

"Hello!"

"Hey Jimmy, you old bugger, what's the story on this team seven ... the referees' team," demanded Hank. "Cripes, the league only had six teams .... the last I heard about it."

"If you would stay around town more, you would know what's going on," came James's rapid response.

"What the hell are you talking about Jim," Hank's voice getting a little annoyed and rising along with his blood pressure.

"Relax Hank," responded James, "I was just stringing you a line ... and you bit. The good news ... for you ... is that you're playing with me again ... and most of the other guys from last year. A few guys got traded but we're still stuck with you and your stinky old gear."

"So I get to carry you for another season ... yipeee!!! I can hardly wait. Mentioning weight, how much do you weigh now ... 300 ... stones!?, retorted Hank.

"Nice talk, Hank. You know how sensitive I am about my physique ..."

"Your what, Jimmy? ... physique ..... you must be kidding," guffawed Hank laughing heartily.

And so the jibes, banter and blather started along with the rest of another hockey season for the Joxville Old Boys.

The season really begins when the Old Boys play their first game --- just like the previous poem says. That is when the handshakes, increasingly like milkshakes (soft, mushy and cold), are made and the warmth of camaraderie is renewed. That's about the time when the musty, moldy or downright raunchy old gear gets sorted and aired out from an over-stuffed bag of equipment, some of which dates back to medieval (or was it maxievil?) times. That's when the funny stories, jokes and pranks begin ... within the socially secure and comfortable confines of a dressing room and a rink.

But Hank couldn't wait for the first game. He was keen to shoot the breeze with some of the Old Boys before then so he phoned his old buddy Jack, a dour Scot who liked to be called Jock. Jack is so old, he remembered a guy named Methuselah or maybe it was one of his grandchildren. Jock was a great old guy with lots of life experiences, mainly related to his career as a salesman and a dry sense of humor that he liked to share. He also was blessed with a lot of homespun or, being an old farm boy, some barn yard philosophy.

Such down home rhetoric seemed to flow from Jock. He frequently made the tired old comment that "Playing hockey is just like riding a bike! There's really nothing much to it ... put on your gear, go out and skate around, pass the puck, shoot it into the net .... it's an easy old game".

Hank would reply with an equally profound comment like, "Balderdash" or words to that effect. "At the start of each season I have to figure out if I have my skates on the right feet ... they never seem to fit right..."

"Hank, you always seem to have two right feet ... or was it two left ones," retorted Jack.

"Probably left ones .... I'm a liberal," came Hank's reply.

The chatter brought back a pleasant recollection to Hank; of his son playing his first hockey as a Mite or was it a Pee Wee, 30 odd years ago? His young son claimed that he was a "big boy" and wanted to put on his own skates. But sometimes he put his little-too-large skates on the wrong, small feet. So, with a felt pen, his mother very discreetly put L and R under the boot of the appropriate skate. Hank thought about doing that for some of his mates - just to see their reaction and get the season off on the right foot, so to say.

Into the inner sanctum --- the dressing room

During these tales of deep intrigue, Hank will take us inside the mysterious, shrouded in secrecy confines of the oldsters' dressing room and provide an "expose" of selected and somewhat censored, yet intriguing activities as well as pass along much, but not all, of the spontaneous, sometimes funny if not gut-busting hilarious, witty repartee. (Remember the tongue in cheek!!) He will expose what he can of the "great unwashed", even defying the sacred precept of "what's said in the dressing room ... stays in the dressing room." Through his astute observations and perceptive senses, peeks or, more likely, squints will be provided into the mystique of old timers' really not-so-unusual, activities, events and behaviors. Due to long-standing norms and oaths of secrecy (like a secretive sect or cult), too much cannot be revealed about the verbiage and behavior of his team, the Old Boys. Hank is still an "active" member and does not want to betray the codes of conduct and trust of the cult, be deactivated, ostracized, wiped out or taken for a ride down a dark, winding, windy road and left out somewhere in the prairies during a freezing snow storm in mid-January.

Through Hank, we will hear some of the banter, usually censored especially for the "F word". The "F word" and a few other naughty vulgarities do slip out occasionally from Max, a rather foul-mouthed fellow, who uses it as a noun, pronoun, verb, adverb, adjective, subject, predicate, conjunctive and in every other way imaginable in almost every one of his utterances. Take the "F word" away from Max and he would be tongue-tied, which would not be a bad idea.

What's in the Bag?

Since this book is a "mixed bag" of tales, anecdotes, other forms of prose, and poetry, the hockey bag (much like a woman's purse) and its contents are very revealing about hockey players ... especially old geezers who may have accumulated a whole raft of "treasures" in their decades-old bags.

Passing references have been made to the odorous, over-loaded, maybe even toxic hockey bags that old guys use. Believe it or not, they are an issue of some concern, not only in terms of individual hygiene but also in terms of team and maybe even public health. Plagues could have started from such bags of bacteria. Doctors, nurses and other health experts should have recommended that many of the bags be condemned and destroyed.

To the old guys, their hockey bags are rather personal and not to be messed with. In effect, "keep your nose out of my bag!!!" Old timers' hockey bags are like women's purses (repetition is for emphasis). Hank thought of Heidi's "suitcase purse". She could carry an enormous variety of "things and stuff" in that modern day version of the long ago settlers' saddle bags. But that is another story for another time but it does provide some useful perspective.

Certainly there are more reasons than privacy to keep one's nose out of an old boy's hockey bag. While reports or rumors of mice, rats, other rodents and various vermin have circulated, no actual evidence of such creatures has been found or reported in any geezer's bag of gear, yet. Notwithstanding (like the controversial clause in the Canadian Constitution), some actual, factual scientific research, of recent vintage, has been conducted at a real Biotechnology Training Centre in a major Canadian University on "what's living in your hockey bag?"[7]. What, pray tell, could any university research have to do with old timers' hockey bags???

It seems as though some curious researchers in the field of microbiology were interested in finding out what kind of bacteria and contagious diseases might be present, germinating or whatever in real (young) boys' hockey bags. Their findings were scary. Bacteria with long, unpronounceable names like *staphylococcus epidermidis* and *streptococcus viridans,* were just two of the organisms that were identified. There were related *aureus, faecalis,* yeast and environmental bacteria also found in the boys' bags. 8. While the long, difficult names for the bacteria might be impressive, some of the adverse effects of these "little devils" were not. Various skin and blood infections, mould and pneumonia could be caused by the "staphies" and the "strepties". Can anyone even imagine why kinds of *"occuses, lises, ies, mides"* and their relations might be found in old timers' bags with their many more years of gathering, germinating, mutating and otherwise developing in strength and ferocity ... maybe even some potential sources of pandemics. Who ever heard of old timer hockey players suffering from a pandemic or even an epidemic unless it was eating or drinking too much? Those old buggers have probably developed an immune system that a stallion would be proud of.

So what's the big deal about the bags?? Old timers, like some fathers of the young hockey players, might say "Shake your head! These are hockey players ... not ballet dancers!!!" The big deal is that serious ailments can happen ... like with Eddie Belfour and Mikael Renberg of the Toronto Maple Leafs a few seasons ago. Before the "big league" lockout, goaltender Belfour missed four games from a "mysterious infection". Renberg, another goalie, cut his hand while lacing up his skates. An infection caused his hand to swell up like an inflated balloon and led to talk of amputation and even death –that's pretty scary!!

Incredulously and ironically, in the analysis done of the hockey bags, there was nothing dangerous in the worst smelling ones. "The bugs weren't that gross but the bag was vile" stated Duncan MacCannell, one of the research scientists. 8. He said, however, that the smell was among the worst he had ever experienced. "It came off the bag in a wave." Shortly after the report came out in the media, some of the Old Boys were discussing the disgusting discoveries. One of them wondered if the researchers had ever tested one of their former teammate's bag --- Whale's was enough to send strong men to the farthest corners of the dressing room or even into the shower stalls to dress. "That bag was really deadly", moaned Gentleman Jock, the epitome of cleanliness and hygiene on the Old Boys. Maybe that helped to explain why he was so vital ... at 78 years of life. "Cleanliness is next to godliness", he used to say as if the clean old codger, or artful dodger, could be related to the Lord.

When Whale would come into the dressing room (or any enclosed space, including an arena, for that matter) there was a nauseating odor that ranked somewhere between rotting fish and that hydrogen sulfide stench that comes from sour gas wells ... "'nuff to gag a maggot" as Max used to say. Before Whale would arrive for a game, other players would group together, like pioneers "circling the wagons", and take up an area as fully as possible to protect their breathing, digestion and immune systems from the smell and the threat of nausea or infection. Despite all of the subtle and exaggerated complaints, gagging sounds and other disgusting noises, the affable old geezer seemed oblivious to his "fragrances". So much for poor old Whale. He's no longer with the Old Boys. At last report, he was contaminating the shinny environs of Cowtown.

According to various reports, some of which have been confirmed, the old timers' gals do not want anything to do with those hockey bags. That's reasonable and prudent. Some fellas who play one night will zip up their bag after a game, throw it in the back of their pick-up truck, van or car, then grab it before they play their next game, haul it into the dressing room, unzip it and put the gear right back on again ---- even if it is frozen from a few nights and days of sub-zero weather. How primitive is that?

Obviously, a lot of bad habits accumulate over time. Besides, hockey bags and their contents are kind of "sacred". Hockey players are a superstitious bunch .... they don't like people digging around or snooping in their bags. In fact, some old guys are quite sentimental about their hockey bags. Read on!

****

Lament for a discarded hockey bag

"I would like to play hockey again, but I can't. In an effort to make more room in my parents' basement this summer, my father threw out my old hockey bag --- the whole thing. Saying it was mouldering like fungus in a darkened cupboard ... downstairs, he tossed it on the back of a trailer and, with other unwanted family junk, trucked it over to the dump. On that day I lost my antique CCM Super Tacks (size 7), my precious Ferland hockey gloves, my shoulder pads, my jock ---- and a part of my childhood.

The hockey bag was bright orange. I received it when I was about 9, so my name and address were scrawled in magic marker on the bag, my parents' idea, as though they already suspected that it might be left behind by a distracted son.

When I was a kid .... my father always made me carry the bag to the rink. It wasn't that heavy, but after some hard-fought matches it felt like shouldering a Volkswagen. There were usually stiff winter winds whistling across the parking lot and my hair was damp with sweat and pride.

We never grumbled much about the cold. During the winter of 1977, I was in Grade 6; that year there were about 15 snow days. My best two best friends, Dave and Claude, took advantage of every cancelled class; I did too. We trudged with our canvas bags over deep snow drifts, walking right into the teeth of those historic, towering storms. We stomped across open fields like campaign mercenaries, knowing that the boy in front would never give up. His stride wouldn't lessen, even though we all felt the intense pain of cold on our faces.

For $2, we could skate for the whole day. We played shinny together as an all-star line against older guys working the graveyard shift.

Losing my hockey bag last summer has turned me despondent, perhaps because I've lost one touchstone to the past. Worse, it forced me to think of how others are making decisions for me. Four years ago, I was diagnosed with bipolar disorder and I now live at home with my parents. Until now, I have not told many of my old friends about my illness.

I really have to look after myself, like good hockey equipment. Most hockey fans don't understand how much attention goes into its maintenance, even for house-league players. When I played, I emptied the whole bag in the basement, where it lay and dried out like beef jerky. And I still remember the lessons of leaving a bag of wet equipment overnight in the trunk of a freezing car. When it is put on later, it feels like jumping into a cold winter lake.

I can never wear wet equipment again. But it might not really matter. I may never play hockey again.

I hope the man sitting on the earth-moving machine at the dump took a moment to look into my orange bag that day last summer when it appeared. Before burying, he might have found new shin pads for his son. My helmet ---number 16 --- was still in good shape, although a little battered. Somewhere I hope a whole team of youngsters are using my stuff. But I know that will never happen. My hockey bag is gone forever. 9.

****

Shortly after reading the article about the bacteria-laden bags and dwelling on the prospect, Hank became kind of curious and concerned about his own gear. Wonder what's in my bag, he mused? So, one sunny summer Saturday afternoon, Hank decided to haul his hockey bag up into the light of day and inspect it in the family room.

"Oh, my goodness, what are you doing?", shrieked Heidi, as she saw Hank start to take his gear out of his bag. "... trying to contaminate the house!". Holding her nose in jest, she retreated to the kitchen.

"Hey baby, I'm just checking my gear .... to see if it is in good shape ... might need some repairs," replied Hank, not daring to tell his wife what his true purpose was, lest she get the idea that some items in that bag might be contaminated and should be washed, otherwise cleaned, discarded or destroyed. "Heaven forbid such an idea", muttered Hank to himself.

"What did you say, Henry?", queried Heidi from the kitchen. When his wife called him Henry, Hank knew that she was serious, even very serious, about what she was saying. Hank was smart enough, well at least had enough experience, to know that this was a matter not worth pursuing with Heidi. So he did not respond which, at times, can be a dangerous decision --as most husbands, lovers, partners or "significant others" can attest to, quite readily. Instead, Hank started to take each item out of his bag and inspect it with a mixture of concern, curiosity, bemusement and some misgivings.

On top of his gear was a sample piece of carpeting that Rocco, the flooring shop owner, had given him years ago. "Hmmm!, mused Hank to himself, "that's kind of ratty. But, it's not as bad as that thing that Max uses as a rug ... for the floor, not his head. That's so scuzzy ... must have come over with the Vikings ... it's bloody awful. It should be quarantined ... or better still, exterminated. Oh well, that's his business ... so long as the rest of us aren't contaminated. Wonder what kind of bacteria and crud are hiding in my own rug? I haven't had it too long ... let's see ... Rocky gave that to me ... when was it? ...... when we put in the new carpeting ... was that four or five years ago? Hey Heidi," Hank yelled impulsively and regrettably because he knew that her curiosity, at least, would be aroused and he did not need to be hassled. "Never mind," he shouted before Heidi could respond, "I found the answer to my question".

Right under the grungy piece of rug was a soiled towel that he used to dry off his face and the rest of his body after each game's shower. His thoughts then wandered to Boom Boom. "..that guy is sure clean ... he seems to bring a clean towel, shorts, the whole nine yards for every game ... and even deodorant for after his shower ... he's one clean dude ... maybe too clean ... he makes the rest of us seem like slobs." Returning his thoughts to his own towel, Hank wondered "... when was that washed last?" ... probably not a good idea to have the rug laying on top of it ... could be kind of unsanitary.... to say the least ... guess it should be washed..." as he threw the towel toward the laundry room.

"Yuk" Hank thought as he picked up his "long johns". He never did like white long johns. "Too bad those red ones kind of fell apart. These are bloody ugly ... wonder what some of those stains are? They really need to be washed too," He threw the underwear on top of the towel.

"What's next?", he pondered skeptically as he peered into the bag. "Voila, my Murray U sweat shirt..... had that sucker for a long time ... let's see .... since 1958 ... the year we won our first NCAA championship ... that was a great year ... sure made shirts well back then ... let's see ... how many years is that ... holy cow, he exclaimed half aloud as he did the calculation of the years ... nearly 50years ... that's a long time. Other than a few rips, tears and some fraying, it's in pretty good shape ... but it's kind of stinky. Wonder how many pounds or gallons of sweat that shirt has soaked up?", Hank muttered meditatively as he sent it flying on top of the growing pile of dirty and probably bacteria-laden laundry.

Momentarily, Hank gazed at the old sweat shirt and recalled the "Coach" and various members of the team of '58. What a great coach --- learned more from him in my first week than I had from all my previous coaches in eleven years of minor hockey. Then, immediately, he thought of some of his old team mates; Dogger, a little guy who skated like the wind and never gave up ... just like a bull dog ... hence, his name. And Muzz, another buddy who he used to play pool with before the games ... an anemic, bookish-looking guy with "Coke bottle" glasses ... couldn't see three feet without them but boy could he hit a speedy winger thirty or forty feet away with an accurate pass ... he said he couldn't break a pane of glass with his shot ... he looked so frail but never missed any games. And there was Brewster, flying down right wing ... he could shoot while he was churning down the ice ... amazing ... most players had to get set before they shoot ... he could be driving along and let go helluva of a shot ... deadly, too. What about Zem? Boy, could he even hit, especially with that hip check. Maybe not as hard as old Bill Juzda but he sure nailed a lot of guys ... especially with their heads down. With a smile coming to his face, Hank remembered Johnny Mac and how fast he could skate ... never saw him with his head down ... hell, he could skate faster backward than I could forward ... no wonder he made it to the NHL ... back when there was only six teams ... and Willy ... another one of our captains who made it to the big leagues ... and what a tragedy ... killed playing for Minnesota ... and then there was Big Barry who died after being hit by a puck in the temple that Sunday night during our practice. Oh such tragedies ... along with the good times ... what a mix of memories ... amazing what memories come out of a guy's old hockey bag.

"Hey Hank, what are you doing in there", came the cheery voice of Heidi. "It's awfully quiet ... are you snoozing?"

Hank, being brought abruptly back from his reminiscing, replied "If I was snoozing, I'm not anymore ... but I wasn't ... I was just remembering some of the good old university days."

"When are you going to be done with your equipment? I have some little jobs for you to do", Heidi asked more sweetly than usual.

"Not sure, baby, but you will be the second to know", replied Hank with just a hint of sarcasm.

"Wonderful, I can hardly wait", came the slightly caustic response.

Hank resumed his equipment "inspection" efforts. "Phew, those socks are kind of filthy", he thought to himself, "... and a little stinky too", as he lifted them toward his nose. Then thinking about one of his outstanding college teammates, Hank recalled how George used to play without any sox on this feet. "Yah, we used to tease him about coming from Flin Flon and their junior team being so poor that it couldn't afford sox for the players. George would agree and let the subject go but really we knew that the real reason that he did not wear socks was. He wanted his skates to fit tightly --- 'just like a good glove', he would say, repeatedly. He was so fussy (fastidious, might be a more appropriate word) about his skates fitting tightly, that every season when he would get a new pair of "Tacks", he would take them back to his apartment, put them on, sit on the edge of a bathtub filled with water and soak them right through the leather. Then, he would take his feet with the skates still on them and spend hours letting them dry so they would fit "just like a good glove." Some of us tried that routine but we did not seem to have the commitment or else we did not do something right because we ruined a few pairs of very good and expensive pairs of skates, unfortunately.

"So much for the sox ... they've seen better days", thought Hank as he pitched them onto the pile. ".... probably should throw them out --- with all of the holes they have in them ... maybe I could duct tape the holes like Duffy does with all his gear". Hank smiled as he pictured Duffy, a huge old guy, who had duct tape holding together his hockey pants, shoulder pads, can holder, gloves and other pieces of his equipment. His pants were a special 'work of art', notably in the crotch area ... where Duff did various designs, from time to time, as the tape had to be replaced. What a waste of such creative genius," thought Hank with a grin.

"Oh, damn", smirked Hank as he reached for his crungy old "protective cup", commonly referred to as a "can". This little item was a "hand me down" from his son Alexander after he stopped playing hockey a few years earlier. "Hmmmm, that was about six years ago when he gave me that can", mused Hank. "I wonder where he got it ... maybe from a garage sale ... or, more likely, from one of his buddies ... never did fit properly ... the jock part of it would fit Whale or Big Gerry ... and it is so bloody scuzzy ... lucky I have those old long johns ... might catch something that would really infect the old crotch. Probably should get a new one ... this one has pretty well had the biscuit ... ." Hank dropped the can beside the bag while making a mental note to find a replacement, as soon as possible or remembered to do so.

"Ah, at last, some equipment that doesn't look like it's a hundred years old and falling apart", Hank thought as he looked at his shiny shin pads with the molded plastic guards over the technology-based suspension structure. "Now, there's some hand-me-downs that don't look like a hundred years old ... sure like them ... best shin pads I ever had ... bar none ... better than the ones they gave me at Murray U. Well, the lore of hockey is that back "in the good old days", old Eatons' catalogues, held on with rubber sealing rings, were used as shin pads. I don't remember anyone ever using catalogues but my Dad swore that he and his buddies did ... and that painter and writer, Shostak claimed that he and his hockey playing friends used catalogues... must have been so. My first ... and worst pair ... of shin pads, although I was happy to have them, were made out of blue felt, with some small sticks covered by leather, very thin leather ... or maybe it was leatherette or vinyl ... I don't know. But they helped to protect the shins, even when the little sticks broke ... they were better than nothing ... and probably better than catalogues... . But these are beauties ... nice of my son Alex to give them to me ... when he gave up playing hockey because of back injuries ... suffered while skiing and mountain climbing ...damned fool kid, as my father used to say," Hank thought as he reminisced about his son.

And so it went for Hank and his Old Boy team mates as they, each in their own way, prepared for the season forthcoming. He knew that little Max would likely come into the dressing room, muttering about who knows what, shake every body's hand, ask how they where, how their summer was, "how's it hanging", then open his hockey bag and discover that he had left his skates, can, shin pads or some other essential item at home or, maybe with a little luck, in the trunk of his car. Similarly, Charlie Hustle would come prancing into the room, a big smile spread across his face, his eyes sparkling and shake hands all around the room, stopping and chatting with some of the guys about who knows what. The rest of the team would come trooping in, drop their bags with a "thump" on an open spot on the floor and sooner or later, open their bags, put on their gear and be ready for another season.....

II. The Old Guys and the naturally younger Gals

"Hello hockey fans in Canada, the United States and Newfoundland. Welcome to Hockey Night in Canada."

Remember Foster Hewitt's rousing welcome to the National Hockey League's Saturday night game broadcast on CBC *radio?* And do you also remember the introductions of the starting line-ups for those games, the following one for members of the "original six" National Hockey League teams?

Starting in goal, three times Vezina Trophy winner, five times Stanley Cup winner, from the Toronto Maple Leafs, number 1, Walter "Turk" Broda;

On defence, the guy who made the mistake of challenging Gordie Howe ... and suffered serious consequences, from the New York Rangers, number 8, "Leapin" Lou Fontinato;

At the other defence position, arguably the greatest of all time, nine time NHL All Star and the first defenceman to win the NHL scoring, the pride of Parry Sound and the Boston Bruins, number 4, Bobby Orr;

On left wing, the "Golden Jet", 10 times first team NHL All Star, four times goal scoring leader, from the Chicago Black Hawks, number 9, Bobby Hull;

At center, 14 times NHL All Star and the longest serving captain of Les Canadiens du Montreal, number 4, Jean Beliveau;

On right wing, the big likeable guy from Floral, a man who has played for 26 seasons, is the highest scoring right winger in the history of professional hockey, member of 11 different Halls of Fame, the recipient of many other honors, from the Detroit Red Wings, number 9, Mr. Hockey ... Gordie Howe.

Well, as you will see, the Old Boys get no such illustrious introductions.

The Line-up (need a way of sorting out these "motley old men")

In true "big league" style... here is the line-up for the Old Boys. Profiles of this august group could be found later in the introductions.

In goal, wearing #00 ... the pride of Montreal's east side, the incomparable *Andy;* also playing goal ... either later in this game or some other time soon, Mr. Moneybags, ooops, sorry, the guy who struggled from abject poverty to prosperity, *Wonderful Willie*....his number is a dollar sign ... . (More later about the wacky world of screwed up goal tenders).

On defence, like many politically correct folks who don't want to be offensive ... the jawbone of the team ... #77.... Henry Hillhouse ... who will at least maim any body ... if he is not called *Hank* or Hunk... but not Henry;

Another guy who claims to be a defenceman ... some of the time ... a player known as *Rover* because he is all over the ice, in more ways than one ... also known as *Boom Boom* because of his not-so- powerful shot, #66 ... *Ronny* ... and you might notice the resemblance to Santa Claus ... without a beard;

Here's an all around player, like a keg, straight from the Calgary Flames' farm team ... he can really shovel it ... a guy with a great sense of humor ... a candidate for the M.F.P. (most funny player), #55 ... the not-so-little *Mikey;*

A relative newcomer to the old timers, a guy who would still be a rink rat if he did not have a family to support ... a guy who would play hockey 25 hours a day if he could ... the balding guy with the big mustache, #69, *Bobby ...* sometimes referred to as *Bozo* because he acts like a clown or *Bull*, like in a china shop**;**

One of the strongest men in the league, a guy who used to climb poles for a living but got tired of being referred to as a monkey, a guy who is as smiling and affable as they come, everybody's favorite team mate, #7, big *Billy*;

Last ... and surely not least ... on defence ... the largest man on the team, weighing in at somewhere around 18 stones ... doesn't sound as heavy as 250 pounds ... #44, the man who aspired to be another Bobby Orr ... but couldn't stop growing ... *Gerry,* the giant;

Turning now to the forwards ... in contrast to the previous guys who are referred to as the backwards or the backsides .... it is my great pleasure to introduce to you, the guy who personifies (whatever that means) perpetual motion ... a man who is always moving ... he puts all of his gear on while standing up ... including his skates (just kiddin', like the grandson says) ... the first guy on the ice and into the shower ... and the first guy to start sucking up the suds, #14 ..... *Charley Hustle;*

Last year the Old Boys acquired ... through stealth, graft and a lot of whining ... certainly the fastest guy on our team ... if not the planet ... a player who is all over the ice but usually takes the face-offs, from St. Boniface, Manitoba .... a candidate for MVP, #10 ... a guy named *Guy*;

Playing on the right side, despite his politics..... is the oldest, slowest player we've got ... a guy who plays most of the game between the blue lines ... the team's spiritual leader, in part because he takes care of the beer supply ... one of the best that Kenora has had to offer or so he says ... the "Might Mite" ... number 9.9, *Maxie ...* sometimes called the Knife because of his heart operations ... and that popular song of years gone by;

On left wing, the man who is our captain ... not because of any great scoring prowess or leadership qualities ... but because he does all of the dirty work ... like scheduling games, phoning the players, taking care of the sweaters and socks, etc., etc., etc.... the indispensable #007, Jimmy..., more formally and commonly known as *James*;

Another left winger, who plays with great gusto and hands cast in concrete .... the pride and joy of Loon Lake .... a player who needs no introduction because he will tell you all about himself when he gets the chance ... #16 ... big, bad *Barry*;

The next player needs plenty of introduction because you might not see him on the ice ... for several reasons. One ... he seldom plays because he is so busy!? ... second .... he is very small ... third, he skates like an osprey ... and sometimes makes the same kind of whistling noise... it is a pleasure to acknowledge his presence for the coming season ... #11 .... Lightning *Larry;*

Another player who is often more conspicuous by his absence than his presence and has a name that rhymes with what he does most ... work. If only his wife would save some of his hard-earned money, he could retire ... buy the Old Boys team ... or at least play with it more often. Yes, the joy of his mother and west side Joxville ... #22 ... usually on left wing ... *Dirk*;

One of our favorite players ... and it has nothing to do with him owning a great pasta restaurant in town ... or the fact that he provides some special libation for our ever thirsty team ... a guy who is almost as big as Gerry ... but is 10 years younger, with some more time to grow ...#88 ... just call him *Sal,* even *Sally* but never *Salvatore*;

One of the ... no, really the most versatile guys on our team is #13, *Sammy Clement* ... we call him Sad Sam because of his outward appearance or Cement because it rhymes with his surname, he is so solid and his hands are made of it. Really a good guy who has played every position on the team, including goalie with his 1940s heavy leather and horse hair filled pads;

One of the very special players on the Old Boys team is a fine fellow known as *Doc*, because, believe it or not, he is a medical doctor. Not only is that comforting to his team mates and other players but he is a terrific hockey player. Despite being a Liberal he plays right wing;

Another terrific hockey player ... a very congenial guy who hails from La Belle Province ... has similar gentlemanly traits and the same first name and number as the great Beliveau, of Quebec Aces and Montreal Canadiens' fame, #4, le gros *Jean Pierre*;

No team would be complete without a "Mr. Everything" ---- this guy plays every position with equal ability ... lousy as he would say modestly if you could hear him ... usually one of the first in the room and on the ice, often brings the beer and other goodies, has extra towels, sox and pieces of gear, always upbeat despite being beaten down at times, a great guy and everybody's favorite, whatever number the team gives him, *Denny;*

(In even more hushed and reverent tones), one other man who needs no introduction because he has been around for ever ... reputed to be older than Methuselah or Moses, the pride and joy of Pigeon Lake ... the Beau Brummel of old boys' hockey ... *Gentleman Jack* or for the Scots, *Jock*, sometimes called the *Coach* because that is his symbolic role and challenge with this bunch ... of "uncoachables."

From time to time in the profiles and episodes that follow, various other characters will appear in all their majesty or, more likely, in just their plain, everyday, down-to-earth ways. So, at this point, we take a brief interlude from the mundane, hackneyed intros of non-descript guys to bring you, the dutiful reader, some less mundane, less hackneyed, more exciting, even titillating exposes of the weird ones of the hockey world ... goal tenders.

Goalies! Goalies! Screwed up Goalies!!!

As anyone familiar with the game of glorified shinny knows, goal tenders or net minders really are "flakes", "strange ducks", idiosyncratic to be more discrete, and commonly are treated accordingly, especially by the older, more mature players. Goal tenders definitely do receive more than their fair share of verbal abuse in old folk's hockey --- but no crashing the nets or other such physical pain and suffering ... just some teasing or mild trash talk. Maybe it is a result of being treated like fine crystal or china, tin gods or little Lord Fauntleroys in their prestigious roles. However, when players reach the age and status of a true old timer, there are no "sacred cows", including goalies, on the teams.

All the old guys seem to have tough skins or hides ... at least on the surface. Almost without exception, every player gets his share of cheap shots and other verbal abuse, especially in the dressing room, before and after the game ...and sometimes, even on the ice ... especially from such mouthy guys as Max or big Gerry ... both of whom have a problem with excessive yapping. Players with "thin skins" or low self esteem are better off playing ping pong, curling or bowling in the winter time. Those are more gentile games and less likely to result in serious psychotic or neurotic consequences.

Putting aside that diatribe, a key question is: what motivates a guy or gal to be a net minder; to put on a heavy helmet and a cage-like mask, a lot of cumbersome equipment, including a pair of awkward, thin-bladed skates, bulky gloves, elbow and shoulder pads, a "belly pad", heavy, large leg pads and try to handle an over-sized stick or shillelagh that would have made proud many an ancient Samurai, Celtic or Roman warrior?

Then, and here is the essence of such strange behavior, goalies go out and try to get in the way of very hard frozen rubber disks that are shot at speeds which might exceed 90 miles an hours, although rarely with that much velocity in old fella's hockey... unless some ex-pro is trying to impress his teammates or work off some aggression, frustration, whatever. Who, in their right mind, would want to be in front of a goal, doing almost everything that they can to keep a piece of black rubber from going into it? Good question.

For an answer, Hank dug back into his memory bank and remembered playing three games of goal during his Juvenile hockey-playing days. That was before helmets and masks were used by goalies. He also recalled that he stopped one puck with his mouth which loosened his teeth, puffed up his lips into a dark reddish purple color and made kissing his girl friend painful ... for both of them. But he got a shut out that night and that's what was important to his team ... and to himself. By way of some other form of explanation, maybe such weirdoes have something in common with Puck, the mischievous sprite or goblin believed to haunt the English countryside in the 16th and 17th century, about the time goalies evolved from apes or was it orangutans?

What ...? No goalie!!!

Obviously, goalies are key players on a team. If one or two of the dozen or so forwards do not show up, well there's plenty more to play. Even if a d-man or two doesn't show, a team can get by with four or even rotating three defenders. And some forwards "wanna be" dmen. Maybe they could if they knew how to skate backwards. But no goalie --- that is a big time problem!!!

As a long time defenceman, (sounds like a penal sentence for some kind of crime), Hank knew very well about the difficulties of communicating with goalies, as much on the ice as off the pond. So he was not surprised when neither Andy nor Willy showed up for the game against the Bloozers. As a matter of fact, neither were most of the Old Boys. However, the lack of surprise did not lessen the felt anxiety of not having a goal tender for the game, especially for Jock, the dour Scot in charge of the Old Boys' team.

When he heard about the goalies' screw-up, the usually unflappable coach, manager and good old guy in charge of player personnel, looked like he had just lost his best friend. His face seemed to sag down to his belly. He was really worried about who was going to play goal that night. And it was just a regular game; no playoff game or Stanley Cup final ... just bragging rights ... temporarily.

It was about an hour before the game was to start and no goalie. Now you have to know Jock to really understand the gravity of the no-goalie situation. Not only was he a classic Type A personality, he planned diligently, was very well organized, punctual and did not like screw-ups. To have no goalie in the dressing room or en route an hour before the games was just a little short of an earth-ending catastrophe for the successful, retired ex-sales manager. In hockey, like in soccer or lacrosse, nothing condemns the "management" of a team as much as not having a goalie, preferably the best possible, available for a game ... any game ... at any level. Talk about being caught with your pants down! Not having a goaltender is like having no pants at all.

Sad Sam to the rescue

Given the team's imminent disaster, Jock and James, the captain, went "scouting" around the arena, including the parking lot and local pub, trying to find a goalie. While they were out scouting, Sad Sam sauntered into the Old Boys' dressing room. With exuberantly expressed relief, several of his team mates immediately started asking him, all at once like a bunch of kids, if he had his goal equipment with him. "No, I don't have it with me," came Sam's casual reply. "Oh, damn" and other, more graphic words of concern and disappointment were uttered by his teammates. "Would you go get it"?, asked several Old Boys, almost in melodic harmony. (Hmmm, the Old Boys' Chorus --- rather difficult to imagine.)

Sam looked a little stunned, then dismayed. He was in a dilemma. On one hand, he did not want to let his team down. Evidently, the Old Boys needed a goalie desperately. Obviously, there was no other goalie in the room or else they would not have been asking him to play that position. On the other hand, he had "filled the breach" just two nights earlier. The sad man was still recovering from that game. His body ached and he was not very keen to play goal again ... so soon. And he had had a long day at work and was really tired. In fact, Sam did not even really want to play hockey at all that night. He was there more out of a commitment and a sense of duty to his team than he was looking forward to a rip-roarin' night of fun and frivolity.

Being the good guy that he was, Sam agreed to play goal. He trudged back to his car, drove home and returned a while later, dragging his decrepit old gear behind him. As amazing as it may seem, his outstanding play that night was largely responsible for the Old Boys eking out a tie with the Bloozers. Mind you, the rest of the guys put out some extra effort ... in appreciation of Sam's good sportsmanship.

Sad Sam, he's the man!!!

Sam was tagged with the nickname Sad because he always looked unhappy. Sam rarely smiled. He seemed to have the weight of the world on his broad shoulders --- probably due to his many years as a policeman. Most cops tend to take life far too seriously but then that's easy for non-police folks to say because they don't have to put up with many of the challenges that our gendarmerie do, day in and day out, year in and year out, *ad infinitum*.

Sad Sam kind of reminded Heidi of a Shar-Pei breed of dog her family owned years ago. That was not to be disrespectful (of the dog --- that's genuine sarcastic old boy humor) because Sam was really a fine guy and a good teammate in the fullest meaning of the words. And he was not a bad goalie, especially when no others were available. Three years ago, he had a perfect record: one win and no losses. Two years ago, he had a less perfect year: one win and one tie. Last year, he slipped to 500: one win and one loss. Despite his trend downward, over the past three years, Sam had an enviable record: 60 percent wins and a 3 to 1 ratio of wins to losses. Even Turk Broda or "Gump" Worsely would be happy to have that kind of win-loss percentage.

Sam was a "traditional" KISS (Keep It Simple Stupid) goalie --- stand up, watch the puck, get in the way and keep it out of the net. He might have been the last of the stand-up goalies ... in part because he couldn't get back up on his skates very well after he did go down. He was a man of many hard years, old injuries and numerous aches and pains ... yes, that's our Sammy. For him, there was no "butterflying", "flopping" or any of the other acrobatic antics or gymnastics that Hasek, Turco or other modern day net minders do.

Similarly, the sad man's goal equipment was very, very "traditional", even ancient in the opinions of most Old Boys ... and by golly, in addition to death and taxes, one other thing is certain with oldsters. They have opinions about almost everything whether they know anything about the subject or not. But when it comes to hockey equipment, old pucksters usually know something about that. Most of them have had the experience of using numerous pieces of gear during several decades, ranging from strap-on skates and Eaton's annual catalogues for shin pads to present day molded pads and skates with replaceable blades, light-weight gloves and composition "sticks".

None of the modern developments had anything to do with Sam's gear. His old horse hair-filled, heavy leather pads reportedly came to North America about the time that Cabot or Columbus arrived. None of it was "light weight". Au contraire!!! Oh how the guys used to kid him: "Did your great grandpa really make those pads out of his favorite old horse ... like a keep sake?" "Horse hair (padding) covered in leather gets kind of heavy when it's wet, doesn't it Sam?" or "Sam, are those gloves made out of leather or wood?"

Well, you should have seen Sam's other sad goalie equipment. First of all, he did not own or use standard goalie skates -- skates that have heavier, thicker boots and blades than regular hockey skates. His goal stick must have come to North America about the time the Vikings first arrived on the continent. They must have discarded it as scrap lumber. In gentle terms, "it has seen better days" but then, haven't we all ... and so had the rest of Sam's equipment. The leg pads were rumored to be from the '50s ... some suggest the 1750s. They were thin in places because the padding had shifted or, more accurately, sunk. Both pads were held together with duct tape, the favorite mending material of old timer hockey players. The chest protector or belly pad, was in somewhat better condition --- a little tattered around the edges with a few splits in it that had been patched with duct tape.

Sam's gloves were the saddest pieces of his gear. First of all, they were as stiff as kiln-dried boards. (In present times, it is a major achievement to get construction lumber that dry.) You would think that such stiffness would be a handicap to a goalie. Not according to Sam. He claimed he could hold his stick and catch a puck, by his own admission, "if it is shot at the glove" ... otherwise "I am going to miss it anyhow." Not only were Sam's gloves stiff and unwieldy but there were more holes in the fingers and palms of those gloves that most fishing nets. Honest to goodness, each finger in the glove had holes in it. Inserting your fingers into gloves was a challenge for most dexterous people. Not to stoic Sam. His fingers slid into those gloves like they were programmed --amazing.

As the old saying goes, "beggars can't be choosers". Behind all of their kidding, the Old Boys were happy to have the doleful one between the pipes, especially when no other player wanted the thankless task of stopping their opponents shots. And Sam could take the jibes and old timer "humor' with the best of them. He was a tough "old boot". He even had an "old boot" award to prove his toughness. Remember, he had been a policeman for many years and had "taken a lot of crap" from drunks, whores, petty and other criminals. He could give as good or bad as he got, his eyes twinkling although rarely did he smile. Usually, the expression on his face was like a dour Mona Lisa, not really like a Shar-Pei!!!

Communications with those masked men --- mal? mis? or missing!

As the Sad Sam situation suggests, one of the big problems with goalies relates to them as dysfunctional communicators. What does that fancy term mean? Simply stated, it means that their brains often are disconnected from their mouths or their thoughts are expressed dysfunctionally, at various and unpredictable times, like some women during their pre- post- or menopausal years. In effect, many times, especially in the heat of a game, goalies are illogical and lacking in good hockey sense when they are hollering at their teammates. (During a hockey game, who every heard of a goal tender or any other hockey player speaking in a well-modulated voice, like our grade school teachers used to tell us to do?)

Consider the following malcommunication situations. Two or three opposing forwards are barrelling over the Old Boys' blue line and the goalie hollers "stand up" or "take them there" to the sole d'man. Or, an opposing forward is bearing down on a defenceman as he is skating full speed for the puck in his own zone --- with his back turned to the onrushing, menacing, fore-checking forward. What do the goalies do? Some stand there like a sphinx --- stone cold silent. What a rotten time for a goalie to be quiet. The d'man could use some intelligence about the opposing forward(s). But no, there the goalie stands: mute. Damned fool!! Idiot!!! Both!!! Worse!!!

Then there is the "happy wanderer" type of goalie. Although the "new rules" limit nomadic goalies from confusing and frustrating their d'men and other team mates, some net minders still like to "handle" or play with the puck. Most players, especially old timers, are challenged enough to play with a regular stick with a 3 inch blade much less the larger bladed, heavier goal sticks. But some goalies think they are the Great One, Magnificent Mario or Sid, the Kid and want to dazzle their opponents by stick-handling with their big paddled, unwieldy stick or by making "tape to tape" passes. Ya, right ... in their dreams or some other fantasies. It rarely happens, especially with the geezer goalies. Most of them should have a shovel as poorly as they handle the puck with their goal sticks. Or the goal tender might go behind the net or Lord knows where. Brings back memories of that old, old song: *The Happy Wanderer* ... some of the words of which were "I love to go a wandering along the mountain track and as I go I love to sing my knap sack on my back ... ."

The "real beauty play" as those "hosers" Bob and Doug Mackenzie would say is when the goalie, in his infinite wisdom or a demented state of mind, shoots the puck away from their defencemen or toward them but misses the target by a dozen feet, more or less. No wonder special prayers of dispensation are said for goalies, especially during playoffs or other times when they might be more distracted than normal ... whatever that is ... which led Hank to recall the sign on the door of his daughter's room: "Why be normal?" Normal and goalies are words that do not belong in the same sentence.

Well, as suggested above, the Old Boys' goalies really miscommunicated or just plain failed to communicate for a game following New Years' Eve one season a few years back. Historically, Andy and Willy had an understanding that if one of them could not play, then he was to contact the other puck stopper so that one of them would be available or find someone else to "tend the nets" for each game. Somewhere along the way Andy and Willie did not communicate effectively. Maybe they were hung over or forgot to look at their new calendars or schedules, check their Blackberries, listen to phone messages or whatever.

In this era, there is no lack of high-folluting, high tech communications devices. Maybe they were still in a snit with each other, drunk or hung over so badly that they forgot their duty to perform ... in goal? Surely they were not balking at their "contract". In terms of compensation for their efforts, each year they were offered twice what they had received the year before. And they were not being discriminated against. Every Old Boy had the same contract: no contract.

Superstitious Eddy

Hockey players, especially goalies, have some really quirky characteristics, including some strange superstitions that ordinary folks find very difficult to understand. One of the quirkiest goalies Hank ever knew, and he knew a bunch of them, was a long time teammate and friend, who was super-duper superstitious to the point of various kinds of mania or phobia. His long time buddy, Ed, was a goalie and a pitcher --- talk about a double whammy --- he must have been whammed very hard sometime back in his youth, maybe dropped on his head as a baby --- a goalie and a pitcher and very good at both. Hans Erhardt Gust was so good back in the '50s (of the 20th Century), that he had opportunities to go to universities in the Excited States of America on a hockey or a baseball "scholarship". (From a purely academic perspective, the word scholarship was often prostituted when used in conjunction with athletics. Back in those days, some of the "meatheads" that had football, basketball and other athletic "scholarships" for playing their sports and maybe getting some education made a mockery out of many U.S.A. academic institutions. The term was turned into a misperceived oxymoron away back in the '50s, '60s, and continues today. Athletic grants are a more appropriate term. Please excuse the opinion but I have been there and observed the anomalies.)

Well, anyhow you thought about him, Eddy was superstitious, probably to an exponential extent given that he was very bright, a pitcher and a goalie. In fact, he was so superstitious and eccentric, as a teenager, he would cross the street rather than meet or talk to a very pleasant, beautiful and voluptuous young blonde that most "normal" testosterone-driven young lads would have "killed for". Not young Eddie. Not only did he take an inexplicable disliking to that young beauty, he eschewed all girls while he was in high school. As Heidi would say; "Go figure". Superstitious Eddy had other extraordinary eccentricities. He would walk around telephone poles on the road side rather than the sidewalk side. And there is more to come. The ultimate in being of questionable sanity came during his pre-game "routine" as a college goalie. His process of preparation, odd pre-game antics and behavioral machinations were fastidiously meticulous, sometimes volatile but usually predictable and timed, almost to the minute.

Eddie would arrive precisely 60 minutes, before the game was to start. He expected the stick boy, Danny, to have his goal pads propped up on the floor against his chair. (Eddie had a chair, the rest of the team sat on benches that went most of the way around the dressing room.) Eccentric Ed also expected that his chest protector would be propped up against the back of "his" chair and his shoulder and arm protection gear would be placed over top of the shoulder and arm equipment. In effect, the chair symbolized Eddie, sort of. His skates were to be placed next to each goal pad on the floor. His gloves were to be placed on the shelf above his chair so he could slide his hands into them easily and simultaneously. His helmet was to be placed on the top of his shelf, nearly to the ceiling but he liked to stretch. His goal stick was to be propped against the wall, an arms-length to his right. How eccentric is that?? And there is more.

After Eddie went through his routine of undressing from his normal (which was quite conventional) attire and dressing in his goalie gear, he went through another sub-routine. He would stand up, without his gloves, stick or helmet, and go into the bathroom. On his way, he would reach up and touch the water pipes suspended from the ceiling. Then, he would look in the mirror and with his fingers push any stray hairs out of his eyes or off his forehead. (Eddie did not want any distractions, no matter how minute. He was one very focussed dude.) Then he would go into the stall, clear his throat and spit into the toilet. He would wash and dry his hands, look in the mirror again, touch the water pipes, very carefully put on his helmet, slide his hands carefully into his gloves, sit down, reach for his stick and then shout at the young stick boy, "Danny, where's the puck?"

Danny was expected to appear in the doorway leading to the ice, stop, hold out a brand new, never used puck and wait for the "OK" from the eccentric one before he lobbed the hard, black rubber missile across the room to the oddball goalie. Obviously, nobody --- coach teammate, manager, Chancellor or whomever --- was to get in the way of the "puck throw". And, the puck had to land in Eddie's catching glove a certain way or he would throw it back to Danny, like he was pitching a baseball, over hand and hard. After he had been hit a couple of times, Danny would be "on his toes" and ready to jump aside, let the puck hit the wall, with a loud "whack", pick it up, get the OK and then throw it back to Eddie. And there is more to the superstitions of Eddie, the goalie but that's enough ... for now, and probably forever.

Moody Mo

Maurice Jacques (MJ) Langevin was not one of those "weirdoes" mentioned previously. He rarely played with the Old Boys but was enough of an odd character from around the league to include in this epistle. Maybe he was screwed up from being given the name of Maurice during the N.H.L. playing career of the famous, sometimes infamous, Joseph Henri Maurice (Rocket) Richard of Les Canadiens du Montreal, the fiery forward who scored so prolifically, especially during the years of World War II while a lot of good hockey players were off fighting for freedom from fascist tyranny. Or maybe it was because he was given the name of Jacques after the famous and innovative goal tender for Les Canadiens, Jacques Plante. As a young goalie, maybe MJ was expected to play like the famed masked man, and that does not mean the Lone Ranger.

Be that as it may, many years ago Maurice Jacques was nicknamed Mo. Despite his happiness with the nickname he had personality similarities to Jacques and the Rocket. Mo was behaviorally inconsistent; hence the nickname adjective of Moody.

As might be expected or suspected, one of Moody Mo's more common traits was his sporadic, inconsistent goal tending. As Jock, James and others often wondered aloud: "Which Mo is going to show up" (for the game). Many Old Boys' games and one tournament game in particular illustrated the rather schizophrenic behavior of the troubled goalie. During the Friday evening contest of the annual Joxville tournament, miserable Mo let in the first four shots at him by the less-than-powerful Ponoka Puckduckers. None of the shots were particularly difficult. Mo just was not into the game. Hank, Boom Boom, Mikey and other team mates tried to reassure and encourage their tempestuous goalie but with little apparent effect. By the end of the second period, the score was 8 to 1 for the Ponoka Puckers. Most old timer goalies would have let in about 3 or 4 of the 8 goals. Eight goals against was very disappointing and demoralizing, almost traumatizing, for the Old Boys. The Puckduckers played the last period at half speed and still scored two more goals. Final score: Puckduckers 10; Old Boys 1; one of the worst trouncings ever experienced by Hank and most of his teammates.

Two days later, another Mo showed up for the last game of the tournament. Before the game, he was more yappy (cheerful) in the dressing room, to the point that Max chided him about being an "f'ing" big mouthed goalie. A few minutes later, James said that Mo's banter reminded him of the line from Hamlet about "a tale told by an idiot, full of sound and fury signifying nothing." Mo responded to the chidings with more blustery blather laden with vulgar expletives.

In an effort to tone down the chatter, Hank nonchalantly asked Mo if he had "brought his A game to play?" Mo's cryptic response was "I don't have an A game!" However, during the following hour or so, Maurice Jacques played like one of his namesakes, making incredible saves with his gloves, pads and stick. He stopped two or three breakaways, bullet shots from the slot, stacking his pads and virtually doing somersaults in goal. It was Mo's best performance in years, clearly reminiscent of his 5 periods of shutout goal tending two years previously in the Joxville Tournament. Needless to say his team mates were puzzled but very appreciative of their erratic puck stopper's performance during the championship game. Maybe he needed the pressure of the game to enhance his performance. Maybe a lot of other factors bore upon his play. Whatever it was just added to his reputation for inconsistency and unpredictability, hardly positive traits for a goal tender. But, one must remember, those guys really are screwballs ... as Hank's ex-father-in-law used to say.

Andy the Performer

Occasionally, like on various patron saints days, like Andrews, Patricks and Valentines, Andy would do some gigs for local places of entertainment. He also performed with his band in local dives and small hotels. Andy was *not* a member of the Boston Pops or the Joxville Symphony Orchestra. He was a down-to-earth, country and western, with a little bit of rock and roll thrown in, kind of musician. Mainly, he played an electric guitar but also could play the harmonica. Sometimes he played them together which was a bit of a feat, requiring rather extraordinary skill, coordination and concentration; useful traits when playing goal.

Every now and then, Andy would spontaneously perform part of a "routine" or whatever it was called for the Old Boys, usually in the dressing room. Two of the all time (well, last year or so) favorites were his novel renditions of "happy birthday" and "puttin' on the dog." Written accounts do not really do justice to Andy's performances. How can mere written words accurately and adequately describe him pretending to play his guitar or singing his songs with all of the facial expression, suggestive gyrations of his limbs and other body language that a real "performing artist" uses? A picture would spare a few thousand words and convey a much more lucid depiction of Andy in action. Alas, no such picture exists. Such is life --- we can't have everything so we have to do the best with what we have. Amen!!! How's that for a little bit (or byte) of old timer sagacity?

So, here's the scene for Andy's "improv" performance. Picture a dreary dressing room of sweaty, tired old guys "huffin' and puffin'" as they take off their gear and start sucking on a can of beer or pop. Some, like Charley Hustle and Guy, have had their showers already and are into their beer-drinking with the same gusto that they have for playing hockey. Various conversations, mutterings, burps, farts and other uninhibitted noises pervade the room. There is some serious conversation and grumbling to be heard, if you want to bother listening to it. Much of the din is upbeat chatter and laughter. And some of it is just downright entertaining, like Andy's rendition of "Puttin on the dog".

"Puttin' on the dog". One night after a vigorous game against the Bloozers, Hank and Andy were sitting next to each other on the dressing room bench. The d'man was telling his puck stopping mate how much he enjoyed Andy's recent tribute to Jean Pierre's birth of 60 odd years ago, particularly the creative, unique words and how well old Andy had remembered such a lengthy recitation. Just like he had flipped on a light switch, Andy's face beamed. He jumped up, went into his geetar-playing stance and started yellin' and tellin' Hank, Max, Mikey, Big Gerry, Guy, Charley Hustle and others within earshot about the new song he was working on ... called "puttin' on the dog". The words, in part, go something like this:

"Well, my wife and I have been married for many a year...
and guess what I am starting to hear ...
about wanting a fur coat
so she can put on the dog
(blah!, blah! blah! melodically ......)

Well, sure as hell is my fate
one night when I was out late,
I hit a dog with my car
and right then and thar
I figured my wife would have her coat
about as easy as skinning a goat.
(blah! blah! blah! melodically...)

coat turned out as nice as you please
went right down to her knees
but after a while she started to sneeze
said something about itching, like she had fleas.
(blah! blah! blah! melodically).

While his teammates roared with laughter, made rude sounds and gestures, Andy continued to strum his make-believe geetar and sing his little ditty about "puttin' on the dog". Just another performance by one of those unpredictable puck stoppers.

Too bad, all of the testosterone-charged, uptight, road raging, stressed-out, violent men of North America's society couldn't be in that old guys' dressing room to "kick back", have a hearty, healthy laugh and enjoy living in its most basic form. What is more basic to living in North America than 12, 15 or 20 guys from all walks of life, with a vast amount of life's experiences, attired in their scuzzy underwear or birthday suits, having a good laugh? As the little known local philosopher Dwight Dee would say: It doesn't get much better than this ... does it boys?" "No Dwight, it doesn't!!!" And, thank you Andy for your humorous contributions to our good life.

Andy's "pissed off" (but as Confucius supposedly said, "tis better to be pissed off than to be pissed on")

By almost any measure Andy is a good guy ---- talented, naturally funny, successful, etc, etc, etc. But he is human and he does play shinny intensely and competitively, sometimes even hyper competitively. And, like most competitive people, he likes to win and, above all, not make dumb mistakes. So he was hard on himself... very self-critical, chastising himself when he let in a goal that he thought should have been stopped. Andy would mutter to himself, sometimes cussing his mistake and other attributes, even grumping after a game was over. (His up-beat, humorous entertaining was much more enjoyable. But then, if every day was sunny and warm, the weather would get kind of boring, at least for old timer hockey players.) Remarkably, for a goal tender, he was very tolerant and uncritical of his team-mates. He was unlike other goalies who critically and loudly swore, screamed and threw various objects, including equipment, sticks, pucks, water bottles, cans or whatever they can get their hands on, at their teammates, usually d'men who, due to happenstance, tended to be close to the nets being protected by the goalie.

Now remember, Andy was and still is human. So one night, in a game against the Ghosts, a team that wore all-white uniforms, Andy "exploded" at Hank. Well, the situation was something like this. The Ghosts had stormed down the ice with three attackers on two Old Boy d'men. One of the Ghosts let go a "wicked shot" (remember these are old timers) and Andy stopped it. So far, so good! Hank "picked up" the rebound in front of his net and then took a look where to pass it. Still, so far, so good! But he took about three nanoseconds too long in his looking around and had "his pocket picked" by one of the Ghosts (which naturally he could not see, in part because the nebulous soul was behind Hank and in part because he was invisible). Well, that dastardly ghost passed the puck to his winger beside the goal and the puck was in the net faster than Andy could say "damn you Hank"!!! Needless to say but then old guys usually make lots of needless statements, Hank felt badly enough at being so careless but almost mortally wounded when he heard Andy's exclamation. As soon as the puck was dropped at centre ice the matter was forgotten ... and the game went on ... to a satisfactory conclusion. The Old Boys won 5 to 4, despite Andy and Hank both being on for all four goals against, a matter that Andy did not let Hank forget after the game and weeks after that ...the miserable old sod.

In hockey lore there are countless goal tenders who would make interesting subjects of discussion and ridicule. In the episodes to follow, a couple of weird, irrepressible goalies, known fondly as *"Suitcase"* (*Wally*) and *"Clown"* (*Joey*) will appear from time to time. Suitcase's "significance" comes from the way he picked up his nickname more than for any other attribute, especially his goal tending. Stated succinctly, Wally was a "well travelled man". Moreover, he is the only known goalie in the history of Joxville's old timers hockey that had a goal scored on him after it was shot from the other end of the ice and off of the side boards. It was a zone clearing, slowly sliding shot by a tired opposition player that poor old Suitcase "whiffed" on badly ... very badly, much to the chagrin of his cheering fans, jeering team mates and his embarrassed self.

Then there is *Clown* ... our pal *Joey* ... truly unique for being the only hockey player known in the annals of old timers shinny to wear a clown outfit onto the ice for a game ... and actually play the game in such goofy garb.

Profiles of the Old Boys and their Gals

Note to reader. If you are tired of reading about the oddball characters in this tome, skip the next few pages and check out some of the "action" in the following set of stories. OK?!

Hank is the guy telling the story; the "talking head". He was a good player "in his day" (whenever that was). During his three years of university eligibility he played on two national championship teams. Now he's in his 60s, has had a wide range of work and management experience, travelled extensively and has had a career as a teacher, consultant, businessman, politician, community activist and international development volunteer. His appreciably younger wife, **Heidi,** is a beautiful blonde, blue-eyed woman with a sweetness that seems unreal at times. She thinks old timers are the "nicest gentlemen" she's ever met --- how's that for being naive?

Until he suffered some heart problems, **Mike** was one of the most naturally funny people that trod the floors of old timers' dressing rooms. His persona reeked of humor and, quite often, of garlic, also. Like most old timers, he liked to eat lots and lots ... of whatever ... usually poly saturated trans fats, preferably in French fries, pizza and other heart-challenging foods. He was overweight, kind of a "roly-poly" with a round jovial face and a light-hearted disposition. His heart attack led to some big-time losses of weight as he had to change his diet dramatically. After his heart attack, he quipped that he had two lists of food to eat: the one given to him by his doctor and the other with the foods he liked on it. Typically, he talked with enthusiasm and the lilt of an Irishman, which coincidentally was his gregarious mother's ancestry. Mikey was bright, energetic and a top flight salesman who had done well during his career. At 62 years, he is too young to retire. Besides, his wife "didn't want him around the house, getting into her hair" ... whatever that meant but one could well imagine. **Marie**, was a beautiful brunette and a very quiet, pleasant lady who was busy with her career, community activities and grandchildren. She rarely appeared at old timers' events, unfortunately.

Max has had a tough life. As a child he had rheumatic fever and spent six weeks in hospital (that was back in the times when hospital care was readily available and patients were given enough time to recover and feel like a real human being before being "released", like so many cattle being chased out of a pen). That childhood ailment left him susceptible to other health problems, notably a heart attack that he suffered one night toward the end of an Old Boys' game. Fortunately, two of the other players were paramedic firemen who kept him alive with CPR until an ambulance arrived with its trained personnel. From that moment on, numerous doctors, nurses and other specialists kept the little man with the big heart alive. Maxie was divorced about 13 years ago while he struggled to quit smoking, stop drinking and keep a regular job, all of which he succeeded in doing. Max was one tough dude, greatly admired, maybe even revered, as he hit the ripe, some might say rotten, old age of three score and ten.

Ronny, a.k.a. **Boom Boom, Rover** and some nasty names not fit for family consumption. Boomer was probably the ideal old timer hockey player. Just into his fifties, he had a great mix of talents and personality. Like most old timers, he was seriously overweight which will hurt him as this story unfolds. He was a strong skater, had a quick snap shot and used his weight to great advantage, especially in front of the goals, both in his own end of the rink and the other end, where he was more likely to be; thus the apt nickname of Rover. Both Ronny and his wife, **Rhea,** were pleasant and affable. They were fun people who liked to travel, party, tell stories and jokes, laugh and consume a lot. One of the standing (or sitting) jocular questions around the dressing room and wherever Boomer happened to be was "whether or not he spent more time travelling than working", to which he would feign grievous injury, insult or other harm and claim that he was one of if not the hardest working guys in the "gummit" as that guy Kelly of Pogo fame, used to write.

Big Gerry was a serious man who took old timer hockey the same way he took most other facets of life --- intensely, although he had been known to laugh, occasionally, especially after a few beers and not around his wife. **Patricia,** who would not countenance being called any other name than Patricia, was a stern, stereotypical retired old school teacher. Maybe her 37 years of teaching grade school had something to do with her readily apparent cold, impersonal persona. That's what most of the Old Boys sort of figured, especially since they could recall their incorrigible behavior during early years in school --- "seems only natural that she should be a tough old broad", said one of the Old Boys, rather impetuously. All that irreverency aside, Gerry was a power forward who liked to line up at defence so he could get more playing time. To Hank and other members of the Legitimate Defencemen's Association (LDA), Gerry and other old forwards who were "playing back" were imposters and should be charged with impersonating a d'man.

James was Mr. Steady Eddy, Mr. Reliable, Mr. Nice Guy. He was soft-spoken with a friendly demeanor and a ready smile. Rarely did he miss a game. He was the team's "iron man", who ran marathons in his spare time. Jimmy was a leading candidate for the MVP award because he religiously brought the boys' booze to the games. That duty involved more than just picking up a couple of boxes of brew before each game. Some of the *prima donalds* wanted certain brands of beer or "hard stuff", like Chivas Regal, Crown Royal and dark rum which also required mix. Some even wanted ice, like in cubes, as well as mix for their drinks. Jimmy never grumbled; only smiled. He and his wife **Anne,** were both busy professional people. Their family life was very important to them. They had three adult children and several grandchildren.

Charley Hustle. Charley was one of, if not the most popular guys in the league. He was an outstanding player who was not only one of the fastest skaters but one of those "dipsy-doodling" guys that drive the opposition, especially the defencemen, crazy, like stark raving bonkers. He was an unselfish center iceman who passed well and scored occasionally which is probably one of the reasons he was so popular, especially with the opposing teams. **Betty** was Charley's girl friend. She was a raucous lady whose laugh can be heard throughout any arena built. She was also built with hooters that were reported to be bra-busting when she laughed or became angry. Betty had what Charley refers to as a "dynamic personality". Others, who knew her well, said that it was volatile much of the time. Just goes to prove another one of Newton's laws that "opposites attract." Unlike Patricia who wanted to be referred to by her given name, Betty did not want to known as Elizabeth. Seems she was not a big fan of the Queen.

Guy, rhymes with flea, was one of the smallest players on the team and in the league. Guy could "skate like the wind", sort of like his namesake, the famous Guy Lafleur.

He and Jimmy were the two quietest guys on the team. Guy let his outstanding play on the ice do the talking for him. Not only did he skate very fast, he scored often, often getting his "hat trick" and then being required to score no more in a game, lest he be penalized by more than just buying a round of beer for the boys after the game. Like Guy, **Annie,** was very quiet, a tiny little lady who rarely attended games or any activities related to the Old Boys. C'est dommage!!!

Barry Since Old Boy Leo was elected to the Legislature, Barry took over the role of Mr. Intensity on the team, maybe even for the entire league. This guy had his own small construction services business and "worked like a dog", often putting in 12-14 hours a day (and night). Rather than relax and "kick back", Barry brought his work ethic and intensity to playing old geezers' shinny. Sometimes he got a little too rambunctious, knocking over other players, which is a "no-no" in seniors' hockey. Barry seemed like a prime candidate for a heart attack. His wife, **Loretta, "**just call me Lottie", was cut from the same bolt (of cloth or lightning). Not only was she a mother of three but she worked in the business almost as much as Barry. But, when she partied, she went "whole hog" as the saying goes, like wild and crazy.

Lawrence Samuel **(Sad Sam)** Clement was one of the real characters of the Old Boys. He was a slender, even frail looking, guy who always seemed to be injured. Maybe that was why he always had a sad sack look on his mug and the nickname Sad Sam given to him. As one old timer said, "He has a face like a mud fence ... a frozen mud fence." Sam's serious facial expression seldom changed. It was like a mask, covering a guy who had a really good, although very understated, sense of humor. Without "cracking a smile", he would make some of the funniest comments. About all that changed were his eyes; they would twinkle like multi-caratted diamonds and then, maybe, just maybe, the right corner of his mouth would turn upward into a subtle smile, sort of like that mystic lady, Mona Lisa, after she had been "goosed". By contrast, his partner **Charley**, derived from

Charlene, a hefty female of Sam's height and about 30 or more pounds heavier was an imposing woman. Her persona was mercurial. It would change while you were looking at her and she was not pretty. She could be downright scary, even intimidating.

A long-time teacher and school administrator, **Larry** was a "cool dude". He was popular throughout the community, the old timers' league and on the team. One of the few players of Japanese ancestry to play hockey in Joxville, at any level, he was cerebral, pleasant and a pleasure to be with, be it in the dressing room, on the ice or in social settings. His moves on the ice were as quick as his mind. Despite more than his fair share of chances, he did not score many goals. "Old Lar" had some of the most ingenious and amusing "reasons" (really excuses) for not scoring. "I felt sorry for the goalie", "we're already seven goals ahead" (rarely was that a fact) or "I'm not going to buy you guys any beer and contribute to your delinquency" were three of his oft-used, tired old excuses for missing open nets. **Michelle,** his petite wife and a doctor, was a "China doll". She was quite quiet, had a smile that radiated warmth and enjoyed cultural activities which did not include hockey. Pity!!!

Le Gros **Jean Pierre (J.P.)** is another big old guy who used to be a good, even outstanding, hockey player, once upon a time. After finishing junior A, J.P. was good enough to have a cup of coffee or two with one of the "original six" of the NHL. That achievement speaks for itself. But he had a motivation different from most of the hockey players good enough to make the National Hockey League back in the '50s and '60s. J.P. went on to university, became a college instructor and returned to hockey as an old timer when he became eligible, circa 1975. Along the way, he gained weight, slowed down and his joints ground down until his knees were lacking cartilage, tissue, gristle or whatever it is that keeps the joints from wearing out and breaking down. When the temperatures drop and the snow falls, he dons his gear and plays the odd game with the Old Boys and maybe in the annual Joxville tourney if his knees are okay which they seldom are, even with his recently replaced knee joints. His feisty, red headed wife, **Colleen,** is really a spark plug for J.P.'s and his laid-back persona and life style. She has enough energy for both of them and is the "life of a party", who resonates with a very hearty laugh, especially for such a little lady.

Andy. This character of characters has already been introduced and featured in his roles as a quirky goal tender, entertainer inside and outside of the rink and old timer personality. Somehow he just did not seem like a successful investment advisor. As if his job did not have enough stress and strain from unsatisfiable clients, he had a challenging family life with a son who had social problems, strained relations with his estranged wife, **Maggie** and a brother-in-law who Andy commonly referred to as a "nut case".

Willy. Why is it that old timer goalies seem to have neurotic wives? Willy's wife, **Susan,** was a case in point. She had more ailments than were included in the Encyclopedia of Medicine or any internet equivalent. And Willie had a few health problems of his own, including a recent heart attack, which was attributed to living a highly stressed life. Injuries from playing goal added to his miseries. Despite his own physical woes and the psychic and neurotic ones of his wife, Willie was an upbeat kind of guy with a ready smile and a great sense of humor. Following a "golden hand shake" by a life-sucking corporation which cared little about its long time employees, he struggled to adapt to being "let go" ... at least temporarily. Being entrepreneurial, he started his own computer services company. That venture kept him very busy and caused him to miss numerous games. While he lamented the missed camaraderie, he did not miss his wife's chronic complaining.

Gentleman **John**, a.k.a. **Jock** was the consummate hockey old timer. He was one of the "founding fathers" of the Old Boys as well as the league in which they played. Last year he was honored with a "Life Membership" in the old timers' association. He played well into his 70s, had been President and informal leader of the association and various other organizations in Joxville. The saying "let Jock do it" was appropriate to this fine man because he did almost every thing that was to be done in Joxville's old gafffers' hockey. Jock was almost always a gentleman, rarely ever raising his voice or expressing vulgarities. Clearly, his demeanor reflected a strong Scots' upbringing and a career in business, culminating with a senior management position for a large international corporation. His wife, **Anne,** beautifully complemented George. She was a pleasant, gracious lady with a warm smile and a very engaging conversationalist. Anne was one of the most ardent supporters of the Old Boys, rarely missing a tournament or social activity.

Other Old Timer Characters

With the odd exception, the Old Boys were a great group of guys. Each one had his own unique personality that was more or less compatible with the other old guys. Each was a "character" in his own unique way. ("Character" meaning that they had unusual, eccentric and distinctive attributes.) Some, like Andy, Boom Boom, Big Gerry, Mikey and Max were conspicuous by their mere presence. They were more gregarious, louder and more humorous than most old guys. By contrast, James, Sad Sam, Larry, Guy, Jean and Gentleman Jock were quieter, introverted, even shy, guys.

Various other interesting old guys from different teams and places often "popped up" from time to time, commonly at tournaments. A few of those old characters are profiled in the following lines.

The Clown. Every now and then, usually at an old timers' tournament, a guy named Joseph (Joey) Elder, would show up dressed and made-up like a clown, complete with a multi-colored, billowy suit, a orange wig, red bulbous nose, sometimes very large false ears, plenty of garish make up on his face and a hearty bass laugh. Joey was a natural clown. He really did not need clown's clothes and make-up to be funny. His portly persona bubbled over with genuine humor, laughter and fun. Joe was a good guy who was not only funny but generous and a good goalie "to boot", as the old saying goes.

Ernie was a big pleasant, laid back kind of guy like Ernie Ells, except that he once used to be a good hockey player. Now he is a bionic man. He has had more operations than the average surgeon. Let's see: one or two for heart problems, one for cancer, another for hip or was it a knee replacement and numerous other hockey injuries such as broken bones, concussions and damage to various and sundry other parts of his mind and body. The point about his surgeries is exaggerated but he surely has had more scalpels and other unfriendly instruments stuck into him than the "normal" old bugger (whatever normal means) during the past couple of decades. And, here is the "grabber". A few years ago Big Ernie had the giving spirit, gumption, intestinal fortitude and whatever else it takes to roller blade the 300-odd kilometres between Oiltown and Cowtown on behalf of the cancer society or was it the heart and stroke foundation or both? Now that he is forbidden by his wife **Julie**, his doctor and his good sense from playing the glorified game of shinny, he organizes and manages all kinds of old timer events and other hockey teams for tournaments, charity week-ends and who knows what all. Undoubtedly Ernie is Mister Good Guy Old Boy Puckster in the fullest, richest meaning of the term. Bless him!!!

Cheap skate **Chuck** a.k.a. The Chiseller. This dude (or is it dud?) is a real estate agent and laundromat operator who rumored to take bags of coins from the machines and forget to pay income taxes on them. With the Old Boys, he is also known as "56 cents" because one of the few times he paid for his pop after a game, he put 56 cents into the can, rather than the $1 every other pop drinker paid. This slime-ball is not a bad hockey player. He is just a bad person who happens to play old timers' shinny every now and then, further indicating that he is unreliable as well as being short of integrity. As the old saying goes, "every barrel has a bad apple."

Genial **George** personifies Mr. Nice Guy. According to his wife **Amy** and associates at work, he is always smiling, pleasant and courteous. He is a very generous man who sponsored an old timers' team back in the years when the association was struggling financially to survive. Coincidentally, he was also a real estate agent but at the opposite end of the ethical spectrum from chiselling Chuck.

Mario, the Magician, is not to be confused with #66, the Magnificent One or Mario from the Ocean City and other tournaments. Magical Mario is at least 20 years older, can skate all night, although not very fast and not necessarily toward the opponents' goal and has a "million moves" in his repertoire. He is "a dipsy doodler" who is well known for performing magical maneuvers with his stick, the puck and his body.

Turk, was nicknamed after Walter "Turk" Broda of Maple Leaf fame back in the '40s and '50s. Turk is a roly-poly kind of guy with a perpetual smile. Maybe he was just happy to be alive after surviving intestinal cancer and is still playing organized shinny 12 or 13 years after his life-threatening scare. Turk was a long time Old Boy, one of the "originals" and an Honorary Life Member.

One of the funniest and most interesting old guys to play sports is a robust looking guy with a "brush cut" as such male coiffures used to be referred to "back when", i.e., in the '40s and '50s. **Hans** is his name and almost any activity is his game. This rather large, meaning that he probably weighed more than 250 pounds, handsome old "kraut" really liked the sauerkraut, wurst and all that went with it, was originally from the Bavaria region of Germany. Despite his strong, aggressive style of play, his eyes twinkle, his face is smiling and he had an endless stream of jokes, funny sayings, one-liners and anecdotes, both on and off of the ice. As a former high school teacher, he reportedly had great rapport with his students, just like he enjoys with his "jockular" cronies, on and off of the ice.

Dr. Phil, the dentist. Phil is not related to the tv personality who offers advice to people with social-psychological and other personal problems. Our Phil is always pleasant and smiling (cynically said to be promoting his dental work, although when you think about it, he does not work on his own teeth, does he???). This guy is a "gung ho" player who is a good skater. He skates miles but rarely scores or even makes a good play but he is there, doing his best, having a good time and a great contributor to Old Boys camaraderie.

Zak, the occasional Coach. Zak usually comes out to "coach" one of the older teams in the annual Joxville tournament. Well into his 70s, he is very vital, gregarious and has a great sense of humor ... one of those pleasant people with a perpetual smile which breaks into an easy laugh. Zak makes others feel so good just by being there ... wherever. Despite being relatively small, about 5'6" and about 160 pounds, his laugh can be heard around an arena. This cigar chewing, former defenceman is an avid fan of hockey at all levels, especially kids hockey to which he is known to be a very generous, although anonymous donor.

Rex. This big, old outdoors guy is a former rodeo performer and champion bronc rider. In his "second life", he became a gifted hockey player and painter (water colors and oils). Watching him use his hockey stick and his paint brushes is quite a contrast but he is very skilled with both.

Oddie or **Aud** are take offs from Audrey who, like Hank, detests his given name. In fact, he strongly, even vehemently abhors the name and can be inclined to anger, rage and violence (often feigned and greatly exaggerated) against anyone who calls him by his given name. Since he is a rather large, strong man, most old timers refrain from antagonizing the Odd guy. He is another naturally funny man and a clever prankster when he is not being antagonized. Even when he is playing hockey, which usually requires some intensity and concentration, old Oddie is smiling ... sort of like Garfield, the comic strip cat. He is having fun and it shows all over his face. Like Max, he chatters a lot while he is playing. But he is a good guy --- the prototype old timer ... solid player, enthusiastic and funny --- a great combination.

Thinking about prototypical old timers, Joxville was blessed with several of them, most of whom were involved in forming and sustaining the Old Boys and their association over the years. There was old Wes and Leo, two former N.H.L.ers who played for years in "the bigs" before returning to their "old hometown", to work, raise their families and have a civilized life style which included playing old timer hockey twice a week. A few years later, Jimmy joined his former New York Ranger team mates after he had established his ranch near Clear Creek and had the time to commute for the glorified shinny games in Joxville. Big Stan, who had had a couple of "cups of coffee" with Les Canadiens back in the '50s, or was it the '60s, also joined the Old Boys and played beautifully for years.

The four ex-N.H.L.ers brought a certain classy elan to playing the game. They did **not** go charging around the rink like runaway bulls, bumping and crashing into others, grabbing and hooking with their sticks or waving them in the air, up around the other players' eyes. No, these classy guys skated and handled the puck so beautifully, minimizing their efforts and maximizing their results. Those "originals" and their classy play are missed. Fortunately, they are still alive and able to share some of their stories with the Old Boys, usually at the odd league event or, almost always, in Tim Horton's coffee shop. Coincidentally, all four of them played against Tim in the NHL.

Thus endeth the intros to most of the old geezers who play for and against the Old Boys. As the stories unfold, the odd other old guy will come in and out of the lore. They all add to the fun of the game and its "action". So, as one bumper stick states, "get in, buckle up and let's go!".

III. Where's the Action? Off the Ice!!!

Like Nathan Detroit's "oldest floating crap game" (of Guys and Dolls infamy), it could be anywhere!!

When it comes to ruminating about "action" for most shinny-playing geezers, one has to be creative, to think dynamically and well "outside of the box", to borrow a trite old "saw", like in a saying. Being an old boy hockey player can be much more (or less) than actually playing organized shinny. These fellows find their "action" in many different places, like arenas or rinks, restaurants, coffee shops, pubs, bars, golf courses, ball diamonds, strip joints, gambling casinos and other emporia of sin, vacation spots, doctors' offices, hospitals, at work (maybe) and only the Lord knows where else. So, to make some sense out of the "comings and goings" or meanderings of the oldsters, an effort will be made to look at their activities, selectively and discretely, both off and on the ice. In effect, the generic, not geriatric, answers to the basic question "Where's the Action" are: Off the Ice (this segment) and On the Ice, (the following selection of eclectic thoughts and mutterings).

True, "dyed (hopefully not died) in the wool", legitimate old blokes find that most of their action time is spent off of the ice, in any number of places as just mentioned. However, given the intensity of playing hockey, especially if the puckster is into his '60s, '70s or beyond, the action is greatest when they are playing and recovering, like when gasping or hyperventilating, from their few minutes of actual play on the ice. For their typical 20 to 30 minutes of ice time in a game, most old gaffers who play hockey will spend half an hour getting their gear together at home and putting it into a vehicle. Then they will likely need the best part of an hour (or more) to commute (some socially responsible old guys even "car pool") to the arena and another good while to haul their gear from the parking lot into a dressing room. Note: None of this preparation schedule includes time out for a snooze, coffee, tea, love-making or other distractions.

That hour and a half will likely be exceeded following the contest. Very few Old Boys hurry away from the dressing room, unless they are a doctor, utility service man or somebody else "on call". To begin with, most old guys seem to need a lot of time to take off their gear (especially their skates for obvious reasons such as advanced fatigue, big bellies and short arms), shower (some even shave, probably because they have a "promise" awaiting them), dry off (and there's a lot to dry, some of it in hard-to-reach places), put on their clothes, put in their false teeth, brush their receding hair, pack their stinky, soggy gear, have a few drinks, relax, shoot the breeze and return to their abode ... oftentimes via a friendly bar, pub, restaurant or other place of libation, eats and conviviality. Fun times ... you betcha!!!

Roughly speaking, old timers need anywhere from three to five hours (or 180-300 minutes) to play "their game" for 20 - 30 minutes, give or take three standard deviations if one is statistically inclined. Taking that time is fine with them because time is *not* of the essence for most old guys, unlike their younger, more driven, up-tight, overly stressed, hyper-efficient and productive days of yore. Old geezers come to realize the importance of being alive, in the fullest sense of the word, and enjoying life. They might want to plant, tend and pick the roses as well as smell them. They can hear the clock ticking, the gong of the hours on the grandfather clock and know that time is running out. So they are going to enjoy themselves as much as they can or are able. That is why all of the activities related to the game, especially the priceless camaraderie, are so important, probably even more so than actually playing the game. After retiring as a player, that youngster, Wayne Gretzky, discovered how much he missed his team mates and others in the dressing room, the joking, teasing, story-telling, laughing and other fun activities, the exciting times, super-charged atmosphere and all of the electric interactions and irreplaceable camaraderie of the game after he retired. The Great One did not take much time to became part of the struggling ownership of the Phoenix Coyotes (which really sounds like it should be spelled as Kiotes), getting involved with the management of Team Canada and, ultimately, coaching the Kiotes. And why not?

For most aging guys, the importance of camaraderie grows stronger with each passing year, to the point that some of the old guys are really quite happy and satisfied just spending their evenings in the dressing rooms ... "coaching", filling water bottles, passing around the beer and soda pop or just "hanging out" as the kids say ... as long as they are having some fun with their old buddies. Oldster bonds are strong and enduring. That's the main reason that the Old Boys see Jock, Zak, Freddie, Matty, Colly and other odds and sods from time to time, especially when the Joxville tournament is being held. With increasing age and decreasing physical conditions, actually getting out on the ice and playing the game becomes a pain or a series of pains --- in the back, the hips, knees, legs, arms, shoulders, head, various and sundry other parts of the body. Who needs that kind of misery?

Within the inner sanctums

Dressing rooms provide the predominant places where most of the off ice "action" happens. Once they are in the dressing room, most of old guys' actions become more focused with most of their energy and effort devoted to putting on and taking off their gear. While the sounds will never be heard in a symphony or even a rock tune, they are sort of a strange "music to the ear" of an old timer. In their inner sanctum, grunts, groans and other manly and sometimes disgusting, sounds are heard as the old guys put on their gear. Some gentle huffing, puffing and muttering will be heard especially when the old fellows are bending over trying to put on and lace up their skates. The heavy huffing and puffing is heard when they are trying to get those *&#+?>*?! skates off their feet which for some reason or other seem further away each year. Seriously speaking, some old guys have difficulty seeing or cannot see their feet because of the massive bellies that block their view. Imagine putting on skates, boots or shoes without being able to see one's feet! Getting their skates on and off are two vital challenges of many old players. And there are other physical and perceptual hurdles that have to be hopped before the Old Boys are ready to play ... on the ice.

If anyone is interested, each player takes the gear out of his bag, those sensually and ecologically repugnant bags, and puts it on in various, often unique, ways. Some take their gear out and put it on one piece at a time, like my long ago boyhood friend's father counting inventory, such as cans of paint, tools, nuts and bolts, in the family hardware store fifty years or so ago. Others virtually dump their gear out on the floor, like a dump truck driver dumps a load of rocks. Then they decide what they are going to put on, rummage around for the item and put it on. Oldsters repeat such a "process" until such time as they think or maybe, more precisely, feel or sense intuitively that they have all of their gear, more or less on the appropriate parts of their body.

But, it is not uncommon for old guys to remember that they did *not* put on their can, girdle (for their Cooperalls and looking svelte), shoulder pads, suspenders or some other item(s) as they stand up, get their balance and waddle, hobble or stagger toward the ice (surface, not cubes). Worse still is the fully dressed hockey player who feels the pressure to pee just before he heads toward the ice. Now that is a choice for expert decision analysts to ponder. "To pee or not to pee? ... that is the question! --- sounds sort of Shakespearean. Then there is the matter of remembering to take out the false teeth or plate, put in the contact lens, take some pills or whatever else is essential to playing the game ... and surviving.

After the pain and suffering of getting dressed, playing the game and then taking the gear off their tired, old aching "bods", it seems only natural and logical again that the old fellas head for the coffee shops ("hockey brother" Tim Horton's is a big favorite), restaurants, cafes, pubs, bars and wherever two or three are gathered in the name and spirit of hockey and related activities. That covers a multitude of sins, mostly of a verbal kind.

Wherever the old guys locate there is bound to be many stories, opinions, quips, jokes, anecdotes, a rare wise comment and lots of laughter. Based on non-scientific observations over many years, one can conclude that old timer hockey players (or pretenders) probably laugh and enjoy life more than any other group of people, with the possible exception of clowns, well-fed babies, giggly young girls and boys. As will be evident, hopefully, in the following quips, anecdotes, stories and what have you, old timers' "action" happens almost anywhere they come together in twos, threes or great multitudes.

Celebrations and other joyous occasions

Some Old Boys consider just living, "being on the right side of the grass", to be a cause for celebration. Most people, if they have lived and survived six, seven or more decades, readily agree. Every morning when they wake up and get out of bed they celebrate life and living, often one day at a time, more or less like Buddhists. Better still, and an another reason to celebrate, is being relatively healthy, having happy, meaningful relationships and truly good friends as well as interesting acquaintances, like most of their old boy buddies. Anything beyond such generic (or geriatric) celebrations is a huge windfall. Remember the old shinny players' mantra: life is simple: eat, drink and play hockey.

Birthdays (not death or dying days)

What is more special to most people, especially for children and old folks, than celebrating a birthday, although for greatly differing reasons? Like older folks, youngsters love birthdays because they are the focus of attention from family and friends. Where the two age groups differ is that the kids look forward to and relish the occasion, especially for the "loot", i.e., gifts, cake, drinks, entertainment and other materialistic consumer items showered upon them. By comparison, old guys and gals just treasure the fact that they are still alive and hopefully healthy and happy. The kids dig the tangible; the old folks enjoy the intangible. Be that as it may, birthdays are special, some moreso than others, like Max's 65th, Big Billy's 60th and Jean Pierre's 55th. What made these occasions special was the fact that they were celebrated in unusual places and unconventional ways ... as you are about to discover.

The anniversaries of old timers' birth are a mixed blessing. While most old geezers are happy to be alive and looking for more good days and nights, like in sound sleeps, there is the nagging thought that each year is one closer to the inevitable. So, different guys have different attitudes and take their own approaches to birthdays. Given his heart attack and other personal problems, Max was just thankful to be alive and able to enjoy another hockey game, day, month, year. Most of the Old Boys share that view, realizing that at any time they, a hockey buddy, friend, relative or someone else important to them could pass away. "Die" is an uncommon word in the vocabulary of the Old Boys. They tend to use symbolic words like "passed on" (no pun is intended), "left us", "gone to meet their Maker", "be with their family, friends or loved ones" or other discrete terms. So, the celebration of life and each annual anniversary of it is special to old guys and gals.

Warning: what follows may not be suitable for some readers. Parental guidance might be advisable

Max's "exotic" 65th

For most people, reaching the age of three score and five is something of a milestone. Maybe that age is when people who have worked for many years are ready to retire, get their pension, "kick back", relax and do what they really want to do, like travel, bird watch (on the beach, in the trees and elsewhere), tend their garden, paint landscapes or the back fence, sing, dance, read or whatever else meets their fancy (whatever that means). In effect, they have lived long enough to gain their freedom from the duties and obligations of being a "bread winner", a parent, grandparent, a responsible member of the community and other roles self-imposed or bestowed upon them by family, friends and society at large. And, if the government and other organizations with which they have been employed have managed their pension funds wisely and that's a big "IF", then the old guys and gals may reap the fruits of their labors at ages when they do not feel like or are unable to labor any more. Ah, the joys of "freedom 55", 60, 65, whatever age!!!

Well, poor old Max was not so fortunate to be "foot loose and fancy free" when he reached 65 years of age. (Years later, he is still "working like a dog") As his previous introduction revealed, the little guy with the wonky heart had had a tough life. His road through life had been filled with lots of potholes, bridges washed out and some serious detours. He had grown up in poverty during the "dirty thirties" and started working to support his family and self at the ripe old age of 15 years. His education in the "school of hard knocks" prepared him for little more than low level jobs that had devolved into menial labor as he aged. Yet, he never complained about the cards of life that he had been dealt.

Even after losing his best job because of drinking problems, being divorced by his wife, estranged by his oldest daughter, her husband and children and suffering a near fatal heart attack, the gutsy little 5'8", 165 pound trooper "soldiered on". Following his heart attack and that's another story for later, he went back to his job with the Department of Public Works, changed his life style, especially his eating and boozing habits and returned to playing for the Old Boys. And, pardon the pun, what a heartfelt welcome Max received from the guys upon returning to his team.

So, when dear old Max's 65th was approaching, a few of the Old Boys started planning an event while sucking back a few brew one cold, miserable night following a spirited shinny contest, Guy, Big Gerry, Dumbo (a non-playing oldster) and some other Old Boys were "brainstorming" and *scheming* for a celebration that would be very special for their aging friend and team mate or, in their words of endearment, "the old bugger". The question was: what would be really unique and meaningful for Max ... an event that he would never forget, even through the dementia years of his life???

Well, the mental machinations started slowly with some rather feeble ideas like buying him a present or two, like a hockey stick "with some goals in it", a used Maple Leafs' sweater (he was a long time Toronto fan --- damn fool), a kid's sized can (for obvious and not-so-obvious reasons), some used long johns and/or a birthday cake. Bingo!!! Some eyes lit up, brains started to whirl and creak. The Old Boys were on a roll. As more beer was soaked up, increasingly wild and crazy ideas came tumbling out of their mouths. The idea of a birthday cake sparked more creative and interesting suggestions, like a big birthday cake with a chick (young female) jumping out of it ... better still a nude chick jumping out of it. Such provocative suggestions led Big Gerry to suggest that maybe a stripper could be hired for a brief appearance at the hockey game on Max's 65th. "YA!!! now we're cooking", thundered big old Dumbo, his massive girth shaking with laughter and merriment. "Ya!!! that's a damned good idea ... let's do it. Yaaaa!!!".

So the idea was hatched that a lady who shucked her clothes "professionally" would be hired for a while before the Old Boys played Les Rouge Rogues on the same night as Max's birthday. Big Gerry would be in charge of arranging for the lady's appearance, its timing and the nature of her brief performance. James, the serious-faced engineer but mischievous fellow that he really was beneath his mask of professionalism, was in charge of arranging for the two teams to be in the Old Boys' dressing room just prior to the highlight of the night. Dumbo, Max's best friend, would be certain that "the birthday boy" came to play that night after they went to dinner with some of the boys --- no gals allowed. This was a special boys' night out ... and the women were only too happy to oblige. Besides, they had better uses for their time and did not want to inhibit their Old Boys ... wise women!!!

For the next few weeks, an unusual amount of excitement, even electricity, was in the air of the Old Boys' dressing room. A lot of whispering went on as more and more of the team members got wind (not the flatulent form) of the pending performance. In truth, old timer hockey players are really a bunch of conservative men. They are not overly adventurous or risk-taking in their thoughts, words or, especially, their deeds. Hiring a stripper to appear in their dressing room was about as much risk as many of them could have imagined, much less actually been involved in during their lifetimes. Concern was expressed about some hearts, notably Max's, not being able to take the excitement, stress and strain. But Big Gerry, Dumbo and others were "really into" the event and were not to be deterred. And they were not. The "critical mass" was moving forward or, more appropriately, the snowball was rolling.

On a very cold night, like minus 20 odd degrees, in mid-December, all of the Old Boys turned out for their game, the late one for the evening. Normally, 20 percent, more or less, would not have shown up for a regular game in such conditions. But that game was a special event. The complete turn out by the team was notable itself because usually, Sam, Jock, sometimes Doc and the odd other old guy would be too tired, too lazy, getting laid or just watching tv and would not be there for the "late show". Not so on that miserable night in 2002. As sailors say, "All hands were on deck". The pre-game routine went fairly routinely, except so many players were there that they were practically sitting on each other in the dressing room. Be that as it was, Max seemed completely oblivious to what might be happening. He was his normal self, complaining vociferously about the %()<^&#@+*# weather, including his multi-grammatical use of the "F" word, yapping away about how miserable working outdoors was and just blathering away, almost non-stop until he went trudging out to the players' bench and ice surface beyond.

A few of the Old Boys lingered a while just to make sure that the activities were proceeding as planned. "Yup, the girl will be here sharp at 10:30", said Big Gerry confidently with a huge smile spread across his face. "You can count on it ... like money in the bank ... my son is seeing to that!" The reference to his son led the others to a series of questions about what the son did, was he a pimp, did he "know" the girl, etc, etc, etc. Gerry ignored his buddies except to say "that's his business!" which left the Old Boys with more questions, quizzical looks and smiling faces and twinkling eyes.

"How are we going to get Max and the others back off the ice and into the dressing room without him being suspicious?" asked Guy. James replied instantaneously, saying "I've talked to Hughie, the captain of the Rogues. When we start to skate off the ice, he and his team will follow, taking Max with them... gently ... to our dressing room. We will all sit down around the room ... or as many as can find some space and express best wishes to Max ... and start singing Happy Birthday to him. That will be the signal for the young lady, we hope she is young and not some old hag, to make her grand entrance. She will take it from there ... she's the pro."

And so it came to be. After a few minutes of warming up on the ice, the Old Boys skated off the ice, leaving Max looking bewildered and quizzical. His looks changed almost immediately as Les Rogues surrounded him and then escorted him off the ice, down the walkway and into the dressing room. He was ordered to sit down on the bench. A cascade of best wishes descended upon him from around the room as the old guys let out a great variety of happy expressions related to Max's birthday. Some of the utterances were joyous and pleasant, others were somewhat sarcastic and rude, even crude. But all of them were sincere, more or less reflecting the personalities of the men in the room. After a few minutes of such raucous banter, Dumbo and James started singing "Happy Birthday". Others joined in the rather flat, monotonic, uninspiring rendition of the song. Pavarottis ... they were not.

Just about the time that the durgey, draggy version of Happy Birthday was completed, into the room came two very large young men wearing black leather jackets, black pants, black boots, black gloves and dark sun glasses. "My gawd", blurted Mikey, "who are those thugs?" "The mafia", replied Sal. They really looked rather scary, like the Mafia types that Hank had actually encountered in a clients' office in Almaty, Kazakhstan.

An ominous silence fell over the room. Max and several others looked just a little bit uncertain and wary, if not down right fearful. For a few seconds, Max really looked frightened when those two monster men walked, more like marched, straight toward him. Then some nervous chuckles, laughs and a few other mixed sounds of merriment broke the tension. The joyful sounds escaped from the old guys nearest to the door. They could see what, actually who, was behind the "honor guard". Following the two huge guys was a petite little lady in a raincoat. Her chaperones, guards or whatever they were stepped aside and she started dancing slowly and provocatively toward Max. "Holy shit", exclaimed Max as he squirmed on the bench like a "cat on a hot tin roof." He was twitching and wiggling around, his face becoming pinkish and the closer the dancer came, the deeper the red flush on his face became.

Let there be no doubt about the performing abilities of the young lady. She was singing Happy Birthday very softly and seductively as she slithered so smoothly and gyrated gently toward Max. Hank was getting concerned. He had been with Max through his heart attack and was not looking forward to a repeat performance by his team mate and friend. But all he and the others in the room could do was watch ... and they did ... eyes fixated intently on the young woman who then slowly let her rain coat open and slide off her bare shoulders and body. She was nude except for a miniscule piece of wedge-shaped material that covered the pubic, not public, area of her crotch. Then, she sashayed slowly, evocatively toward Max.

Tension filled the air as some of the old guys in the room wondered if Max's heart would withstand the strain. The young lady kind of cooed at Max as she stopped right in front of him, slowly turned and then gently sat on Max's lap, who was completely encased in his hockey gear. She teased Max, by sensuously saying "Is that the way you welcome a lady wanting ... to wish you a Happy Birthday?" Max, for the first time in the memories of the Old Boys was speechless ... temporarily. He opened his mouth but no words came out ... just a few gurgling sounds that probably he had not uttered since he was a baby in his mother's arms.

Like they had been coached, the old timers around the room started chiding Max about his unwelcoming behavior. "Gee, Max is that the way to greet such a nice young lady?" "Hey Max, give her a hug ... or a kiss." "Wake up Max, you're not dreaming!" "Let's see all that charm you've been boasting about" ... and on and on and on. Soon the room was in a state of uproar as the comments, laughter and other noises filled the room and spilled out into the hallway.

Slowly, seductively the almost totally bare-naked lady bent over, closed her eyes and kissed Max on the lips for what seemed like an unduly long time. Max's eyes never closed or even blinked. In fact, they seemed like they were frozen open, like you see dead people in some grotesque movies. Then very slowly, gently the young lady withdrew her lips from his, looked kind of coyly at the slightly smiling face of the Old Boy and said softly, "You're kind of cute ... what are you doing after your game ... like two-thirty or so...?" While old Max stammered to reply, a chorus of responses came from around the room, like "he's going home, he needs his rest", or "he has a bad heart and can't take too much excitement" or "he's taken, will I do instead?"

Then, one of the enormous men dressed like a gangster bent over and picked up the stripper's coat, signalling an end to her exotic performance. Slowly, she rose from Max's lap, turned gracefully to face him, smiled sweetly and then took a few steps back into the awaiting coat. With one last wink or two, a few kisses blown to the birthday boy and some words that no one could hear over the raucous din of the room, she slipped between the two human mountains dressed in black and danced lightly out of the dressing room and apparently out of Max's life ... although he claimed he met her later, several times. But that is what a lot of old timers' stories are made of; fantasies, fluff, falsehoods and fun.

Needless to say, nothing in the known history of old timers' hockey in Joxville has come close to the celebration of Max's 65th. If Hank and the others had not experienced the event, they would have doubted quite strongly that it happened. But it did and Max still smiles when he is asked about the experience. Keep smiling Max, it makes people wonder what you're thinking.

"Chairman" Billy's 60th

By comparison, Billy's 60th was dull and really a non-event. But what it illustrates is the range of initiative and creativity that goes into the caring and thoughtfulness that old guys have toward their shinny playing brethren. Compared to the tough life that Max had endured, Big Billy's was "a piece of cake" or, more precisely, a cupcake. Seems that the Old Boys involved in planning the "low budget" celebration of the big guy's birthday claimed that they were concerned about his weight ... close to 300 pounds on a frame that was not built for such a load. Even heavy duty machinery and trucks break down when they are overloaded. Since the oldsters did not want to contribute to Billy's breakdown, they decided not to lay on a lot of grub or even a big cake. So they decided to present Big Billy with a cup cake, which metaphorically is a symbol of endearment. The presentation was made with much pomp and ceremony ... like on a paper plate with an honor guard of roguishly attired pucksters accompanying the presentation ... and, naturally, an Old Boys' rendition of the traditional happy, happy, happy song.

What made Big Billy's birthday a little unique was his grand entrance onto the ice for the pre-game warm up. Dirk, one of the big guy's best friends and a bit of a prankster, thought it would be a good idea if the birthday boy was driven around the ice for all to see and acclaim. Hiring a limo was out of the question, if for no other reason that it cost too damned much. Try as he might Dirk and a few other Old Boys could not convince the rink attendant to drive Big Billy around the rink on the Zamboni ... the driver had some hang up about it being against city policy, possible legal liability, insurance and other rather lame, although technically strong, excuses. So James, in his infinite technical wisdom brought out a chair from one of the rooms and proceeded to position it beneath the big guy's behind, pushed it gently forward until Big Billy plunked down onto it and then, with help from Dirk and a couple of others, proceeded to push the birthday boy around the rink to a chorus of Happy Birthdays and various hoots, shouts and waves of laughter. The small chair holding the huge man was symbolic of the contrasts found in the old geezers and their related activities and antics. And, the ultimate irony of the hijinks was that Dirk and Big Billy both received delay of game penalties from miserable old Mel, the referee without any sense of humor.

Guy gets a funky Happy Birthday serenade

One night in the inner sanctum, after another hard fought loss, someone said something about birthdays. In his affable, low key, laid back way Boomer mentioned that Guy had a birthday soon ... like maybe tonight. There's Guy, the tired old speedster sitting in his "long johns", looking bedraggled and mostly undressed, getting ready to finish that task and head for the shower, one of the purest joys for most of us, especially after a hockey game. (In years gone by, that joy would have been a result of "getting laid" after the game. Oh, how the sources of joy change over the years.) Guy was in a rather pensive mood, his mind off somewhere in space or the past, who mumbled something in the affirmative and apparently that was a cue for randy Andy. Still in his sweaty, stained, scuzzy underwear, Andy jumped up and strolled over in front of the startled Guy and started singing and reciting a version of Happy Birthday, unheard of by the Old Boys until that moment --- truly a scene to remember ... or to forget.

First, you have to picture the scene: a room full of tuckered out, sweaty old shinny players wondering what the hell Andy was going to do. Was he going to kiss Guy, berate him, sit on his lap like the hooker did for Max. The Lord only knew what that flakey goalie might do. And Andy sure had the Old Boys' rapt attention. Then he "strikes a pose", sort of like Elvis or any one of the many other rockin' 'n rollin', hip swingin', crotch grindin' "geetar" players ... and he started strumming his imaginary instrument and singing. Well, the song seemed to be endless. Two or three times, when Andy took a pregnant pause, appropriate term for fat-bellied people, some of the Old Boys started to clap, hoot and holler. Andy continued on enthusiastically with his unique rendition; partly singing, partly reciting the words. The raucous laughter grew in volume and range, like a person experiences while walking toward Niagara Falls and its thunderous roars as the water cascades over the rocks into the abyss below.

Here are the words that Andy sang, recited and otherwise uttered to the bemused birthday boy:

> "Once a year we celebrate with stupid hats and plastic plates
> The fact that you were able to make another trip around the sun
> And the whole clan gathers round and gifts and laughter do abound
> Then you let out a joyful sound and we sing that stupid song
>
> Happy Birthday, now you're one year older
> Happy Birthday, your life is still not over
> Happy Birthday, you did not accomplish much
> But you didn't die this year ... I guess that's good enough

So let's drink to your fading health and hope you don't remind yourself
Your chance of finding fame and wealth decreases with every year
Do you feel like you're doing laps, eating food, and taking naps
Hoping that someday perhaps your life will hold some cheer

Happy Birthday what have you done that matters
Happy Birthday you're starting to get fatter
Happy Birthday its downhill from now on
Try not to remind yourself your best years are all gone

If cryogenics were all free, we could live like Walt Disney
And live for all eternity inside a block of ice
But instead our time is set, this is the only life you get
And though it hasn't ended yet sometimes you wish it might

Happy Birthday you wish you had more money
Happy Birthday you life's so sad its funny
Happy Birthday how much more can you take
But your friends are hungry ... so cut the STUPID cake

Happy Birthday, Happy Birthday, Happy Birthday tooooooo ...
Guy babeeeee!!![10]

Although the words were laden with "dark humor", Andy's performance made the song "a hoot" for the old guys in the room, especially for the birthday boy. Every one had a good laugh but no cake. James forgot to bring the cake; not even a cupcake. Oh damn!!! No problem for the Old Boys. They were clappin', hootin', hollerin', laughin' and expressin' various forms of good wishes to Guy, some joyous and others kind of crude but then that's the true nature of old timer "humor". There was the birthday boy, figuratively sitting about ten feet tall on the dressing room bench, smiling and blushing like a kid ... on his 55th ... happy as a pig in a dung pile or words to that effect. May he, like all of the other Old Boys have many more healthy, happy days if, for no other reason, that they are fine fellows and deserve them.

Other fun times

Next to playing shinny games and "makin' love" (for the high testosterone types), eating and drinking rank highly in the fun preferences and priorities of the Old Boys. After a few years, some of their eating and drinking events become kind of institutionalized ... meaning that they are done at the same place, about the same time of year, every year. Other activities, like tail gate parties, are more spontaneous in nature. For the guys who had been with the Old Boys for several seasons, a feat unto itself, the annual Chinese dinner was a special event, in part because they could stuff themselves 'til their eyes bulged and not gain any weight ... permanently. In part, it was special because they would go to the China Gardens where Henry Ho always "took good care of the boys." Over the years, the new wave of Old Boys were more interested in pizza and chicken wings than they were in Chinese food. Even old timers change over time, believe it or not!!! C'est dommage ... what a shame ... Henry Ho's Chinese food was so much better than any sauced-up skinny wings or spicy pizza.

When it came to decision making, the Old Boys were a very consensual group, much like the Inuit of northern Canada. No acrimonious, conflict-laden, hard nosed negotiating had to be done. Anytime from mid-October until the end of the season, upon some player's initiative or query, the Old Boys would check on the funds they had in the "beer and penalty fund". Max, who would make any accountant or controller proud, would announce, with great pride and gusto, that the fund was flush or words to that effect.

To the great unwashed, the nature of that fund might not be obvious. So, a few words of explanation are in order (whatever "in order" means). The Old Boys pay a premium for their beer after each game. For ten years or more, the price was 3 beers for $5. Last year, it was increased to 2 beers for $5; an increase of roughly 50 percent ... highly inflationary and a cause for protest, if not rioting. (No wonder the Bank of Canada was raising interest rates.)

Be that as it may, the "profits" were accumulated until there were enough for some kind of a "bash". Additional contributions to "the beer fund" were made when Old Boys were given the occasional penalty. They contributed $2 for each trip to the "sin bin". Some, like Big Gerry, Bad Barry, Dirk and even Boom Boom, contributed more frequently to the fund because they had a propensity for penalties. Oh, and one other source of beer fund revenue came from "buying a round" for the team when an Old Boy scored a hat trick or performed a miracle and had a shutout. To the great unwashed, that may seem like a penalty rather than a reward for outstanding performance. But you have to understand the convoluted culture and perverse psyche of old shinny players. Buying a round is really an honor. It symbolizes exceptional performance and is recognition of such performance. Some guys who do not play goal or who are not prolific goal scorers yearn for the time when they can buy a round --- it's a real status symbol, despite the phony grumbling about having to put out $20 (cheap round) to buy beer, other booze or pop for a "bunch of slackers", etc, etc, etc.

So, before, during or after a game in early November, just after the effects of over-indulging during (Canadian) Thanksgiving and before their stomachs had shrunk, one or more of the Old Boys would raise the question about money in the beer fund. On one such occasion, Max who was in charge of bringing the beer and managing all of the proceeds from the beer and penalty fund, "figured there was about 400 bucks in the kitty". (Question: how many female pigs and male deer does it take to make half a million dollars? Answer: 500 sows and bucks!) Sorry but it just kind of popped into mind and it never hurts to repeat one of your dear mother's old jokes, does it? Seems fitting for old timers' tales!

Annual Chinese feast

In years gone by, before the onslaught of chicken wings and pizza devotees, the Old Boys used to open up the "beer fund" and count their nickels, dimes, quarters, loonies, toonies and big bills. Inevitably, they would decide it was time to have a "boys' night out" and go to Henry Ho's. One of the expressed reasons for this special event, which usually took place in mid-November, was to fill the gap in over-eating and boozing between Thanksgiving and Christmas. A more genuine reason was to enjoy the camaraderie of the team. And what better way than sitting around a large table, yakking away, laughing, hootin' and hollerin' and just having a good, old-fashioned fun time? Another reason, sort of like the icing on the cake, was the wonderful hospitality of the China Garden's owner, Henry Ho. Henry was the always cheerful, happy little man with a huge, omnipresent and infectious smile. Sometimes it seemed like he had no ears because his smile spread from 'ere to 'ere'. Like many owners of Chinese restaurants and other eating places, Henry had come to Canada from China as a child. Like many other Chinese immigrants, he worked hard, studied diligently, lived frugally and became a success in "this wonderful country".

Max or some other Old Boy would phone Henry to reserve their special room for the annual fete. The room was special for several reasons. One, it isolated the boisterous oafs and their antics from the rest of the restaurant's patrons. And it provided enough space around a table with large "lazy susans" for efficiently serving the copious, excessive quantities of food that Max ordered. Max was a clever little devil. He would have the uneaten food boxed up and take it home for his evening meals during the coming week(s). The Old Boys didn't mind that rather insignificant transfer of wealth because Max really did have a hard time making ends meet on his laborer's wages.

So, one night in November, usually a Wednesday, the Old Boys would amble into the China Gardens in ones, twos or threes. They were always met by a petite, smiling lady who knew by their appearance and demeanor that they were the old guys who were to be taken to the Shanghai Room. There, in the modest splendor of a room decorated with bamboo plants, rice paper, hanging silk scrolls, some ornate pieces of furniture and oriental music playing softly, was the large table around which the old guys would set themselves. Max usually sat at the head of the table not only because he was the most senior geezer but also because "he was in charge of the dinner", which meant he ordered the numerous dishes of food, served the beer and paid, usually haggling ritualistically, over the bill with happy Henry.

About half an hour before the feast was scheduled to begin, all of the Old Boys "would be in their places with bright shiny faces", as the children's song of yore said. Punctuality was no big deal so long as there was beer to drink and other guys to shoot the breeze with. Camaraderie reigned supreme. Greetings were exchanged, stories were told, jokes were cracked and an evening of joyful conviviality was underway. All too soon, it seemed to Hank, the food was being served. Plate after plate of steaming rice, vegetables with tender pieces of beef, pork or chicken (Henry said "no dogs") in them, sweet and sours, egg rolls, wonton soup and umpteen other dishes were set before the Old Boys who became strangely quiet with the parade of food to their table. One could almost see the brains grinding away, trying to decide which serving would be the most preferred, the second most preferred, third, fourth, etc, etc, etc. Then the meal's melee began. Clean plates were given to the salivating old guys. Platters of food were attacked. Silence descended as the Old Boys "dug into" the mounds of food in front of them. Most used forks to eat with but, a few, like Big Gerry and Larry preferred chop sticks, in part to show off and in part to maintain their dexterity ... or so they said.

After the first onslaught on the mountains of mouth-watering grub, the conversations re-emerged. The anecdotes, stories and jokes came bubbling out. But there were some serious conversations, even discussions, going on, too. Larry and Big Gerry continued their never-ending discussion of the local education programs and funding. Doc, Andy and Sal argued about the health care system. Sooner or later that evening, most of the Old Boys complained about government and the politicians, although none of them except Hank had run for or been elected to a political office. What's that old saying about "walking a mile in another person's shoes" before you criticize them???

Consuming large quantities of food and beer energized the Old Boys, at least temporarily. After they finished gorging, if not drinking, was when they became rather noisy, even boisterous. Discussions, even arguments raged. Voices rose in volume, arms were waved and fists were shaken, solely for emphasis. The old guys' intensities increased along with the body language. Occasionally, buns were thrown, notably when some guy stood up and tried to make a speech. One night Bad Barry had the bright idea that the Old Boys should stand up and say some nice words about then-Prime Minister Mulroney and his government. That was a divisive topic for the Old Boys. Most of them were conservatives but had developed a strong dislike for Mr. Mulroney, his cronies and their devious government. While Barry was going on about the good government the Tories provided, bigger Sal became so annoyed that he started throwing buns at Gerry. One crusty roll smacked him Barry on the forehead. Not only did he sit down promptly but it stopped the unappetizing discourse and brought roars of laughter from the old guys.

So it went each year for several years before the newer Old Boys expressed a lack of interest and enthusiasm for Chinese food and lobbied for a change in venue and grub. While change is supposed to be good, discontinuing the annual Chinese dinner was not a good decision for a lot of reasons. The main reason was the Old Boys no longer enjoyed the hospitality of Henry Ho.

Barney's Sports Bar

In Joxville, a few small social joints met the exacting decision criteria of the Old Boys. Barney's Sports Bar was one of those establishments. Barney Bjornsen, a fifth generation Canadian of Scandinavian ancestry was crazy, literally and figuratively, about sports of any season and form ... especially hockey. Barney's, as his place was fondly known, was more or less like an English pub. It seated about 50 or 60 people but then others preferred to stand, walk around visiting or could not find an appropriate piece of furniture upon which to set their more than ample bums.

Barney's was located about half a mile or metric equivalent from the Joxville Sportsplex which included the rink, indoor soccer arena, tennis and squash courts, swimming and diving pools, wall climbing, weight rooms, running tracks, gymnastic rooms and Lord knows what else in it. The odd story of sexual activities were heard from time to time but they were only rumors ... no first hand accounts. By almost any objective standards, the complex was a first class facility. But that has bugger all to do with Barneys except that the "plex" attracted a lot of people almost every day and night who inevitably became tired, hungry and THIRSTY. Since Barney's was the closest watering hole with a sports ambience, that was where the players and their buddies headed for ... naturally... like swallows returning to pastrami or whatever that island was called. Barneys was proof of the first principle of successful retailing: location, location, location.

Barney's was the Old Boys' favorite "watering hole". After most games, some or all of the oldsters, along with the team they just played and teams from earlier games, congregated for post-game patter, banter and blather. Often they moved some tables together, just like they owned the joint. Considering how much they had "invested" in the place, they probably did own a good "piece of the action". But that's beside the point. The point is that they went to Barney's for a good time which is relatively simple to do ... have a few beers, eat some grub and shoot the breeze. Like the t-shirt slogan says: "Life is simple -eat, drink, play hockey". (Seems like that has been said before ... damned oldzheimers.)

Usually, the chitter-chatter was about hockey ... the game just played, its highlights and lowlights, outstanding and depressing plays, good goals and bad goals and on and on and on ... ad nauseum. But old timers, at least most of them, were not limited by tunnel vision. They got the big pictures, especially on jumbo-sized televisions. At Barney's, they simultaneously watched several huge tvs attached to the walls, pillars, stands, ceiling or wherever while they talked, sang, whistled, ate, drank or smoked. Who says oldsters can't walk and chew gum?. "Wow!!", "helluva play", "what a shot", "super save" and other exuberant exclamations escaped from the more impetuous geezers as they watched and carelessly expressed their emotions and impulsive thoughts about what was happening on the "boob tube", another oxymoron in the age of flat screens.

In a similar vein, some of them were not reluctant about mentioning the outstanding features of the waitresses. Call it sexism or whatever, the old guys figured that anybody who was making such a display of themselves expected to have various observations made and views expressed. So much for political correctness. Let the radical feminists and politicos be bothered about such matters. Old timers have other interests ... like different levels of hockey, other sports and some serious concerns about the environment and its degradation, pollution, waste of resources, health care, personal, family, community and local business, economic conditions, politics, government, international relations, wars, pandemics, space exploration, fun vacations and umpteen other topics too numerous to mention or remember.

For sports nuts or "animals", Barney's was a great place to be. Barney was a jovial, effervescent host. His staff were clones, sometimes clowns. The place had loads of ambience ... a mix of mellow, not raucous, excitement, down-home charm and comfort. There was even some distinction about the place, especially if one was a sports-oriented person. Posters or photos featuring superstar athletes like Wayne, Mario, Sid the Kid, Pinball, A Rod, Steve Nash, Becks (soccer striker, not the beer) and numerous other players, banners, sweaters, caps, sticks, pucks, you name it were stuck on the walls, hanging from the ceiling, taped to the bar and anywhere else Barney and his staff could find space to display sports-related items. Most chairs were padded to comfort the weary, often bruised bodies that set upon them. A few tables were large enough to get the gang around. Food was passable without any dysentery. No stomach pumps were needed ... or available. Various brands and types of beer were cold, served in big jugs and good-sized mugs, with a "deal" for the Old Boys, usually three jugs for the price of two. Service was cheerful and effective; not too fast and rushing, not too slow or inattentive, just right ... call it the Goldilocks service, despite the presence of some very attractive brunettes and red heads ... male and female.

At Barney's and places like it, the old guys have a damned good time. That's "what it's all about", the "bottom line" and other old clichés that express the same idea, only in different words. So it goes for an hour or *more* ... a few fellows were not too keen to go home. Some wait "until the last dog is hung" or Barney cuts off the drinks. But they're old enough, if not smart enough at times, to know when to call it a night. Sooner or later, they ate their last bite, finished their drinks, bid "adieu", "ciao" "adios" or "cheers" and headed for the door, stopping along the way to pee, share another story and shoot the breeze with the omnipresent Barney as they passed by the long, darkly stained, carved oak wood bar and out the front door into the cold dark night.

Bar-b-qs

"Barbies" as the Aussies and Kiwis refer to outdoor cooking and related activities around a barbecue pit or grill, are a big favorite with the old guys and their gals. The ladies don't have to make a meal and the guys have an opportunity to be with the boys, have a beer or three, eat too much without momma yapping at them, shoot the breeze, enjoy the great outdoors and generally have a damned good time. The Old Boys usually have two barbies a year; one in the Spring and the other in the Autumn; usually in the same place, Pope's Park and with the same menu; burgers, "smokies", cold sloe and potato salad, buns, "butter" which was really margarine, relish, mustard, ketchup, cookies, coffee, pop and BEER. In the fall, fresh corn was served. In the spring, extra veggies like carrots, cauliflower and broccoli buds or whatever they are called were being served. All in all, they were great times. How could they not be, considering the fact that they were held in a beautiful natural setting at prime times of the year, families were welcome, the food was very good and there was no charge, except for the booze. As Max so repetitively and so tiresomely says, "It doesn't get any better than this". For the dear old bugger and many others, that's probably quite true.

House parties or other get-togethers

Question: Who are the "biggest party animals" – the old guys or the gals? While most old timers enjoy getting together with friends, the gals seem to be even more strongly motivated to do so ... for almost any kind of social activity. Maybe their social propensities validate the stereotype of women as social mammals. Be that as it may or any other month (sorry for the bad pun), the oldsters did get together for a variety of activities during every season, if not month, of the year. Pick the month and there was at least a house party, dinner, bar-b-que and various other kinds of social gatherings.

Gentleman Jock and his charming wife Anne were two of the most frequent and most gracious people when it came to hosting social activities. And they covered the whole gamut, one of the real highlights being their Stanley Cup bash during the first Sunday of the final playoffs. Their youngest son, Stan by coincidence, made a replica of "the Cup" out of tin and aluminum foil. It looked quite authentic, except no one would dare drink out of it like the NHL champions do. Having even a replica of the Stanley Cup was like having a shrine or an altar at which to worship. Ardent hockey fans consider Lord Stanley's magnificent mug to be worthy of worship. For many Canadians and growing numbers of Americans and Europeans, hockey has become a religion in the generic meaning of the word and the Stanley Cup is its holy vessel. Play-off time is its annual celebration.

Each Spring cum early Summer, a mild form of playoff fervor would infect the Old Boys. Over the years, what started out as a cozy little party in the Coach's basement steadily expanded throughout their home. As the N.H.L., true to its corporatism, kept increasing the number of teams, extending the season and playoffs from early Spring to Summer, the Stanley Cup Party overflowed the house and ended up being a barbie, mostly outside of their good-sized house, although subject to the vagaries of the "summer" weather.

That was fine with the Old Boys who preferred the great outdoors to the more claustrophobic confines of houses and other buildings, especially during the non-winter, poor sledding months, likely June through August. Other than predictably unpredictable weather, about the only problem with having a bar-b-que outdoors was the quality of the tv picture. Jock only had a small television for the outdoors and was "too dam Scotch" to buy a larger one for only a few hours each year. Besides, the bright light of a sunny summer day and evening detracted from the contrast needed for the best quality picture. So, some of the really keen hockey fans and hungry oldsters, especially with fading eyesight, would go back and forth from the house to the yard, much like tennis balls during a match. No problem, "Hakuna Matata", as they sing in the Lion King.

Everybody was happy and having a good time except for the genial host and his even more genial wife. They seemed to get stuck with doing most of the work, although over the years Jock, citing age, fatigue and seniority declared that volunteers need to bring some salads or deserts and do the bar-b-quing. Again, no problem: umpteen old guys volunteered to cook the steaks, chops, burgers and whatever else there was to bar-b-que. In fact, some Old Boys, like Big Gerry, Dirk and Boom Boom preferred to cook their own meat (so to speak). Otherwise, if they let those "hide tanners" cook the meat it would end up being like shoe leather; tough and tasteless. Besides, there were some very experienced, if not expert, chefs in the ranks of the Old Boys. But that should not be surprising, given the fact that the best chefs in the world are of the male gender. How do you like those apples: Eves???

So, there they were ... about 15 or 20 old guys and their companions out in the McKays' backyard on the soft green grass, among the rose, peony and potentilla bushes, cherry and apple trees, various and sundry other flowering plants with the sun shining brightly and warmly upon them. How good was that? As the afternoon went on, it got even better. There was plenty of beer and other libations, snacks of all kinds, some of which were even nutritious like veggies and the mouth-watering, drool-inducing fragrances of baking potatoes and sizzling steaks, chops, burgers and sausages. Yummers!!!

The ebb and flow of camaraderie pervaded all of these activities. Jokes and funny stories were being told about hockey, various other sports and umpteen personal experiences, some too dicey, spicy or confidential to reveal. Such story-telling was almost certain to evoke raucous roars of laughter. Gentleman Jock, Mikey and Andy were great, even captivating, story tellers. The dour Scot was especially entertaining. He was a walking, talking history book and as a former travelling salesman, a super teller of tales. Almost certainly, Mikey's jokes resulted in spontaneous outbursts of raucous laughter. Naturally, there was Andy telling jokes, singing songs and even strumming a real guitar. In sharp contrast, some of the more serious guys and gals were involved in topical discussions, their faces masked with solemn expressions, eyes squinting, brows furrowed and voices muffled as they talked about investments, politics, health and other matters of concern.

Then there was the crew of cooks who were happy to relieve Jock of that task. Some really enjoyed cooking or, at least, bar-b-quing. As Willie would exclaim, usually about once an hour, "It gives me an opportunity for creative expression" to which any number of responses would come, like "you think your big belly is a creative expression", "burning a hot dog is creative?" or "maybe you should try painting ... your back fence". And so it would go, all too quickly, through the pleasant afternoon and evening until the game was over, the food was eaten, the mess was cleaned up and the gals started to remind the guys that "they'd had enough to drink", "it was time to go home" and "I'll drive". "Yes ma'am", muttered the odd Old Boy.

Similar "get togethers" were held at Grey Cup or Super Bowl time, to honor the saints, like Patrick and Andrew, celebrate Al Capp's (of Little Abner cartoon fame) and anyone else's birthday, Oktobrefest, Halloween, New Years and as many other occasions as the old guys and their gals could conjure up. While the themes varied, the social activities, interactions, benefits and costs were similar. For a few bucks, a subsequent gut ache from over-eating and a headache from over-imbibing, the fun times were immeasurable. Most of the party animals and the rest of the oldsters could hardly wait for the next one.

Vacations - whenever, wherever, you name it! Let's go!!!

Taking time off from one's job, regular routine of mundane duties, onerous responsibilities and even from the Old Boys' team was fine with most of them as long as they could relax, have a good time and return sooner or later to their "normal way of living". Most of the old folks liked to travel and find new or different place to recreate and enjoy themselves with family, friends and "significant others", whatever that meant. Others, especially the really keen tournament types, went to several such events each year, especially to "The Snoopy" and Ocean City as well as slow pitch ball, golf, lawn bowling, chess, checkers, cribbage, tidily winks and any other kind of tournament they could arrange and afford. Some, like Boom Boom, Doc and Big Gerry, mixed some vacation time into their work travel and ripped-off their unsuspecting fellow taxpayers while they were at it. But that's another issue for another time.

During the "normal" hockey season, meaning the time from early October to the end of March or the six months of good sleddin' in the Great White North, about one seventh or 14.285714 percent of the oldsters headed for warmer climes. Historically, and sometimes hysterically, most of them went to the southern climes of the Excited States or what some Canadians viewed as the world's largest amusement park. Other, more discerning types, took off for Mexico, South America, Caribbean countries and other hot spots around the world, like Fiji, Tahiti and Kookamonga. As much as they loved Canada and playing hockey, warm weather was a strong attraction, especially for those old crocks with the arthritic or rheumatoid ankles, knees, hips, shoulders, elbows, wrists and other joints in their bodies.

Boom Boom, Big Gerry and Hank were the "big travellers" on the Old Boys' team. They really enjoyed traveling and sharing travel stories, intelligence and whatever else they could think about with each other and any other warm body who was willing to listen, whether or not they were interested. Listen in on one of their animated conversations about recent travels.

Hank: "Hey Boom Boom, nice to see you back! Where have you been for the past month or two ... going around the world ... and I don't mean in a naughty sort of way?"

Boom Boom: "Look who's talking ... squawking ... about being away. Seems like you were gone most of last season ... sure helped our win-loss average ..."

Hank: "I was away on business ..."

Big Gerry (interjecting): "Ya, monkey business ..."

Hank: "Hush your mouth oh big Buddha. I was in Romania doing a volunteer development project ... in fact, I did two of them while I was there ... saved the taxpayers lots of money.. and made a greater contribution to the well-being of the world."

Boom Boom: "Cow paddies ... Hank. What do mean a volunteer project ... development? Off you go on taxpayers' money ... having a good time ... eating and drinking ... living it up ... and we pay."

Hank: "Wouldn't that be nice ... that sounds like what you do ... when you go to those gummit conferences ... vacationing in all those warm, sunny places ... in January and February. Talk about ripping of the taxpayer!"

Sal (thunderously): "Give it a rest you guys. You make me sick with all your travel stories while some of us stay home ... work like mules and then support your running around the world ... spending our taxes ... that stinks!.

Tournaments as vacations

Shinny games often provide the focus, rationale and/or destination for mini-vacations for old guys and gals. Old timers' hockey tournaments are held almost any month and almost anywhere in the whole wide world. In the "Great White North", to borrow a term from those hosers, the Mackenzie brothers, the Canadian Adult Recreational Hockey Association (CARHA for short) listed around 270 tournaments in the early years of the 21st century. That number included a few tournaments for the gentler gender. Whoever heard of an old timers' tournament for women? The term "old timer" is incongruent with women. As wise or, at least, highly experienced old guys know, there are no old women --- in hockey or elsewhere in the universe. Maybe a few have gained "senior" status but any person who is 90 years or older isn't likely to be playing hockey anyhow or any way. How's that for being discrete ... or patronizing?

So, back to the tournament trail we go briefly (an entire chapter is devoted to such events later on in this meandering narrative, a common practice for old teachers which prompts the need for another quiz.

* *

QUIZ TIME

There are scores of shinny or hockey-related tournaments held annually.

Question: In which provinces are the following sets of tournaments held???

Chetwynd and Lillooet? Elmvale and Manotick? Grand Prairie and Red Deer? Neguac and Fredericton? Brandon and Flin Flon? Biggar and Saskatoon? Corner Brook and Gander? Maniwaki and Val D'Or? Whitehorse or Inuvik?

If your Answers to the above question were British Columbia, Ontario, Alberta, New Brunswick, Manitoba, Saskatchewan, Newfoundland and Labrador, Quebec and the Yukon Territories respectively, then you deserve a case of brews. If you missed one or two of the answers, you merit a six pack. If you missed three or four of the provincial locations, you might get the booby prize. If you missed five or more, then a Grade Six Canadian geography course would be appropriate.

* *

As interesting as the names of the locations may or may not be, there are some rather creative names of the tournaments. Some of them are seasonal like the Harvest Hockey Jamboree, Halloween or Valentines. Isn't the latter a romantic touch? "Hey Charlie, old boy, what are you doing for your sweetie on Valentine's Day?" "Man, I'm taking her to the Valentine's Cup tournament in Tatamagouche (Nova Scotia)!!!" Now doesn't that sound like a winner with the ladies? Methinks they would much prefer breakfast in bed, dinner out, a dozen roses or even a box of chocolates. No? **Yes!**

Mentioning the gentler gender, a growing number of senior tournaments are for women. There's the Ripley (believe it or not?), the Sunshine Coast Ladies and the Archives Women's tournaments. Other tournaments are memorials to noteworthy people, like the Carlos Paolinelli Memorial in Prince Rupert, British Columbia, the Paul A. Thompson Memorial in Bobcaygeon, Ontario and numerous others, mainly in Ontario. Creativity and merit abound in the names and purposes of some tournaments. Tourneys are held to support worthwhile community and national charities including Easter Seals, minor hockey, children's foundation, food banks and emergency services. How about such tournaments with names that include Wiser Guys, Hogtown Hogs Hoggy, Old Cat Cup, Paint Your Wagon, Baby Boomers and Grumpy Old Men? No foolin', they actually have been held!

Jocularity (jokes? stories! "cheap shots", humorous antics, other forms of old guys' fun)

Almost inevitably, any time or place that old timers interact, jocularity is bound to happen ... in some form or other, especially with guys like Mikey, Andy and Joey the Clown. Almost immediately and so naturally, like steam and hot water bubbling up from geysers, some semblance of humor occurs when such old guys interact with one and other(s). Maybe it's a silly grin spread across a tired, wrinkly old mug, maybe it's the out-of-date, out-of-style, out-of-elbow or out-of-something shirt that one or more are wearing, maybe it's a clown outfit like roly-poly Joey, the jovial goalie from Cowtown wears or maybe it's just the naturally humorous persona of guys like Mikey, Andy and Boom Boom. Whatever it is, many of the old guys are just plainly and simply fun to be with. Almost inevitably, their fun kind of persona and its inherent talk, actions or both ooze out of their pores, mouths, gestures and other body lingo.

Capturing Mamood somebody or other (with no ethnic offence intended)

This dressing room performance was given one Thursday night in early March of a recent year. It was a cold and snowy night --- sort of like the hackneyed old line that Snoopy (of Peanuts cartoon fame) often used when he started to write a story. Old Boys trundled into the dressing room, bundled up in warm coats, toques, mitts, gloves, boots and what have you to keep warm. As might be expected, they were grumbling about the cold weather, slapping their hands together or blowing in them for warmth, stomping their feet for some reason or other, maybe to warm them or knock the snow off their boots or just an expression of disgust with the cold weather or whatever. The usual banter and blather was going on about the weather, how cold it was and how nice it would be to see Spring "pretty damned soon."

Well, in comes Mike, snortin' and fartin' like an old bull, kind of shaggy with his hair protruding from under his ball cap in various directions. He was blathering about the cold weather, snow, winter, "colder than hell", on and on and on. Most of the Old Boys tried to ignore him. But Mikey was not an inconspicuous man. He was rather large at 6' 2", 230 pounds and, at times, had a persona that was loquacious (you know, like Cassius Clay, a.k.a, Mohammed Ali), gregarious and liked attention ... immediately, if not sooner. And he had "presence". So Mike commanded or, at least, got the others' attention when he starts yakkin' about "Mamood somebody or other."

Some Old Boy: "Who the hell are you talking about, Mike"

Mike: "You know that guy they found in Pakistan or Afghanistan or one of those places over there ... one of Osama's boys ... one of his high honchos."

Max: "Ya, that must be good news for Bush ... maybe he will get the "F" out of Iraq... ."

Andy: "Ya, maybe it will help the stock market..."

Hank: "Don't hold your breath. Bully Boy Bush has his own agenda for the Iraq Invasion and occupation. He wants their oil ... the U.S. is desperate for oil and Shrub is beholden to the oil industry ... they put him into power... pardon the pun ... with 65 or 75 million bucks of campaign funding ...

Mike: "Nice pun Hank but did you see the picture of that Mamood ... like his hair was flying all over the place?."

Max: "What the hell do you expect. He was sleeping when he was arrested. He didn't have time to get an appointment with his beautician ... or even have a shave or shinola."

Mike (fixated on the guy's appearance): "But, did you see that guy? He looked like a wild ... and crazy guy!"

Andy: "Look in the mirror ... when you say that."

Mikey continued with his tirade. He seemed to be fixated with "Mahmood". There he was, standing in the middle of the dressing room, with his shirt off, his long dark hair dishevelled from thrusting his hands through it. He was waving his arms around, especially from his head outward to illustrate how wild and crazy "Mamood's" hair looked. Old Boys were laughing all around the room.

Max: "You know Mikey, you look like that Mamood guy! Maybe we should call you Mamood from now on..."

Andy: "Ya, especially since you're so moody at times. Wonder what Mamood means? ... probably man of many moods ... just like you Mikey ...!!"

Mike: "Go to hell, you guys! Here I am ... trying to keep you old buggers informed ... and you turn on me ... like a pack of wolves ... nice guys..."

Max: "Where's the crying towel? Mikey's feelings have been hurt. You sound like a wussy goalie."

Andy: "Shut up, Max ... of we'll turn your pacemaker off."

As Hank and others learned later that night from newscasts, Mike was rally ranting about Saddam Hussein just after he had been captured. He had been found in a hole in the ground, near his home town in Iraq, not in Pakistan or Afghanistan. That made Mike's story even more funny, if for no other reason than Mikey had been so adamant about the tyrant's name and where he had been captured.

Somehow the routine just does not seem as funny when describing it as it was when Mike performed it. As Heidi has said so often when she is telling about a funny incident and nobody is laughing ---"Guess you had to be there."

What's the big deal about Hank's beard?

For reasons unknown, sometimes but not very often, old guys do something a little out of the ordinary ... like Hank growing a beard. By historical and modern social standards that is not an earth-shaking act. But as has been stated before, the Old Boys are a conservative bunch. You could probably count on one hand the number of "active" old timers with a beard. Bald - yes; mustaches - maybe; hairy faces - not damned likely. So, after being away for 10 days or so, including a week in Mexico, Hank was looking a little fuzzy on the face. He'd looked scruffy before so nobody said much ... that had any meaning or merit. But, after another week or so, the questions and comments started.

James: "Did your razor break?"

Hank: "No, the mirror did!"

James walks away laughing heartily.

Boom Boom: "Does Heidi like it?"

Hank: "That's kind of personal .... isn't it?"

Boom Boom (sheepishly): "I didn't mean that ..."

Hank: "What ...?"

Boom Boom (even more sheepish, to the point of being embarrassed) "Well ...you know?"

Hank: "No ... I don't know what you mean. I'm no mind reader. Say what you mean!"

Boom Boom: "Shut up and drink you beer, fuzz face!"

Mike (joining in): "I've never had a beard ... or a mustache .... or anything like that. My nephew has a mustache . He likes it .... (adding as an afterthought) ... for some reason? Why are you growing a beard?"

Hank (trying to rationalize the hair on his face): "Shaving is a nuisance ... waste of time. I figure that if Mother Nature wanted us to be clean shaven we wouldn't have hair growing on our faces ... you know ... like our fair ladies!"

Boom Boom (rebounding aggressively, at least by old timers' standards): "Nice try, Hank! ... blaming Mother Nature for your sloth."

Hank: "What's this sloth nonsense? Where did you find that word? Sloth ... isn't that a sin? Hmmmmm ... with a snorting sound for emphasis."

Boom Boom (continuing his personal attack on Hank): "Next thing you will be telling us it makes you look wise ... like Einstein, Schweitzer ... or one of those guys."

Hank (kind of detached, thinking about Einstein, Schweitzer, Bell, Freud and their beards and musing in response): "Don't I wish ..."

Boom Boom: "Don't we all wish you would smarten up."

Mike: "That's not very nice, Boomer."

Hank: "Consider the source."

As the old saying goes "small things amuse small minds" and the drivel about Hank's beard returned following a game against the Jolly Green Giants. The yapping was started by Billy, their goalie ... in the Old Boys' dressing room. Fat Billy, as he was known by friend and foe alike, really fit the stereotype of netminders. He was round and kind of squat like a beach ball. Enough said. Consistent with the stereotype of goalies, he was a flake and idiosyncratic. So, he came visiting the Old Boys, just after he had been a big reason for the Old Boys losing. In a word, he had been "sensational", stopping virtually every puck and all of the trash talk the Old Boys could fire his way. Coming into an opponents' dressing room after frustrating their scoring efforts all game was like Daniel walking into the lion's den waving a read flag and shouting, according to one old timer who apparently had been there.

As he sauntered casually into the enemies' dressing room, Billy was barraged with "heat", "flak", other forms of verbal abuse ... you know, cheap shots like "rubbing salt into our wounds, are you Billy", "you've got guts man" or some other original utterances that were so profound that they escaped Hank. Billy shot the breeze with the Old Boys for a while. He was a "nice guy", as least ostensibly. He had been in the RCMP for many years and retired a few years ago as a Staff Sergeant. Like most oldsters, he had had his "knocks" in life, most recently a knee replacement --- seems like it was sometime last year ... or the year before. What difference does it make? Billy was back playing goal, as good as ever. Too good tonight, damn it, mused Hank half aloud.

Billy: "What's with the fuzz on your face? Wife kick you out of the house ... without your razor?

Hank: "Nope ... just growing a fur coat for winter.."

Mike (interjecting): "... like other animals..."

Billy: "You should have started sooner. Winter is just about over"

Hank: "Oh well .... I can always transplant it ... you know like sodding .... Boomer has requested a sod or two for his bald patch"

Boom Boom: "What the hell are you talking about, Hank? I don't want any of your face fur on my head ... even if it does need some."

Billy smiled and started talking rather softly, even seriously to Big Gerry. But nobody paid any more attention to the interloper from the other team. He was an old timer and that made him acceptable as one of the brotherhood, irrespective of what team he was one, even if he was a goalie who might be carrying an infectious, even fatal, disease known as "goalieitis"

Goalies revisited ... ever so briefly

As should be evident by now in this tome, goalies are a common target of stories, jocular jibes as well as pucks and out-of-control bodies. Let's face it, most of the play is directed toward the goalies. Why not the humorous side of the game, also? Most of the time, the "cheap shots" are spontaneous, like the night that Mike made an "off the wall" comment about one of the other goal tenders in the league

Mike: "Heard that Moody got married this past summer."

Andy: "You're joking, he couldn't get a woman to go to lunch with him ... even if he paid for it ... the lunch that is."

Roars of laughter roll around the room, like the guys who walk around it. Boom Boom spews a mouthful of beer out into the room which prompts Hank to say "that damned Boomer, he will never learn to laugh and drink beer."

Tales about wives, other women (usually hypothetically, imaginary, fantastically)

Old timers seem to have an endless supply of quips; some spontaneous and novel, some funny, many of them sick, others are old standards and most evoke some laughter or levity. Often, when the utterances are about their wives, girlfriends, partners or "significant others", they are one-liners or very short, often hackneyed and occasionally repetitious. Usually, much of the humor was conveyed in the body language and, to a lesser extent, in the content. As the communications guru of bygone years, Marshall McLuhan said so profoundly eons, well at least decades, ago: "the medium is the message".

Trite, mundane, disgusting utterances

Some old guys really try to be humorous and rarely succeed. They bomb or, in the vernacular of some curmudgeons, they stink. Despite being the topic of many old fellows' jocularity, there is no Viagra for humor. But some old geezers or gassers, like Max, keep on trying to be funny. Sometimes they succeed. Most times they do not. Maxie might get a few weak snickers or some forced laughter from the hackneyed old one liner, "I saw you with a different woman", especially if he could provoke some awkward or angry reaction from the recipient of a made-up story, to wit,

Max: (to a player on the Bloozers' team, recently divorced and accompanied by an attractive young brunette): "Hey Paddy, did that chick dye her hair? The one you were with last night was a blonde."

Or, how about the sick humor of Mikey and his "in the ear" favorite?

Mike: "My wife likes it in the ear. Every time I want to give it to her in the mouth, she turns her head"

Then there's Guy's "Crisco is her name".

Guy: "Hey Sam, I heard you calling to your wife the other day. You were calling her Crisco. How come ... that's not her name!"

Sam: "I don't dare call her lard ass."

As bad as those snippets of "humor" were, Big Gerry had one that was about as bad it gets. It could have been entitled "My wife wants bigger tits".

Big Gerry: "My wife was complaining the other night about her tits --- she wants bigger ones. She says she has tried exercises but doesn't want implants or anything like that. So I suggested to her that she try rubbing toilet paper between her breasts. She said 'Why should I do that?' And I told her.... look what wiping your ass has done!

Nobody ever said that all old buggers were nice ... all of the time.

"Trash talk"

Most old timers are well-mannered, self disciplined, decent men who limit their verbiage, on the ice that is, to hollering for passes and various and sundry other utterances related to the game. Rarely is there any trash talk like one sees (if they read lips) or hears from "hot shots" in "professional" sports or some mouthy teenagers. But occasionally such verbal garbage, although rather mellow like the men that it comes from, is heard ... like during the "heat of battle" in the Joxville Tournament of '98. The hometown lads, in the 55+ category, were losing a close game to the Old Buffs, a club team from Cowtown.

Desperation set in as time was running out on the Old Boys. Since he became a defenceman, away back in minor hockey, Hank had been a talker. He used his chatter, in part, to distract opposing players. So there he was in front of his team's goal, "tying up" an opposing forward when out of his mouth popped the following exclamation; "Man, you've got bad breath!" The opposing player stopped, looked kind of stunned at Hank and retorted with a hint of snarl, "What did you say?" Hank replied, "You've got bad breath". The opposing forward kind of smiled and said, "You should taste what it's like from inside. It's bloody awful. I drank too much last night". Then both players went their separate ways back up the ice ... both smiling at the exchange of verbiage.

Naturally or, some puritans would say, unnaturally, naughty, even nasty, words are exchanged between players on the ice. Old guys are not offended or even bothered usually, if some body of their age, give or take a decade or two, says: "Hey Max, you ugly old bastard " or "Guy, you stinky old fart" (or French language equivalent). Such utterances are not considered to be trash talk. In fact, they could be words of endearment or, at least, a welcome greeting. What makes the distinction between offensive and affective is the how those words are said --- the degrees of niceness or nastiness that are expressed in the tone of voice, the sneer on the face or the anger in the sayer's eyes. Old guys are human, too.

During games, most of the trash talk results from overly aggressive efforts and contact being made in front of one goal or the other and along the boards when players are vigorously trying to score a goal, gain possession or, at least, control of that elusive little black disc on the ice. Such physical contact often inflicts some emotional or physical pain or frustration upon the competitors. Such stimuli also cause some players to utter words that are not commonly accepted in churches, in public places or courteous company. Rarely, ever so rarely, are such vulgarities taken personally. Old guys tend to have thick skins, poor hearing, selective perception and limited retention, especially for words they don't want to hear. Any of their gals will attest to that. So anyhow, very little of the disgusting or otherwise antagonistic verbiage registers in the minds of the old guys. As the old saying goes, "it's like water off a duck's back" and isn't that just the way it should be ... for old guys and everybody else who is interested in a civil society.

Breakaways

Breakaways are one of the most desired, frustrating and exciting plays in hockey. Even the corporatized N.H.L. has discovered that obvious fact. For the hockey neophyte or the sadly uninformed, a breakaway usually involves player(s), usually a forward or two, sometimes three, who happen to be all alone with the puck, facing the opponent's goal (that's essential) with no other player between him/them and the other team's goal tender. Such a situation is a hockey player's dream, especially if that player is really a "sniper" and can actually score goals. Every hockey player knows how to score goals in their mind ... a head fake and a bullet shot low to the stick side of the goalie ... or a shift of the body, then draw the puck across to the back hand and "roof it" ... making the goalie's water bottle jump off the nets.

Jimmy's many chances

Scoring a breakaway goal may sound easy ... but it is not. While no known hockey expert has ever knowingly stated which is the easiest way or if there is an easy way to score a goal in hockey, even the great ones and lesser mortals will say that scoring breakaway goals isn't easy. Just ask Jimmy. He was a fast little winger who had more breakaways than anyone in the history of Joxville Oldtimers. (Although no records were kept, hearsay or oral history was reasonably valid or at least reliable). Well, no one can count the times that Jimmy would be heading up or down the ice with the puck on his stick and no one else between him and the opponents' goal, except the other team's puck stopper. And no one else was fast enough to catch him. So off Jimmy would go "90 miles an hour", stick-handling the puck and heading for the opponent's goal. Well, it didn't make any difference whether he shot the puck, deked the goalie or tried to "slam dunk" it, Jimmy would rarely score. Most times he would miss the net or, at best, hit the goalie with a shot.

Occasionally, Jimmy scored on a breakaway. Even more rarely was his breakaway goal a "biggie", meaning that it was important to the outcome of an old guys' game. One of those rare "biggies" came during a tough and tenacious tournament tussle between the Old Boys and the long time rivals, the Cowtown Rowdies. True to their name, the Rowdies were a bunch of ruffians on the ice. Lord only knows how they behaved off the ice and quite likely nobody really cared about that. On the ice, they barged around the rink like they owned it, bumping into opposing players, even goalies, like bowling balls banging into ten pins. They carried their sticks around like pitch forks, instead of on the ice where they could be used for passing the puck, shooting and scoring goals. Needless to say but it will be said anyhow, they were an aggressive gang. And they were experienced players who played very well together as a team. They were tough competition.

And so it came to pass that on the final day of the Joxville annual tourney, the Old Boys played the Rowdies in the playoff game for the "G Division" championship. Anyone who knows the alphabet probably knows that G is the seventh letter. Similarly, the G Division was the seventh level of teams in the tournament. Needless to say, but old guys will say it anyhow, the calibre of play was not threatening to the N.H.L. or any other level of competitive hockey, except maybe the over-80 category. Nonetheless, the Old Boys and the Rowdies were locked in "mortal combat" in their efforts to win the final game and achieve bragging rights for the next few days or maybe until the next game that they played against each other.

Midway through the first period Sad Sam missed a wide open goal that a Pee Wee could have scored into easily. But, Sam rose above his miscue and on the next two shifts he scored. Yippeee!!! the Old Boys were ahead 2 – 0. Since the Old Boys were rarely two goals ahead of any team, they must have been in a state of shock or complacency because, guess what, the Rowdies roared back in the second period and tied the game with two "ugly" goals. Historically, the Old Boys have not had a lot of confidence about winning games, especially tournament games when the level and intensity of the competition rises significantly above the normal level for old timers' hockey in Joxville. However, the Old Boys, backed by an outstanding game from their goalie Andy, kept the game tied until late in the third period. That was when Jimmy had another of his seemingly endless breakaways.

As they had been during most of the entire game, the Rowdies had the Old Boys "hemmed" into their own end, charging and barging around, passing, shooting, missing, being stopped by St. Andrew, getting frustrated and ever so desperately pressing for the winning goal. During one of the Rowdies' onslaughts in the Old Boys' end of the rink, Guy got momentary control of the puck and banked a pass off the boards beyond the Rowdies d'men who were "pinching in" trying to score. Out of the blue or somewhere in space flew Jimmy like a race horse heading for the homestretch. He picked up the puck (on his stick) and skated very rapidly toward the Rowdies' goal. To his team mates, Jimmy seemed to be skating far too fast and would likely lose control of the puck, shoot it wide of the net or into the goalies' pad which he had done countless times before.

Such a missed opportunity was not to be. Jimmy skated straight at the goalie, made a little fake move to his left, then pulled the puck across to his back hand and slid the puck between the goalie's pads (the "5 hole") into the net. Wonder of wonders, Jimmy had scored on a breakaway. For the Old Boys Jimmy's goal was an achievement of great distinction. The fact that it was the winning goal against the Rowdies made it a greater source of joy. If that does not seem like a "big deal", it certainly was to the Old Boys as they hugged and mobbed the little man who had scored such a big goal. Who says old timers are not competitive? or emotional? or appreciative of winning goals???

IV. Where's The Action? Old Boys Games!!!

We're cool! We play on ice!!!

Where's the action? As we saw in the previous segment of this epic series of shinny stories, old timers' interactions are more often off of the ice and could be almost anywhere --- in sports shops, Tims and other restaurants, bars, pubs and other libating establishments, while vacationing, during various tournaments, around arenas but predominantly in the dressing rooms. At this point in the evolving expose of old guys and gals, we move closer to the *action*, right into the heart and heat of the battles, more realistically, some of the relatively mild, slow-paced, somewhat skilled, more likely unskilled, even uncoordinated, unglorified and under-hyped shinny contests which could be located in a wide variety of locales with one common characteristic: ice.

This scribbler faced a dilemma in trying to convey a representative sample of the diverse places, people, their interactions, camaraderie, joys and sadness and other meaningful attributes of such a complex set of dynamic elements. So he just said "to hell with such political correctness." Let's just get close to a few games and enjoy what's happening with the Old Boys of Joxville. The setting and people involved could have been almost anywhere in the world ... north of the 36th or 37th parallel of latitude. Unfortunately, limited resources did not support such travel. So we are stuck mainly with some geezers' games in Joxville. Along the way ahead, we venture further afield (or arena) to such exotic places as Santa Rosa, Cowtown, Mountainview, Ocean City and Fruitland. There we will enjoy some games, their players, fans, friends, other activities and more good, old-fashioned fun.

What started out to be a look, listen and learn from a game or two ended up with compelling snippets from five Old Boys' contests. One encounters great difficulties putting bounds or limits on the seemingly endless enthusiasm and energy of old pucksters. So dear reader, skate along, use your imagination and enjoy the high-paced, thrilling, exciting play, the dynamic interactions and priceless camaraderie of highly developed and skilled athletes competing in pressure-cooker games for high stakes, like bragging rights at work or Tim Horton's, at least until the next game is played. (And be sure to remember the tongue-in-cheek sense of humor)

V. Game One (Return of the Old Boys - to their place of refuge)

Pre-game madness

The first game of the season, which could be the last for any one of these old codgers ... ("one never knows, does one", as Fats Waller used to ask???) is probably the most enjoyable one, socially. (Physically, it is quite a different story.) For the Old Boys, it's a time of coming back together, of renewing true friendship and pleasant conviviality that were, for most of the old coots, discontinued temporarily since last season. Aging pucksters slowly saunter, shuffle or stumble into the dressing room with their heavy bags of gear (and Lord knows what else) that they haven't used or even opened for six months, more or less. Jovial smiles and genuine greetings welcome each player. An aura of levity pervades the room. Hands are shook, maybe a few slaps on the shoulder, even the odd hug ... but no kissing. Such interactions spread quite quickly, almost automatically. Camaraderie is readily renewed. The banter and blather begins - lots of chatter about the "good old summer time", the golf or ball games, catching some fish, family fun, especially with the children and grand kids, the vacations, about lots of happy times and some that were not so pleasant ... like business deals that "bombed" or, more significantly, deaths or serious illnesses of fine friends or family members.

Some old guys share heartfelt conversations. Willie, a good Old Boy and a good goaltender at Jack Benny's claimed age of 39 ("and holding" well into his 60s), was telling Hank that his wife was diagnosed with MS ... in addition to her asthma and related health conditions. They had had a tough summer.

"She was so sick that she had to be home from work. She was nearly bed-ridden ... and she's only 55", mused Willie, his face grim with apparent concern. "We couldn't travel ... that "messed up our summer vacation. But what can you do when your wife is so sick?" Willie asked rhetorically.

Hank listened attentively and looked at his teammate empathetically. He knew what Willie was talking about. "His" Heidi had had health problems for years; apparently stress-induced. Her skin condition had "stumped" several doctors, dermatologists and other medical experts for years. Then there had been Hank's house fire that took most of the distressful year to deal with .... and there were the heart attack victims --- Max, "Fiesty" and Harry. Other old guys had shared their personal problems; some being very serious, sad situations. Nobody seemed to escape such miseries. It was part of being an old timer. Somehow they all coped. But being an Old Boy sure helped with the trials and tribulations of life. The camaraderie and support of the other oldsters sure helped if not get rid of the challenges and discomforts of aging ... even for the "rookies".

Rookies or rejects!?

At the start of each season, some awkward moments occur for the new old boys; the "rookies" or "rejects" that are traded. They are the new players on a team. They have either just entered the league or been "traded" from one team to another club in the league. (More about the trying traumas of being traded later.) Naturally, most of the newcomers feel "out of place" with a new group of guys, maybe like fish out of water. Even if they are in their 50s, 60s or 70s, they feel like "new kids on the block". They are replacing some guys who had valued friends and meaningful relationships with the Old Boys. They have to "fit in" and try to become part of the team. For some, that's not so easy.

Even in old timers' hockey, it is tough to do, for most of the players... until one or more of the Old Boys "welcomes them". Some of the team members do that very well --- greet the new guys like those nice folks from Welcome Wagon, shake their hand, ask their name, what they do, what position they play, etc, etc, etc and then introduce the "rookie" or "reject" to other players on the team. Pardon the pun, but that "breaks the ice". Personal relations are established. Often, somebody knows somebody who is a mutual friend or two guys enjoy fishing or whatever and the connections are made; new relationships start to develop. Camaraderie is in bud. It's really quite natural and easy if the players have the right attitudes. And it's amazing what a few smiles, some pleasant words and a sense of friendliness can do to a stranger joining a new team (or any other group for that matter). Most old guys and gals do that very well. They've all joined new teams or groups and felt that discomfort ... at least, momentarily.

An atmosphere of camaraderie is what creates a "comfort zone" for old guys and gals. A good part of the comfort comes from the pervasive, omnipresent and oftentimes latent, sense of humor on old folks. Jocularity has more than one meaning to the Old Boys. As well as wearing it, old timers live it openly. Teasing erupts into jests, counter-jests and laughter, of varying volumes, from quiet smiles to loud roars, of spontaneous, natural joy and amusement. With familiarity comes some sarcasm, slagging and chiding. Typical jibes deal with less hair, more weight, less sex, more hockey.

Hank: "Hey, Mikey... how was your summer??? ... looks like you were on a diet ... a high cal diet ... well, we know where the beef is!!! lots of beer, too... hey big guy???"

Mike: "Look whose talking ... Mr. Svelte. Did your gear shrink ... what's with the big gut?," comes the response.

Max: "Nice tan, Mike. Where were you all summer ... in a cave?"

Mike (feigning hurt feeling): "My skin is delicate. Be nice to me."

Max: "Ya, I'll be nice to you ... if you score some goals ..."

Hank: "...or have learned how to play defence."

Larry ... the ballerina ... or "sugar plum fairy"?

Over the growing din, Big Gerry starts jibing (little) Larry, the Old Boys Mutt and Jeff, only Gerry is much, much larger than Jeff (of comic strip fame) or most other players in the league. So he has a significant presence, spatially and vocally, with his commanding voice, a deep bass with plenty of volume, developed during thirty odd years of teaching ... in junior high school. He is one big powerful, tough dude. So when he starts roaring, most of the Old Boys listen, whether they want to or not. Well, Big G goes after Little L about doing some kind of dancing on a local tv program.

Big Gerry: "Hey, did you guys see Larry, the ballerina the other night on tv? bloody awful, I would say. Lar, old boy, what the hell were you doing ... dancing around in a pink tutu ... what are you ... some kind of a fairy? It looked like a fairy costume! What was the routine ... the dance of the sugar plum fairies or something like that?"

Mike interjects: "Ya, my wife saw him on tv the other night ... and she asked if some guy dancing around in a pink outfit was one of our old boys ... he looked kind of familiar to her ... had seen him at some of our dos ... but wasn't sure where. I wouldn't admit that any of our guys were doin' ballet ... or dressed up in a pink tutu or whatever you call that silly looking outfit. I said no damned way. None of our guys would be doing anything like that ...would we ... like denigrating our manhood ... our macho image ... our very essence? Larry, were you doing something like that ...???"

James interjects: "Maybe we should call him fairy ... instead of Larry."

Laughing heartily and ignoring the defamation of character, the tough little guy responded.

Larry: "Yup, that was me ... I got talked into it for a fund raiser...nice, eh? ... bet you're jealous that you can't do a plie or whatever you call that spinney move."

Big Gerry replies in a falsetto voice: "Ya, you're spinney alright! All you need is some blonde hair ... learn how to chew gum ... and say daha!"

Sobering situations

The laughter rolls around the room and most of the big bellies in it until, in stark contrast, James said "Did you see where that boy in Cloverdale shot himself ... guess he died ... strange, eh?" Max asked "how old was the kid?" Sal responded, "about 17, he was in high school." Guy inquired about when it happened? Jean Pierre replied "It was just today ... this afternoon ... after school." "Ya," James responded, "Seems that the kid got reprimanded by a teacher ... then went home and got hell there ... must have been too much for him." "...must have been more to it than that ... there must have been some history", boomed Big Gerry, the man with so many years of "first hand" experience in teaching and counselling. "So sad ... so damned sad... bet the parents and teacher feel really bad," mused Mikey, half aloud.

Hank picked up on the topic, saying "Dam, you never know what is going to trigger something like that... . I was a counseller in college ... one Sunday night a bunch of us went out to eat dinner at a nearby restaurant About five of us were counsellors and two or three were students. Well, there was a nice young man ... pleasant ... articulate ... seemed quite self confident but kind of quiet. Well, after we finished eating we walked and talked our ways back to the dorms ... and do you know... about an hour later some guy jumped off the top of the building ... it turned out that it was that nice young man. He hadn't show any signs of suicide ... and we had been trained to be alert for such signs ...you know, the introverted, withdrawn loner, maybe showing signs of depression, anxiety ... like that. Hell, that young man had none of those traits ... we all felt so badly about his suicide. We asked ourselves what we could have done ... still ask that question every now and then ... ."

The din had hushed. The room was filled with older men seriously thinking their own thoughts, some remembering similar situations from their past. There is a lot of collective past there ... probably about 750 years worth ... of teaching, counselling, other professions, business, policing, trades and a wide range of experience in many locations across Canada and other parts of the world. Moments of meditation and reflection cast a pall over the room ... temporarily.

Barfy bags

For a few moments the quiet is broken only by the sensual sounds, like some grunting, groaning and like noises, of the old guys unpacking their gear and starting to put it on. When they have to bend over and open those repugnant bags of gear, then the challenges to senses and sensibility begin. Maybe it's the bending over that takes the greatest effort, and even causes a back or a groin strain. But worse still is the fact that some of the old pucksters have have bad bags. You "get wind" or a whiff of it when one or more makes a gagging sound or starts choking. One of the Old Boys has opened his hockey bag and started to "dig out" his gear, sort of like a serious stream fisherman digging maggots out a dung pile. Some of the players' equipment has not been out of the bag for five months or more ... that's about 150 days and nights or more rather than less, or approximately 3,600 hours, during which bacteria, viruses, vermin and other unhealthy, harmful crud have probably been germinating or whatever they do and growing voraciously. Some of it smells downright rank, even nauseating or just plain "bloody awful".

"Oh, my gawd", wheezes Charley Hustle, normally a quiet, pleasant chap, "what died in your bag, Guy? ... or is it some old, rotten Roquefort cheese...?

"Eh, mon ami, c'est un bon fromage, n'est pas?", laughed Guy as he replied, baffling Charley with his response en francaise.

"Don't know about that, Guy but that gear stinks like hell", gasped Charley ... "nearly as bad as Barry and his farts."

"Whoa, wait a minute, Bucko," thundered Barry from across the room. "I heard that and I don't want to be compared to Guy's hockey bag. I've got some pride."

"That", injected Hank, "... would be a compliment ... to you Big B .... an insult to Guy's bag."

"Screw you, ugly one", came Barry's creative and profound retort.

"Ah ha, ... doing without it again, ... eh Barry", responded Charley, referring obliquely to the big guy's sex life, of which, typically, he was rather boastful.

And so the blather deteriorated to the lowest common denominator with fatuous insults and sarcastic rhetoric.

Max's messed-up mouth

Mike, who is rarely quiet for very long, with apparent sincerity, asked Max about his mouth. "What the hell happened to your mouth, Max? Where are your pretty pearlies? Max, who usually had a big toothy smile, tried to smile but he was suffering some difficulty. His mouth was swollen, some of his teeth were missing and his lips were kind of purple and puckered. With a twisted, sort of sardonic smile, the little old guy said slowly and painfully, "Stopped a puck .. last Wednesday ... was playing a shinny game with some young guys ... puck came around the glass ... and smacked me right in the f....g mouth ... dirty bugger." Hank, being a businessman, asked the obvious question. "Do you have any insurance to cover the costs of replacing your teeth?" Before Max could answer, Mikey, who was back to being his "normal" loquacious self, guffawed and said "Hell, he has more money than he knows what to do with ... plus he has insurance with the gummit ... don't you, you Maximillion? Max: "Ya, i do but it's still going to cost me about $800 ... out of my own f ...g pocket ... the insurance doesn't cover all of it. "Those f...ing big insurance companies sure know how to charge you ... but don't want to pay out ... bastards!" Then Big Gerry got obscenely into the conversation, saying something about better blow jobs. For various and numerous reasons, Max's response was not recorded.

Back to the bags

The banter and blather before the first game of the season is much more amusing than most ... because some of the Old Boys forget to check their gear before they came to play. So there was James muttering about "no damned socks", Mikey can't find his "can" and Sad Sammy had soap on the blades of his skates.

Sammy (muttering annoyedly): "Bloody bar of soap broke and it's on my blades..."

Andy: "Who put the soap in there ...?"

S.S.: "Shut up, Andy ... you're not helping matters. How in hell am I going to get soap off my blades ... I've never had soap on them before ... look, it really sticks ... what am I going to scrape it off with? it sticks like .... bloody glue!"

Andy: "Try your personality ... it's abrasive.."

Sad Sammy: "Screw you, you flake..."

Mike: "Be nice to our goalie ... he's a tender little flower... ."

Sammy: "Ya, a stink weed"

Larry (looking serious): "Samson, do you have a stone ... that might clean the soap off. I have one you can use"

S.S.: "Thanks ... can I try it ... I don't know what else to do ... maybe some tape would take it off ... bloody soap ... ."

Larry: "Here's the stone ... catch it!" as he lobs a small black case across the room to his blustering team mate with the soap on his skate blades. Sad Sam takes the piece of graphite out of its container and starts to scrape at the soap stuck to his skate blades.

James (the thinker): "You know, Sammy, if you ever used soap to wash with, you would probably know that you can wash soap off ... especially off of something like steel ... that's what skate blades are made of ... just in case you forgot ... or didn't know ..."

Mike: "Hey Jimmy Boy, you're more than a pretty face .... you're smart, too. No wonder you're our team captain, our leader ... you're soooo smart"

James: "Thanks Mikey ... i love you, too"

Sad Sam jumps up (as least by old timers' standards) and heads for the wash room carrying his skates, muttering as he goes about being a "dumb dumb", "how could i get soap on my blades", "how sticky it was" and "how difficult it was to get off." Minutes later, a joyous yell booms out of the washroom. "Yipee, it's coming off ... the soap's coming off my blades ... yipee!!!" ... like a kid who has just discovered the joys of ice cream.

While Sad Sammy was fussing about his skate blades, James borrowed a pair of socks and Mikey found his can in the outside pocket of his bag, muttering about "that damn kid of mine using my gear and not putting things back where they belong".

Max retorts: "Be thankful your kid plays hockey ... he could be doing drugs."

Mike agrees; "Ya, he's a pretty good boy"

Andy adds: "He must take after his mother ..."

Mike: "Shut up, oh toothless one!"

Hi Ho! Hi Ho! it's off to the ice we go!!

Eventually, the old guys get their gear on and "clomp" out to their players' box. Walking in skates on hard surfaces have their own unique sound, like clomp or, in eastern Europe, klomp. If the ice was not ready, some fitness fanatics will do some stretches, others would stand and yak with other Old Boys or their opponents, others would just sit quietly on the bench with their thoughts ... memories of past games, past plays, past achievements ... and failures. Who knows what goes through the old geezers' minds before the first or, for that matter, any game of the season.

Sometimes while he was waiting for the ice preparation to be completed, Hank's mind would often harken back to his playing days at Murray U. For him, those were the times of greatest joys and achievements in hockey and, maybe, in his entire lifetime. Fond memories would rush into his head and fill him with wonderful feelings - warm, bubbly sensations, kind of uplifting, inspiring - like no others. He would think about sitting on the bench in the old arena (actually, a converted WWII airplane hangar, commonly referred to as the MU Barn and you can guess where the babble went from there), filled with hollering (some mooing) fans, championship banners in the rafters and warm, even intense, feelings of pride ... for his team, himself, his university. Those were such treasured moments; ones that could not be shared because no one else could really appreciate and value them as he did, not even his beloved Heidi. They were so unique and deeply personal. Nobody else could treasure them like Hank did. Besides, every Old

Boy probably had his own treasured moments that he could enjoy all by himself. Hank sure hoped so.

At last, the ice was ready and the Old Boys stepped, stumbled and otherwise got their shabby old bodies onto the ice. Except for Charley Hustle and Guy, who bounced out onto the ice, the others started slowly, tentatively --- it's been six months since most of them were skating. Yes, skating was a little like riding a bike --- with a difference. Bikes have tires with traction; skates have very thin, probably dull (or soapy), blades that slip or slide. So most of the Old Boys were getting the feeling of their skates and "hoping like hell" that they didn't fall on their butts - any hockey player's nightmare. Sammy was hardly moving, worried that there might still be some soap on his blades which would add to the slipperiness of the ice. He skated a few feet and then returned to the bench to use Larry's stone and scrape away the soap that had not been washed off.

By the time Sad Sammy was done fiddling with his skates, the rest of the Old Boys and their opponents were skating around the rink, some in twos or threes, renewing their camaraderie, while others were leisurely skating by themselves - going through their regular "warm-up" routines. A few players stopped, got down on the ice and did some stretches and various other calisthenical contortions. (Try saying those two words three times quickly.) Hank thought they are nuts, getting cold on the frozen ice when you wanted to get warmed up, get the old muscles loosened up and your body moving. "... to each his own", he mused to himself, just as Charley Hustle whizzed by him. Hank shouted, "Slow down Charley. You'll get a speeding ticket..." But Charley did not hear Hank. He was down the ice, zigging and zagging as he virtually flew around the rink. Hank watched Charley skate and said half aloud, "... he can sure skate... kind of reminds me of Paul Coffey ... how he flitted over the ice ... his blades don't seem to cut into the ice ... amazing."

As Hank skated back into the Old Boys end of the rink, Andy was hollering at his teammates for some practice shots. Pucks were scattered around the ice and the players started taking shots at their goalie. Big Gerry fired one high, much too high - like just by Andy's ducking head.

Andy: "You stupid bastard, keep your shots down..."

Gerry (as he skated by the goalie, responded meekly): "Sorry, Andy"

Three or four more players take shots at the goal, all missing and hitting the back boards.

Andy: "Hey, you blind buggers ... try hitting the net ... I need some shots ... too bad you can't bring your seeing eye dogs on the ice ... maybe I would get some shots."

A few minutes later, the referee's whistle sounded. Time for the game to start. Some players took their last shots (could be their only one for the entire game forthcoming). All of the players skated slowly toward the goal and started to shout encouragement to each other, some whacking Andy on his goal pads or a teammates' backside. About then, James asked three forwards if they want to play together on a line. They can "start". The others would get "organized" on the bench. Hank, the senior defencemen, picked Mikey to start with him on defence. The rest of the Old Boys skated off to get their lines "sorted out" and await their turn to play. No body was concerned about who started and how much ice time they would have that night ... probably more than they really wanted, especially for the first game of the season for most of them.

The shinny begineth

The Old Boys first game of the season was against the mean old Mid-Knights, all "decked out" in their solid black uniforms -- "kind of intimidating even for old timers", mused Hank to himself. Old timers do not lack for creativity. It was apparent in many ways, particularly in their team names ... like Huff and Puff, Old Buffs, Puckduckers, Spanish Flyers,

Fallen Stars, Antiques, Goldies, Old Goats, Old Buoys for a team from a coastal city and other monikers of admirable uniqueness.

The Mid-Knights started strongly. On the first shift, Hank and his sidekick Mike had a goal scored ... against them. Mike was out of position and Hank did not move into the spot where he could have kept the scorer from doing his dastardly deed. Back on the bench, Mikey provided some perspective, albeit pretty thin gruel. "Hank, now we don't have to worry about protecting a shutout for Andy." Hank didn't know whether he wanted to laugh or cry at his partner's dark humor. On the next shift, those "bastards" (old timers do get intense when they are playing hockey), got a lucky goal. Hank went out to challenge the Knights' defenceman who had the puck and then shot wide of the goal. As bad luck would have it, the shot deflected off a dormant Mid-Knight standing beside the goal and into the nets. The Old Boys were down by two goals in the first five minutes. As he skated back to the bench, Hank gave a passing thought about calling it a (K)night and heading for the bar. Instead, he muttered, "Guess, we will just have to step it up."

And the Old Boys did. Minutes later, Big Gerry scored a beauty, barging his way through several of the Mid-Knights and firing a wrist shot (old timers are not allowed to use slap shots), like Joe Sakic, that whizzed past their goalie before he made a move for it. Despite playing most of the game in their own end of the rink, the Old Boys "bent but they did not break". After drooping behind by a score of 5-2 midway through the game, they came back led by one of their new acquisitions, Doc, short for M.D., who sniped two goals. He hit the far corner low on one and up high on the near side for the other... like the puck had eyes or had been shot by Wayne or Mario ... very hard accurate shots, especially when you consider Doc's playing history.

Until he started playing old timers, at the "ripe old age" of 53 years, Doc had not played hockey. He was too busy being a dedicated student, professional and parent. When he first came into the league, he did not skate very well, he did not handle his stick, the puck or his body well --- at times, he "was out of control". At well over 200 pounds, he was so awkward that he was something of a menace to others on ice, both to the opposition and his own teams. In recent years, with a lot of determination and some real natural athletic ability, he had turned into an intelligent player who used his size and developing skills at deflecting and shooting pucks into something of a goal scorer. And any team, including the Old Boys, could always use goal scorers.

Larry and Mikey scored along with Max, Guy and Charley Hustle. Andy, after a shaky start in goal, settled down, made several "sensational" saves after letting in five goals (which is no big deal in old geezers' shinny) and shut out the Mid-Knights for the rest of the game. Seems like the Mid-Knights could do everything well ... skate, pass, shoot, block shots, fore check, back check (even in old timers' shinny?) ... except score more goals. Maybe they became too complacent and lost their edge. On average, they were much younger, probably by five years or more. Overall, they really outplayed the Old Boys, some of whom were "dragging" with 20 minutes or more remaining in the game. As Hank said to Hans, one of the referees, "Are we playing slow time? I'm having a hard time keeping my ass off the ice." Hans smiled and quipped, "You're helping to keep the ice clean". Hank just moaned in disgust and glided away in dismay.

After the contest -replays and post-game patter

As the weary players staggered, stumbled and in other ways made their way back to the dressing room, they were in a vibrant, upbeat mood --- lots of happy, enthusiastic chatter. Let there be no doubt, old guys like to WIN. That's fun. Losing is not! Most oldsters still play to win with a desire, if not a passion, even though it may be somewhat diminished by years, lower levels of energy and stamina, aching bones and stiff bodies. Besides, winning the first game of the season was a good omen for the contests ahead.

The Old Boys were in a jubilant, congratulatory mood. Charley was lauding Andy for his "great goaltending". Charley: "Great game, Andy --- you played REALLY well"

Andy muttered his thanks but started griping about "#22" (on the Mid-Knights team).

Andy: "That son-of-a bitch, that 22, he kept coming into my crease ... . Next time, I will cut his 'f ...g' head off ... if he does that."

Charley: "Chill out Andy ... and enjoy the win."

As he comes into the room, Guy also compliments Andy. But Andy keeps complaining about #22.

Andy: "That guy *really* pisses me off. He whacked me one time... I'll get the bastard ... ."

Mikey agreed: "That's the same guy who was doing that to Blackie last year. We'll have to get him ... if we can catch him ... he's so damned fast."

Hank, tiring of the grumbling about #22, changed the subject.

Hank: "Way to come back guys ... we bent but we didn't break ... they must have been frustrated ... playing the game in our end most of the night .... and we beat them."

Charley chimed in: "We had the snipers tonight ... what about that rookie Doc with his two beauties ...great trade we made .... Doc for two broken sticks and a puck ... but no beer ... should have made a better trade." --- laughter rolled around the room.

Doc responded, modestly: "Ya, I got lucky tonight."

Mike: "Ya, so don't count on getting lucky when you get home ..."

Doc: "Right!!! Jill will be asleep."

Hank inquired about Doc's ancestry, musing about his last name. "Hmmm, Immonen ... is that Scandanavian?"

Doc: ".... it's Finnish."

Guy: "you sure had some finish around their goal. C'est tres bien, mon ami".

Hank: "Doc are you any relation to Jari .... Jari Kurri ... he was a sniper too, you know!!!"

Doc: "I can't see any similarity ... he was a good one."

Hank: "Who wouldn't be if you were playing with Gretzky?"

Gerry: "Boomer wouldn't!!! He has a hard time hitting the barn door with a scoop shovel. Hey where is he?

Mike: "He's on another boondoggle ... in Frisco ... going to the ball games ... and getting paid for it ... some kind of public accounting conference he's supposed to be attending ... great job ...how did he get it? ... where do we sign up? ...don't know when he finds time to work

Laughter erupts throughout the room

Mikey continued ragging against the absent Boom Boom: "Hell, he's away so much ... vacations, business trips ... other boondoggles ... that's OK, gives us more ice time, eh Hanky?!"

More laughter ripples around the room

Hank, glowering because he did not like to be called "Hanky": "Yup, had plenty of ice time tonight. The ass end of my pants is wet from dragging it on the ice"

Guy, who takes hockey rather seriously and often thoughtfully for an old timer, figured that the Mid-Knights were the better team.

Guy: "I'm not sure how we beat them tonight ... they are younger ... they skate so well ... they pass the puck well ... did you see their 'd-man', number 4, mon dieu, he could sure shoot the puck ... they were in our end most of the night ... or so it seemed ... we were lucky... tres bonne chance"

Hank: "You might be right, Guy, but we scored more goals ... that's what wins the games ... putting the old biscuit into the basket ... the big difference was in the goaltending... their goalie let in some softies ... and Andy was good ... better than good, he was super sensational ... especially after the first 10 or 15 minutes ... when he quit fighting the puck....

Andy (still in a snarly mood about #22): "Screw you, Hank ... if you bloody dmen would take care of their forwards, they wouldn't have got squat."

Hank: "What the hell are you talking about ... you ingrate? Do you want us to do your job as well as our own ... and ... scoring goals at the other end ... toooo!

Hank was deluged with reactions, some of them rather obscene, from the forwards as well as Andy. The old d'man just sat and smiled with delight.

The banter went on throughout the steamy, odorous dressing room. The laughter was like waves on a large lake, rising and receding, almost always present; truly a pleasant sound ... for old timers. James, the team captain, normally a quiet, low-key guy tried to get the attention of the team. He tried several times and then finally yelled loudly and gruffly "Hey you guys, shut your damned mouths. I have some important information for you!" Those who heard him were somewhat shocked by such an outrageous utterance from the normally mild-mannered James.

Big Billy, the large burly defenceman, who had spent some time in the army shouted, "Listen up boys ..."

Somebody yelled back, "Yes sir, sergeant sirrrrr!"

Then Big Jerry boomed out, in his deepest base voice, "Go to hell, William."

The two largest lads on the team have an on-going macho match which the other Old Boys try to ignore. They would glare at each other ... silently, like two rams in rutting season.

Slowly, the raucous din subsided, giving James a chance to announce that the sheets of paper that he had handed out earlier needed to be read and returned, something that adults should not have to be told. But these aged ones, in chronological years, were really boys when they were in the dressing room.

James: "Hey guys, *please* get those questionnaires in ...."

Some bodies: "What questionnaires?"

Jean Pierre: "Those pages Jimmy just gave you, dummy!"

Max: "Did I get one?"

James: "Everybody got one ... so get them completed ... return them to me ... next Thursday or the next game that you play ... they need them to make up the tournament teams ..."

Andy (still in a funk): "What difference does it makes ... I usually get stuck on the worst team ... anyhow..."

Mikey: "Maybe you wouldn't ... if you could stop the puck every now and then ... and weren't such a whiner."

Andy: "Screw you, you dumb d'man"

Mikey: "Hey, we're not the ones who play with the tools of ignorance.... there's only two reasons why you zombies play goal ....you can't play any other position or ... you're too damned stupid to know better ... ."

Andy: "Get some new material, Mikey ... or are you too dumb to learn ... eh, d'man ... doesn't that really mean ... dumb man?"

Charley was up, getting a beer. "Anybody want a beer", hollering over the din. Several affirmative responses were heard. Most say "ya", "ok" or words to that effect. Looking at Max, Charley said: "Didn't your mother teach you to say "Please"? Maxie replied, sarcasm dripping from his words: "Yes please ... mother ... please may I have a pop?" Charley responded: "I'll give you a pop ... right between the eyes." Max: "The way you were shooting tonight, I'd be surprised if you can see this side of the room." After catching a beer tossed less-than-carefully by Charley, Mikey chimed in caustically, "Thank you ... mother". "Go to hell, you guys", Charley Hustle retorted as he sauntered back to the bench to drink his beer and get into the flow of the banter.

Major issue: who's in charge of the beer?

One of the annual issues of the Old Boys inevitably arose early in the season, like before or immediately after the first game. The issue related basically to ensuring the reliable supply and the fiscal responsibility for the beer fund. Mike wanted to know about the price of beer for the coming year, especially to let the new players know that they would have to contribute $5, as "start up costs", whether they drank beer or not. "Profits" from the beer fund paid for the parties through the season --- usually before Christmas, some other time during the winter and the wind-up "event" in the spring when the team "blows the boodle" or cleared out the beer account.

Mikey: "Charley, was there any money left last spring?"

Hank: "Get serious, Mikey..."

Mikey (ignoring Hank): "Charley, did we spend all the money ... at that windup do ... at the Corral ... or whatever you call that scuzzy place ... with all the smoke and loud noise ... music ... whatever?"

Charley: "Sure did ... every last cent ... if you missed it ... too damn bad"

Mikey: "What are you talking about you old drunk. I was sitting right across the table from you ... couldn't you see that far? No wonder you can't score ... you can't see past the end of your arm ... your short arm at that."

Charley: "Screw off, you d'man ... you dumb man."

Hank: "Nice attitude, Charley, you dork ... good for the esprit des corps ... or what have you."

Guy (softly, hardly audible): "You sound defensive Charley. Did you abscond with some of the money."

Charley: (sitting next to Guy): "Hey, what's this absconded crap ... you could damage my reputation ... talking like that ...."

Guy: "What reputation ... for petty theft ... or grand larceny?

Mikey: "Are we putting $5 in the pot ... to get funds flowing?"

Several responses are in agreement. None object. Consensus reigns.

Hank: "Are the beers still 3 for $5?

James: "Yup ... unless you want to pay more ... you rich bugger."

Hank: "Get out of here, Jimmy Boy. I'm no high-priced engineer ... have you seen what's happened to the stock market since July ... some people are losing their pensions ... or at least seeing them erode month after month ... that bloody Bush and his gang in Washington ... playing war games ... they should come play hockey with us ... we'll give them some war ... with a stick right in the nuts ... check out their threshold of pain"

Big Gerry: "Give it a rest, Hank! ... back to the serious matters ... penalties will cost you 2 bucks .... so put your money in the pot Gerry ... hey Sam you got a penalty too, didn't you", chuckled Max.

Sam: "Shut up, you cluckin' hen ... I'll pay ... sometime ... soon ... maybe. That was a rotten penalty ... tripping ... that guy fell over my stick.

Big Gerry; "Sure, Sammy ... they usually do when you push their skates out from under them..."

Sam (protesting): "What are you talking about ... he took a dive ... he shoulda been penalized ... like in the NHL ... and a thousand bucks ... too ... for piss-poor acting!"

Everybody seemed to be talking again. Happy chatter and noisy laughter pervaded the room. That was camaraderie expressed at its best.

Mikey: "Who's going to handle the beer for the next month?"

The noise subsided. Rapt attention was focused on Mike and the question that he posed. This is an important matter, one of the most important matters that the Old Boys or any old timers' team faces. The beer supply must be assured and reliably provided. That's what helps to bond the old souses, slow down their racing hearts and "raise the water table".

James: "Ya, who's going to take care of the beer .... for next month?

An ominous silence temporarily comes over the room as the Old Boys think about the important matter raised by the team captain. It's too important to be flippant about. Some of the players will be away. Others have brought the beer before and it's a bit of a hassle that they could do without. Others are reluctant to volunteer because they suspect that they might "get stuck" with the job for the rest of the season. But all of the Old Boys know very well that "bringing the beer" is an essential task and not one to be taken lightly. It has to be done and it has to be done right. Not only does the beer have to be brought to every game but it has to be cold, it has to be of at least two brands, Prairie Gold, a local favorite, and any other cheap beer for the guys like Boom Boom, Charley Hustle and Big Gerry who will drink anything in a beer container.

James (growing impatient at the absence of cooperation): "Max, how about taking care of brews....?"

Max (who has done it for years): "Sure ... I'll do it ... and I don't even drink the stuff..."

Larry: "You're a good man, Max ... besides, you drank so much in the past that most of us (pausing to consider what to say next) ... are still trying to catch up."

Max: "Ya, I drank more than my fair share ... and it cost me ... big time .... my job .... my marriage ... my health ... the price of being an alcoholic ... is high ... too f'g high!"

Mike: "Hey Max, that's history. Look at you now ... you're doing okay ... you're playing with the big boys....."

Gerry: "Ya Max, you're playing with us big guys..."

Max: "Aren't I a lucky son of a bitch ... at least I'm still alive...."

Hank: "No kiddin' buddy... I still remember you laying on the floor ... not moving ... hardly breathing ... lucky that Woody and Stan were playing here that night ... great to have those firemen playing old timers ... they saved your life ... that Woody, we got him off the ice ... he took one look and started working on you. He was like a machine. He sure knew what to do ... started pumping on your chest ... then he flipped up to your head ... with his gear on ... held your nose and started mouth to mouth ... he was awesome but it was bloody scary!"

Max (somewhat subdued): "I don't remember much"

Hank: "For sure ... you were out cold. Then Stan came in and shouted at somebody to phone 911. Boy, did those guys ever know what they were doing ... they saved your life old buddy.'

Charley: "Hey Jimmy, who's taking care of the beer?"

James: "Max said he would. OK, Max?"

Max (remembering his brush with death, replied softly): "Sure..."

Big Gerry: "I have a matter of beer policy to raise."

Sam: "Beer policy ... what the hell are you talking about, you old bureaucrat?"

Big Gerry: "You guys are always wanting to buy cheap beer ... like that American horse pee ... remember last year when the government raised the taxes on booze? Well, they didn't raise it on the beers brewed in this province ... so Northern Draft is now cheaper than Prairie Gold ...

by six bucks a dozen ... it's just over twelve dollars a case compared to 18 something for the national brands."

Andy: "Let's try it ... probably won't kill us ... ."

Sam: "Ya, and we'll have mucho money for our parties."

Big Gerry: "What do you say? Should we give it a shot?

Max: "Sure, why not?"

Charley "Easy for you to say, Maxie ... you don't drink beer anyhow."

Max: "Just tell me what you guys want to drink and I'll bring it."

After several more minutes of intense discussion about the pros and cons of switching brands of beer, the consensus was to try Northern Draft for a while and save some money. If the Old Boys didn't like it, they could pay more and buy Prairie Gold or some other brand. The importance of the Old Boys' beer supply cannot be overstated. Other than not getting their regular ice time, making sure that the beer and some soft drinks were available was a matter of high, no highest, priority.

For people not involved in playing old timers' hockey, the importance of the beer supply is probably difficult to understand. Some might think it's kind of immature or even immoral. Those people probably do not understand the culture of hockey, at least for adult men. Drinking beer was not obligatory. Some players preferred soda pop; one flakey goalie just drank water. (But his pipes rusted out and he needed new plumbing.) Some might think that drinking beer kept the old timers from "getting into shape". One response to such a suggestion was simply: "there's more to life than being physically fit".

In regard to physical fitness, old timers were not couch potatoes, sleeping or sitting in their easy chair when they were playing. They were exercising their aging bodies fairly rigorously and that required fluids, especially nutritious fluids like grain-based brews or so some, like Gentleman Jock, claimed.

Sitting around the dressing room after the game, talking about whatever, sharing thoughts and experiences, enjoying the camaraderie was really the essence of old timers' hockey. Normally law-abiding men, the Old Boys just ignored the city's posted policy, in fact, a city by-law, banning the drinking of "alcoholic beverages" in the dressing room. In contrast, when they played at the Snoopy Tournament in California during the third week of July, they had to go outside into the parking lot and drink their beer, shoot the breeze, have some laughs and enjoy themselves. That was "Sparky" Schulz's policy and he owned the arena. But during the winter months in Canada and northern states, drinking beer in the parking lot was not an attractive option.

Other banter, blather and verbosity

Playful verbiage is a vital part of the old geezers' camaraderie. From the time two old timers or more gather, humorous and teasing talk prevails. Oftentimes, the babble is banal, even silly but the underlying current of the blather, the twinkle in the old guys' eyes and their body language is one of fun, of having a good time and sharing it with their buddies. Occasionally, chatter becomes heartfelt. The mood gets somber, like when the chatter turns to serious matters, such as Max's heart attack, personal or financial matters and some political issues which usually become the most heatedly "discussed". But, it does not stay that way for long. Levity rules. So it was not surprising or out of the ordinary for Old Boys to be teasing each other after their first game of the season. Like when Big Gerry started back in chiding Larry about his recent dance performance that was broadcast on the local television channel.

Gerry: "Hey, you guys, did you see the tv special the other night... with our little friend over there in the pink tutu

... dancing like some ballerina ... on tv the other night? ... what a beauty ... so graceful ... nice legs too.. ."

Larry (just a bit annoyed with the matter being brought up, again): "Get off my back, you big bugger ... I was doing it for a fund raiser!"

Sal: "Sorry I missed it..."

Big Gerry: "You didn't miss much ... but I wanted to videotape it ... but we had no tapes for our VCR ... too bad ... could have had some laughs watching replays of our little dancer ... seems like you do a lot of dancing on the ice .... didn't anyone ever tell you you're supposed to score goals with that stick .... not use it as a dance partner ...?

Andy joins in: "Ya, I was watching the local news the other night and this little dark haired guy was jumping around ... some place in town ... for some reason or other."

Laughter rolled around the room

James: "... just so long as he wasn't wearing his Old Boys sweater ... we can pretend we don't know him ... or at least, he's not part of our team ... maybe say he plays for Green River ... they have some wimpy guys."

Sal: "Maybe their goalie saw Larry doin' his dance ... and will start laughing every time he gets near the goal..."

Big Gerry: "Hey, Larry, why don't you wear that outfit the next time we play the Red Rogues ... that might distract them ... they need to be ... they're too damned serious, so intent ... they would probably split a gut if they saw that routine."

Guy joins in: "Hey Larry old boy, why don't you wear it the next time we play?"

Larry: "You've got to be kiddin'..."

Guy: "Sure am ... ."

To Larry's relief, the conversation turned to the refereeing and the penalty that Guy took for tripping.

Guy: "What a dive that guy took ... ."

Max: "Hard not to when you trip him ... he's no ballerina."

Guy: "I learned that from Gerry."

Gerry (feigning innocence): "You didn't learn that dirty trick from me. I'm Mr. Clean!"

Guy (faking disgust and disdain): "Oh, barf!"

Mike: "You can blame the ref all you want ... just put your two bucks in the kitty... ."

Guy: "Ya! ya! I will ... wait 'til I get my pants on ."

Jean Pierre: "Gladly"

Once again the chatter changed topic; this time to the Mid Knights.

Charley: "Did you see that big #4 out there ... he was huge ... I had to skate an extra mile to get around him ... and the reach on him ...... ten feet or more... where's he from?"

Big Gerry: "... from the northwest ...near Lac St. Anne."

Guy: "Oh, one of those big French boys ... maybe we're related, you know... like *famille* ... ."

Mikey: "You must be the runt in the litter..."

Guy: *"Fermez la bouche, vous gros vilain."*

Mike: "Don't swear at me, Guy"

Charley: "What about that other big d'man? He's a big boy too. Where did they get those guys? Guess we better do a better job of recruiting ... .

Big Gerry: "Hey Charley, we've got some big guys ... look at Mikey ... and he's in shape ... ."

Charley (snorting rather grossly): "Shape for what? .... barrel races!"

Mike: "Get out of here ... just because you're anemic!"

Charley: "Anemic ... hmmmm..... look at how pale you are ... you albino!"

Big Gerry: "A big fat albino ... nice pedigree!"

Mikey: "Get off my back. It's a matter of genetics. I wasn't well engineered."

While Charley and others were teasing Mikey about his physical attributes, Hank and Andy were chatting down at the end of the benches. Like most of the Old Boys they sat in roughly the same spots in every dressing room that they used. Probably had something to do with being creatures of habit or superstitions or maybe common interests and some special bonding over the years.

Andy was still grumbling about #22 coming into his crease and what he was going to do the next time they played the Mid Knights.

Andy: "I'll get that bastard ... I'll let him have it ... with my f'g stick..."

Hank: "Forget about it ... it's over. We won. You're not hurt. Give it a rest..."

Andy: "Ya, I suppose you're right. Guess I've flogged that dead horse enough ... but sure as hell I'm going to flog that bozo if he charges me in the next game."

Hank: "Maybe we will have Willie playing in goal the next time we play the Mid Knights ... and let him take care of the s.o.b."

Andy and Willie were slated to share the goal keeping through the season. So Andy wanted to know what was the goalie schedule.

Andy (to James, the team captain): "Is Willie going to be here on Thursday?"

James (assertively): "That's up to you and him. Just make damned sure that one of you clowns shows up for the games ... no screw-ups between you spastics. Phone him and make the arrangements between the two of you. He was only going to be out of town for a week or so."

Andy: "OK! Do you have his phone number?"

James (getting a wee bit perturbed): "Look in those sheets I gave you. There's a team list ... names and phone numbers ... for those of you who do not know how to use the phone book."

Andy (a little sheepishly): "You're a fine lad, Jamie me boy. Thanks."

"Oldzheimers"

Forgetfulness is a common characteristic of all people ... of all ages ... not just of old guys and gals. But there are times when forgetting some of the basic items for a hockey game is really, really annoying. So, give a listen while Hank discovers that he does not have a towel in his bag.

Hank: "Damn it, I don't have a towel. I went through all of my gear, made sure that everything was in the bag ... and then forgot to bring a towel ... what a dummy! Maybe Max has an extra one ... he usually does ... that old Maple Leaf rag ... he probably dries his dog with it.

Hey Max, do you have a towel? I left mine at home ... nice and clean and dry."

Max: "Ya, I've got an extra one". Digging around in his oversized hockey bag, he pulls out a ratty-looking old blue and white towel that is really ragged around the edges and it has a couple of rips in it, also.

Max: "Here you go, Hanker ... it's not much but you should get dry with it ... Hmmmm ... smells kind of funny ... wonder when I washed it last?

Sam: "Probably a year or two ago ... whether it needed it or not ... you don't want to wash it too often or it will fall apart"

Hank: "That's OK Max, beggars can't be choosers. That will be fine, thanks."

Max lobbed the towel to Hank. The old d'man gets up and trudges toward the shower room, taking his beer with him. Hank is one of the few players that took his beer into the shower room. When asked why he did that, he simply answered "because I like to enjoy my beer while showering". But, another reason was to protect the contents of his can of beer. He had seen some old guys' stunts in the past that he would rather not be the victim of ... antics such as one guy peeing in another player's beer can. So he took his beer into the shower to enjoy it and as insurance against pranksters.

Hank returns from the shower room, taking a swig from his can of beer. As he walked by Andy, the goalie asks about the Snoopy Tournament.

Andy: "How was the Snoopy Tournament, Hank?"

Hank: "Good"

Andy: "Who went from here?"

Hank: "Just me... I was the only one .... went with a team from Cowtown ... have gone with them before ... the Old Bucks"

Andy (musing about the team name): "You sure it was the Old Bucks? ... not something that starts with an F...?"

Hank (feigning disgust): "Andy, you're disgusting ... that's a reputable team that I went with ... think there may have been a minister or priest on it .... good team ... we won gold. It was a great tournament ... but we sure missed Sparky ... that's the nickname Charles Schulz liked to be called ... great man ... real class act ... he will be missed but Peanuts and the gang carry on"

With his melancholy memories of "Sparky", the teams he had played with and the many other pleasant experiences of the Snoopy Tournament during the past dozen years flooding his mind, Hank became immersed in his fond recollections ... momentarily.

Respect your elders!

Topics of conversation were always changing in the Old Boys' dressing room. Seldom were subjects discussed in any depth and certainly not after the first game. So, while Andy and Hank were reminiscing about the annual Snoopy Tournament, Guy joined in with uncharacteristic effrontery, remarking about how "old and slow Andy looked out on the ice tonight."

Andy (sarcastically): "Thanks a lot, Guy. You youngsters have no respect for your elders ... didn't you father ever teach you to respect your elders? I should teach you some respect you little shrimp ... clobber you but your're so small ... might get charged with child abuse."

Guy: (sarcastically, aussi): "Mange la merde, vous vieux batard."

Andy: "That doesn't sound very nice, Guy."

Guy: "C'est dommage."

Andy: "You think I look so old ... you should try to get down and up, down and up ... on that bloody cold ice ... it's enough to make a guy freeze up quickly ... especially the knees. Wonder how you would do in goal?"

Continuing his counter attack on Guy, Andy softens his barrage: "Guy, you're such a good skater. Do you ever fall down? When you're that close to the ice ... you can bounce right back up again ... just like our kids used to ... before they grew up to be big people."

Guy (laughing): "What are you talking about, Andy? We sit down on the bench and then get back up again ... no sweat ... but then we're in better shape than you over-stuffed statutes."

Andy (getting just a little annoyed): "Hell, you're so short, we can't tell if you are standing or sitting. Here I am trying to be a nice guy and you f'g whimps are yapping at me. Wait until the next game. I'll be hollerin' at you guys ... get that puck out of here, get that f'g puck out of here!"

Guy (interjecting): "Andy, you sound like Max .."

Andy: "God forbid that I should sound like that old bugger."

Guy (sneering): "Andrew old fellow, what were you saying about respecting your elders?"

More eclectic chatter

Big Gerry: "Hey Andy, do you mean we're going to get Blackie back ... telling us to stand up at the blue line when there's a three on one...?"

Laughter roars around the room as most of the Old Boys remember their former goalie and his frequent, ill-advised admonitions to his d'men.

Mikey (mimicking Blackie, last year's goalie, in a falsetto voice): "Take that guy ... shoot that puck out of here ... get it out ... get it out of our end ... hurry up ... shoot it out .... **shoot it out....**

Again the topic of conversation changes, to talking about Dirk, another new acquisition to the team, who did not come out to play the first game. Dirk is a very intense player, who is also a good skater, playmaker, checker, all-around good player.

Andy: "Where's Dirk ... the dork?"

James: "He's out hunting ... moose ... somewhere out west...! ... maybe in the Rockies."

Sam: "Hope he doesn't shoot himself in the foot ... would serve him right ... out killing nature's wonderful creatures ..."

Mikey: "You tree hugger ... animal lover!"

Sam (seriously, as usual): "Damned right! What gives men the right to kill wild animals ... Noah took them all on his ark ... for forty days and forty nights and didn't have to kill any ... even though they were probably pretty hungry ... did you ever think about that?"

Religion is one topic that old geezers shy away from discussing. So, there was an awkward silence until the chatter began again.

Max (with a big smile on his face): "Oh ya, Dirk, with him we're going to be flying."

Mikey: "You forwards will be getting told how to play forward just like Blackie used to tell the defence how to play last year ... and the year before. Aren't you lucky guys?"

Max: "Ya, we'll be getting his f'g lectures on the bench ... great f'g stuff!"

Jean Pierre: " I would rather play against him. He's so predictable ... always passing ... rarely shooting on goal ... or driving to the net. Easy guy to play against ... but he's good ... he skates hard... gets in the way... he'll help us..."

On the other side of the room, another brief conversation erupted. Big Sal wanted to know why Larry only played one shift on the "production line" and then went to the checking line.

Larry: "I couldn't take the pace ... had to slow down ... you guys are too fast for me."

Burst of laughter reverberate around the room, mainly because Big Sal is very slow on his skates ... sometimes likened to a snow-shoer rather than a skater.

Another matter of great financial importance rose through the din.

Charley: "Who wants to sell some Grey Cup tickets? I only have 50 left. Jock, how many do you want... 10 ... 20!"

Gentleman Jock: "Sure I'll sell some ... give me 5 or 10, whatever you want ... not sure who I will sell them to ... but I will try. Annie and the kids always like some ... tweaks their interest in the game."

Charley: "Here you go."

Mikey: "You know how it works for me ... my brother buys one and I buy the Rest. Helluva deal"

Max: "Get off your lazy f'g ass and sell them. Hell, you're a salesman. Those suckers should sell like hot cakes ... if you make some effort."

Charley: "Hey Mikey, if you don't sell them, you have more chances of winning!"

Mikey: "You sound like the lottery ads ... you can't win without a ticket ... the more you buy, the better your chances, like 10 million to one rather than 20 million to one."

Guy: "I'll take five".

Max: "I'll take ten."

Mike: "Me too.

And so it went until all of the Grey Cup pool tickets were given out to the Old Boys. All of the tickets would be sold, the money returned and put into the league's coffers for winners' prizes, some operating and administrative expenses, student scholarships or whatever.

Andy's entertaining ... again

All of a sudden, Andy, who had been roaming around the room with only a towel wrapped around his midriff, went into one of his routines. One of his part-time jobs was leading a band. (Seems to me that was said before --- damned oldzheimers!) Andy was a natural entertainer. He had a fun sense of humor, captivating stage presence and an extrovert (some would say a "show off") which, every now and then, he brought spontaneously to the dressing room. If the team won, he often put on some kind of comedy routine after the game. (If they lost, he was a real miserable old grump.)

Andy: "Hey man, we were playing down at The River Banks last week .. and in came this chick with biggggg boooobs",

> cupping his hands under his "pects" and moving some imaginary breasts up and down vigorously.

Like most entertainers, he was into his act with great gusto.

> "Well, she struts around the room, with her hands under her boobs, saying something like 'can I give you boys some fun ... give you some cushions for your tired heads .... come on boys, let's play'. Then she sits down at a table and orders a beer. After a while, another broad comes in and she has big ... verrrry big, tits... kind of hanging out the sides of her shirt. She sits down with this other chick ... and they are both pushing their own boobs around ... like they were massaging them ... must have felt good ... I don't know ..."

Andy takes a poignant pause, while he caught his breath and built up his audience's attention and anticipation ---

> "Well now, the first one gets up ... she's a blonde bomber ... and starts to walk away from the table ...... says she's no lesbian ...... she would rather sit with some guy ..... and off she goes ... acting like God's gift to mankind ... maybe she was to some kind of man".

The old fellas are howling with laughter as Andy sashays around the room with his bum swaying, mimicking the "blonde bomber". Andy's performance was rudely interrupted by James, who masked his amusement with a somber face.

"What's you point, Andy?" asked James, feigning sincerity. Like the others, he had been laughing lustily, watching Andy's gyrations and listening to his raw humor. Andy didn't rise to the bait. He was a professional entertainer and knew how to ignore interruptions. Instead, off he went on another, totally unrelated, routine. Big Gerry figured that Andy might have had some kind of attention span disorder; an explanation for some of the goals he let in, from time to time.

Andy starts telling about Guy, the team's speediest and, arguably, best player, learning to play the guitar.

Andy: "Hey Guy, remember when you first started taking music lessons... your old man brought you over to our place so my old man could teach you how to play the geetar? ... and you held that geetar like it was a bathtub full of crap."

Making a contorted face of disgust, which brought more laughter from the Old Boys, Andy continued

"You held that guitar and you plucked one string ... plonk ..... then another one ... plonk ... oh, you were a beauty."

Guy, who was usually quite a pleasant and quiet young man, just smiled and replied sarcastically,

"Your old man wasn't very successful with you either ... was he???"

Andy, still strutting around the room, went over to Big Gerry and said,

"Where are you going to be tomorrow night?

"Why", came a gruff response from the big guy.

"Because we're playing at O'Greers ... thought you might like it ..."

"... and he needs some customers there so his band can get paid", quipped Max.

After the remaining few Old Boys finished their "beers", they headed out of the dressing room, most of them aching and stiff from playing, but feeling good about winning the game, "naturally" helped along with a few beers and spirited camaraderie. Basically, that was the essence of old timers' hockey.

VI. Game Two (the return of Boomer and his prolific scoring)

One of the most worthy features of old timers' hockey is the flexibility or maybe it is the acceptance of situations that the old guys and gals have to cope with. Coping is one trait all old folks have learned ... over the years ... and through their experiences. Unlike most hockey teams where some form of servitude prevails, old timers miss games without the wrath of the Lord or their teammates descending upon them. Like Big Gerry, taking off to play slow pitch ball at the Senior World (actually western North America) Games in St. George, Utah, during a couple of weeks in October. Or Hank's going off once or twice a year as a volunteer to do international development projects in some foreign country or other. Or Gentleman Jock and several others who made like "snowbirds and flock off" south anytime from early December to late March. And then there is the master Machiavellian, Boom Boom, who schemes his various conferences (really tax-paid boondoggles), visits his in-laws somewhere or other, takes sick leave and then, naturally, his vacation times, in various creative combinations. Since he is an accountant, who is surprised at his creativity, given the kinds of tricky or devious services received by an ever-growing list crooked corporations.

Before the Game

Just like old pucksters drift out of a dressing room, they drift in, usually with a little more vigor and vitality. Some actually stroll or saunter in. Naturally, Charley Hustle comes bustling into the room, full of enthusiasm --- great guy to have on a team, so energizing and upbeat. He's talking like he skates, about a mile a minute. "How are you? You're looking great ... ready for a big game tonight? Did you sell your Grey Cup tickets yet? How's your golf game ... you're a good golfer ... I remember golfin' with you a couple of years ago ... at our wind-up party ... you were terrific! Where's Max? Does he have his new teeth yet .. or more importantly, is he bringing the beer?" and so it went as Charley chirped away in a steady, high-paced stream of babble; chatter might be a nicer word, especially since Charley Hustle is about as nice a guy as there is ... anywhere!.

Max entered the room, almost like Charley's mention of his name was an introduction. He was loaded down with his big hockey bag (almost as large as he was if you stand it on end), his sticks and the most important item of all ... (drum roll and trumpets sounding) **the beer bag.** Max's faithful and dutiful custody of the beer bag and its contents for all of the years that he had played on the Old Boys' team, had made him its perpetual MVBP (Most Valuable Beer Provider), a take-off on the illustrious award of MVP. For most players, MVP is an honor bestowed with prestige and dignity. With the Old Boys and other old timers' teams like it, MVP has other inane and irreverent interpretations which we won't go into right now.

Rather let's turn to the chatter that started with the entrance of Boom Boom, to the accompaniment of Mikey "singing" a ragged version of Trini Lopez's old hit song "boom boom! boom boom! ..... going to get along without you now .... boom boom! boom boom! .... been getting along without you big guy...." Roars of laughter reverberated around the room. As a "singer", Mike was no Caruso, Sinatra, Elvis or Trini Lopez!

Boom Boom's jovial presence and the jocular reactions to Mikey were causes for merriment. He was greeted with a hail of comments, most of which were not very nice by common social standards in civilized societies. But there were some exceptions, like Charley Hustle's greeting.

Charley (hollering above the noise): "Hey Boom Boom, welcome back! Why weren't you here last week ... contract dispute ... want more money for your prolific scoring ... and that means on the ice?

As the old guys get the drift of Charley's questions, waves of laughter rolled around the room.

Boom Boom: "Missed me, did ya?"

Hank: "Not really ... we won last week ... not sure you can make the team this year... don't look like you're in very good shape..!

Max: "Did he ever?"

Boom Boom: "What kind of talk is that, you guys? Hey, nice mouth you got there Maxie. What happened to your teeth? Some angry husband punch you out for foolin' around with his missis???

Max: "Wouldn't mind that so much ... as getting hit with a puck .... playing with a bunch of young guys."

Boom Boom: "Can't be talking about our team ... our league. Serves you right for playing with those kids ... they'll get you every time"

Hank: "How was Frisco, Boomer? Great city, isn't it?"

Boom Boom: "Bloody expensive, I'll tell you ..."

Charley: "What did it matter to you ... us taxpayers are paying the bills ... anyhow. Right!"

Boom Boom (ignoring Charley): "Went down to Fisherman's Wharf, went to my favorite restaurant ... Pier 69 ... been going there since I was a kid with my folks ... wanted to have a "Crab Louie" ... my all-time favorite salad ... it was still on the menu ... guess how much it was...?"

A rare moment of silence blanketed the room as the Old Boys contemplated the question and their answers.

Sad Sam: "I don't know ... maybe 15 bucks ... U.S.!"

Max: "Ya, that sounds about right to me .... maybe a little less"

Boom Boom: "Would you believe 24.95 ... in U.S. dollars ... nearly 40 dollars Canadian ... for a bloody salad that used to be less than 10 bucks, U.S. or Canadian ... now it's nearly 40 ... still can't believe it .... had a bowl of chowder instead ... and it was about 10 bucks ... U.S. ... for a glorified soup .... won't be going there again .... after nearly 50 years ... kind of sad .... it's expensive down there ... we're better off here."

Jock: "In more ways than just cost of living ... did you encounter any road ragers or pistol-packing types?"

Boom Boom: "No, but we were coming up to a stop light and I looked in the rear view mirror and what did i see?"

Andy (interjects): "A sleigh with eight tiny reindeer....?"

Another roar of laughter in an already raucous room.

Boom Boom: "Ya, right ... don't I wish! No. There was the biggest set of front tires I've ever seen ... filled up the entire rear view mirror ... I looked around and there was the craziest looking monstrosity on wheels .... like a jeep perched up on these wheels ... they were huge ... like an earth mover or Boeing 747 wheels ... way too big for the cab or whatever you call it ... guy was sitting there, revin' his motor .... thought he was gonna run right over us ... really kinda scary!"

Max: "Did he?"

Charley Hustle: How was your summer, Boomer?"

Andy: "What's wrong with your memory, Chuckles? You guys played summer hockey together. Boom Boom has only been away for a week ... on his latest junket for 'government business'. Now there's an oxymoron!!!

Jean Pierre: "Having a problem with Oldzheimer's, Chucky .... or just short-term memory loss?"

Charley: "Why don't you go away, J.P.? We wouldn't miss you, you dork."

Big Gerry: "Now, now boys ... don't fight. Save your energy for the game ... we're playing those hot shots from Le Grande ... you know those guys who skate like the wind."

Mikey (with his characteristic smirky smile): "You mean they pass wind."

Andy: "Get serious ... this is old timers. How many guys do you know that skate very fast ... in this league?"

Guy (who just entered the dressing room): "I do ... guess you were talking about me, *n'est pas."*

Andy: "Ya, we're talkin' about you and all of those peasoupers from Le Grande ... those poutine eaters."

Guy: "Hey tea biscuit, *mange la merde* .... and mind your mouth!"

Andy: "Look who's talking. I know what you said, *en francaise* ... I saw Mr. Trudeau say that on tv a few years ago and he got a lot of heat for such vulgarity."

Max (tiring of the yakking between Guy and Andy, changed the subject): "So, what the "f" did you do in Frisco, Boomer?"

Boom Boom: "Went to a ball game ... saw the Cardinals beat the Giants ... good game but nothing sensational

... both teams are getting ready for the playoffs ... Bonds got a home run..."

Jock: "Boy, he's sure having a great year ... hitting for a great percentage ... all of those bases on balls .... the highest on-base percentages since Ted Williams ..."

Mikey: "Ya, and he doesn't need steroids to take a walk."

Larry: "What else did you do, Boomer?"

Boom Boom: "We went to the Great Pacific Brewery ... that was the highlight ... the ultimate .... the *piece de resistance* "

Guy: "Hey you anglo, quit messing up our beautiful language!"

Andy: "Looks like you brought a keg back with you Boomer ... in your gut."

Boom Boom (ignoring Guy and Andy, continued): "Man, you should have seen those huge vats or whatever they call those big beer storage tanks ... huge, really huge ... hold something like 250,000 six packs in them ... would take us forever to drink that much beer."

Max: "Or die trying..."

Hank: "Maxie, you damned near died once ... and you weren't even drinking then."

Max: "Ya, i know ... but it was all the "f'g" boozin' I did for the previous 40 years ... that stuff will kill you ..."

Andy: "Don't think so. Look at Boomer ... he must have drank one of those vats. How much do you weigh, big guy ... 250 ... 300 pounds?"

Boom Boom: "What a guy has to take because he is well built ... especially from you little guys ... and a flakey goalie at that."

And so it went; seemingly mindless banter bubbling around the room as the Old Boys got ready for their game with Les Rouge Rogues du Le Grande.

Game highlights (although not on the "big screen")

Boom Boom's performance was the "story" of the game against Le Grande, a small neighboring town to Joxville. All the Old Boys expected that he would be featured on TSN's plays of the day - three goals, the big "hat trick" and his first opportunity to buy a round of drinks for the Old Boys ... truly a career highlight for the big guy from Peaceville. For the "record", it must be stated that Mr. Prolific was very fortunate to be playing with Guy that night. Not only was the speedy little centre iceman flying around the rink, he was very, very determined to beat Le Grande because of some old rivalries and various and sundry uncomplimentary comments that some of their "trash talkers" had made about Guy playing with the Old Boys and not for them. So Guy was out to show "them batard Rouges".

Les Rouges came out in high gear, then shifted to overdrive. "Holleee", yelled Guy, "were they ever moving ... themselves and the puck." The Old Boys were "hemmed in" their own end for most of the first half of the game. Le Grande scored two goals in the first three shifts on the ice; beauties at that, or so it appeared to the bewitched, bothered and bewildered Old Boys. Andy was angry. Mike was mad. Charley was "cheezed off". Guy was furious. And so it went throughout the team.

Andy (hollering like a "banchee"): "Get that #$%& f'g puck out of here .... take that guy!"

An endless stream of "encouragement" to his teammates spewed out of the usually articulate goalie.

Max (huffin' and puffin' heavily): "Screw you, Andy. Hang on to the f'g puck (gasping) ..... so we can get off ... we need a face-off."

Hank (yelling loudly): "Take that guy ... where the hell are the forwards? ... clear it ..."

Mike (muttering madly): "Crap ... they scored..."

Andy (muttering madly and loudly): "Son of a bitch .... should have had it..." Hank (calmly, befitting the senior d'man): "No way, Andy ... you didn't have a chance. They were all over us. Too bad we can't hit in old timers ... there's a couple of those guys I'd like to flatten..." his voice trailing off as he headed to the players' box and some respite from the onslaught of Les Rouges. As he approached the box Big Gerry and Jean Pierre were skating out to line up for the face-off.

Gerry: "Tough luck, guys ..."

Mike: "Get it back, boys...."

Le Grande picked up where they left off. When the puck was dropped, they took possession and into the Old Boys end it went with Les Rouges after it like a pack of dogs after a rabbit. "Holy smoke", muttersed James as the players in the cherry red jerseys flew around, skating, passing the puck, shooting, hitting some legs or sticks, more shooting, Andy stopping the puck and yelling: "Get the f....g puck out of here."

Charley (skating furiously, trying to get the puck): "Ya, ya .... we're trying."

By old guys' standards, the pace was torrid. Another shot, another save, a rebound. Big Gerry took a swipe at the puck. It bounced out to Larry who passed it quickly to Charley who was hustling up the ice toward Le Grande's goal. Max, trying to keep up to Charley, hollered "Charley", for some reason expecting a pass. Instinctively, Charley passed the puck to Max. He skated a few strides, then shot, wide of the goal.

Sad Sam (sitting on the bench): "Bugger ... don't know why Charley doesn't shoot ..."

Mike (panting furiously) "Ya, that damned Max couldn't hit a barn door ... with a shovel!"

Les Rouges got the puck and whirled back up the ice toward the Old Boys' goal. But their right winger got ahead of the puck and went offside. "Tweet ... tweet", (or some such sound) went the referee's whistle. Off the ice came Charley and his line. Out went Guy, Boom Boom and Doc along with Mike and Hank on defence. Guy won the face-off, deked his way around one red shirt, then another, gathering speed as he whizzed toward Les Rouges' goal. He didn't pass or shoot. He kept the puck, skated behind the net, looking for one of his teammates to pass to, soon. Just as he was about to be checked, his wrists flicked, his stick moved and the puck flew out in front of the goal where Boom Boom was positioned (like a pyramid). The puck hit Boomer's stick "right on the tape", he reacted instinctively, pushing (he would say "snapping") the puck toward the goal - (an eternity elapsed) before it slid between the goalie's legs into the net

Doc ("high-fiving" the goal scorer): "Way to go, Boomer ... good goal. Great pass, Guy"

Boom Boom: (panting profusely): "Thanks ... great pass, Guy..."

Guy (smiling with his teeth-gapped smile): "Ya, now we're goin'."

And so it went throughout the game. Les Rouges were virtually flying around the rink, passing, shooting and playing most of the game in the Old Boys' end of the arena. Andy and his defencemen got in the way and kept most of the shots out of the goal. Still, by the end of the second period, Les Rouges were ahead by a score of 6 to 4. Somehow or other, mainly some weak goal tending by the other team, the Old Boys stayed close. The score was 6 to 5, then 7 to 5, 7 to 6, 7 to 7. With just a few minutes to play, Guy got the puck and started one of his "whirling dervish" dances and flights up the ice, his wingers trailing. As Yogi Berra has said before, "It's deja vu, all over again".

Guy skated around a roly poly red clad defenceman, did some incredibly deft maneuvers, skated behind the goal looking for an Old Boy to pass the puck to, ignoring Hank and then spotted Boom Boom cruising "into the slot". With a flick of Guy's wrists, then the flash of his stick and zip went the puck onto Boomer's stick. As Foster Hewitt said so many times "He shoots, he scores." And so the Boomer did, rifling the puck "upstairs" into the upper left corner of the net, past the outstretched glove of Les Rouges' goalie. Boom Boom had his hat trick, the Old Boys were ahead 8 – 7. The Old Boys were in a frenzy almost like a team winning the Stanley Cup, the Memorial Cup, the World Cup, a tea cup or some other momentous occasion in hockey history.

And so the game ended. The teams lined up and made feeble efforts at shaking hands and muttering some inane words like "good game", "thanks", "merci" and thinking other kinds of thoughts ... to themselves. The teams were not the most friendly with each other, even by old geezers' generous standards. After the gratuitous hand shakes, the Old Boys kind of strutted off the ice, feeling pretty damned good and wanting Les Rouges to know it, despite their extreme state of fatigue.

Mike (skating beside Big Gerry toward the players' bench): "Sure don't want those Grande guys thinking that they're in better shape or some how deserved to win ... even if they did..."

Big Gerry (sucking air like a beached whale): "Ya .. wouldn't want that ...."

Mike: "... Andy was the difference ... he played great."

Post game joys

Off the ice, the Old Boys shuffled, stumbled and, with some of the younger ones, almost pranced into the dressing room, filled with the exuberance that comes from winning a game, especially when the other team is not only "good" but better than yours. Les Rouges were a darn good team and the Old Boys knew that Andy's goal tending was the difference between winning and losing. Plus, big Boomer scored three goals, a rare feat in most hockey leagues but especially in old guys' shinny where scoring proficiency is usually limited to fond memories or vicarious enjoyment of feats gone by or others' achievements. When the Old Boys reached their room, there was Boomer sitting on the bench with a smile that looked like a full moon, a "happy face", with a hint of a smirk in it --- like "I showed you buggers" written all over it. Boom Boom wasn't going to be smiling too long because, the Old Boys had a way of keeping their teammates humble.

Big Gerry: (with some sarcasm): "OK, ok, Boomer, so you scored three ... sure lucky you were playing with Guy .... anybody could have scored three ... and a dozen more ... if only they kept their stick on the ice ... and didn't have cement hands."

Boom Boom (feigning mortal injury by placing his hand over his heart) "How can you say that ... you cruel old bureaucrat?"

Big Gerry: "Easy ... I speak the truth!!!

Boom Boom (making some snorting sounds): "Can you spell it?"

Big Gerry: "Ya, *i t* ... Ha! Ha!"

Boom Boom: "And that rhymes with you know what ...! ... that's about as close as you're going to get to the truth ... you big turd!"

Guy (enthusiastically interrupting the dialogue between Big Gerry and Boom Boom): "Yipee, we beat those batards!"

Charley: "What about old Boom Boom? ... getting the 'trick'!"

Guy: "Ya, free beer for us ... pass 'em around Maxie you old bugger."

Mike (talking to Guy): "Boy, did you ever make big boy look good ... with those passes ... right on the tape ... in front of the goal... have you been talking to your old buddy, Mario?"

Guy (ignoring the reference to #66): "Hey, Boomer played well ... he got the goals ... give him credit."

Sad Sam (dolefully): "Hell, all he had to do was get in front of the goal ... keep his stick on the ice ... and push them into the goal ... even I could have scored ... with my cement hands!"

Mike: "Guy, you skated miles out there ... and those passes ... even ham-hands Hank could have scored!"

Hank (feigning self deprecation): "Oh, ... I'm not so sure about that ... Boomer has those soft hands ... like the Great One and Mario."

Mike (making a gagging sound): "Cut the B.S. ... look at Boomer's hands ... they're made of concrete ... or at least plaster ... surely the Lord must have thrown away the mold for those mitts!"

Given the oldsters' limited attention span, dynamic thought processes or some other fluke of nature, parts of the babble drifted to other subjects.

Max (primarily to Larry, but loud enough for others to hear): "Are you going to the Flatland tournament?

Larry: "Not likely"

Max: "Won't Momma let you go with the boys for a weekend? ... maybe bring her along. She'll enjoy my company."

Larry (nearly choking): "You must be kidding. She's a classy lady!"

Mike (interrupting): "What the hell did she see in you ... if she's such a classy Lady?"

James: "Newton's law ... opposites attract...."

Charley: "Come on Larry .... we need you ... for your back checking..."

Another burst of laughter fills the room as the Old Boys think about Larry's lackadaisical efforts at backchecking, rarely a forte of old timers, except for skaters like Guy and Charley Hustle.

Max: "Hey Mikey, remember that red head ... two years ago ... at Flatland?"

Mike: "She was blonde ... are you color blind ... or having short term memory problems?"

Andy: "...or both ..."

Max: "Blonde ... brunette ... who the "f" cares? She was a beauty! Wonder if she's still there?"

Mike: "Better phone ahead and make a reservation ... with her."

Sad Sam (dolefully): "Is she a hooker?"

Max: "Nice f'g talk ... I'm in love with her."

Charley: "What's this talk above love? How do you spell that .... *s e x*!"

Mike: "Don't you have one in every port, Maxie ... no big deal for a bachelor stud like you, baby."

The whole room full of oldsters erupted in gasps, moans, groans and other farm yard noises befitting such blather

VII. Game Three (on a winning streak!!!)

Getting up for the Bloozers!

For the Old Boys, winning two consecutive games was a "winning streak". Winning streaks are important to old timers' teams, just like they are to kids, younger men and women, pros, "rank" amateurs or any one else who plays competitive games or sports of any kind. Winning streaks are rare and to be enjoyed and, if at all possible, extended, at least to three games or more.

The third game would be a tough one. In old timers' shinny especially, easy games are unusual. Old guys can find lots of ways of losing and few ways of winning games. The Old Boys were playing the Bloozers, a tough old bunch from across town. Their team should have been named Father Times. While they didn't play with scythes, they often used their sticks like they were. They did not skate as fast or pass as accurately as Les Rouges but they just seemed to wear down the other team. They played their positions well, let the puck do the moving and had a couple of ex-pro snipers who knew how to put the puck in the net - like it had eyes.

When Andy came into the dressing room, he didn't seem to be his ebullient self. He looked kind of glum even though it was a great day for the stock markets; Toronto was up about 150 points and New York had shot up by 241. Mr. Affable looked more like Mr. Miserable. After a few minutes of kibitzing around the room with the guys he went into one of his "routines", part of which was to talk trivia. Andy was at his trivia questioning best.

Andy (to Charlie Hustle and anybody else who might be listening while they were putting on their gear): "Eight players in the NHL have scored 70 goals in a year. Who are they?"

Charley (looking pretty smug): "The Great One, Esposito, Mario ......" Mikey (with a smugger look on his face): "Those are the obvious ones..."

Charley (looking rather annoyed): "Alright smart guy, who were the others?"

Mikey (starting to look a little apprehensive): "What about Mike Bossy?"

Hank (a non-scoring d'man): Andy, did you say in a season or a life-time?

Andy: "You figure it out, dummy!"

Hank (realizing that his humor was not appreciated at a time when his buddies were thinking muttered): "Thanks, old buddy."

Sam (who usually was silent or, at most, soft-spoken responded to Andy's question): "I'd say Kurri and Messier"

Mikey: "That figures since you're such an Oiler fan."

And so it went until seven of the 70 goal scorers were guessed correctly. The eighth had the Old Boys stumped. After several minutes of random and increasingly eclectic guessing and annoying teasing by Andy, he finally put the frustrated boys at ease by giving them a clue.

Andy: "You'll find the guy in a dime."

Max: "What kind of a 'f'g' clue is that?"

Andy: "For you Maxie, probably none ... because you're so clueless!"

Big Gerry: "Nickels, Bernie Nichols! Is that the eighth one?

Andy: "You got it big guy ... good for you."

Larry: "Guess you were doing something with all of your spare time ... sitting in that big office ... with not much to do ... except shuffle some papers ... go to some meetings ... sharpen some pencils ... collect some ill-gotten commissions ... and read *The Hockey News*.

After their period of thinking about Andy's question, the Old Boys were in a pensive mood. One could almost hear the wheels of their minds, creaking and grinding around the room. Quickly, by old guys' standards, Hank piped up with a question for Andy.

Hank: "Hey Andy, what town is Gordie Howe from?"

Andy (responding immediately and impetuously): "Saskatoon!!!!"

Hank: "Nope"

Andy: "Estevan!"

Hank (with a smug smile spreading across his rugged old mug): "Nope"

Guy (who had just come into the room as the question was asked): "Prince Albert!"

Mikey: "Biggar! Have you seen the sign going into that town? It says 'New York is big ... but this town is Biggar."

Hank (still smiling, in part because he remembered the train ride and going through Biggar on his way to

Saskatoon for the New York Ranger hockey camp many years ago): "Nope"

After several minutes of sporadic and wrong answers, Hank gave the Old Boys some clues. He even mentioned some flowers like roses, daffodils, tulips. Still there was no correct answer. So Hank gave in and said in a condescending way: "The answer to the question ... in case any of you guys forgot .... and that's appropriate for old timers ... is Floral, Saskatchewan." Then Hank went on to tell his story about meeting Gordie Howe to Andy, Boom Boom, Sam and the other Old Boys who were within earshot. (That story can be found in a subsequent segment entitled "Special Times".)

An easy win!

True to form, the Baby Blooze waddled out onto the ice and did their "warm-ups" like a bunch of old guys sitting in a bar or ducks on a pond. Most just sat on the bench and watched the others go skating by. That indifference or complacency kind of annoyed the Old Boys, all of whom skated around the rink, did some stretching exercises and tried to warm up the old bones and muscles. Then they took lots of shots at Andy, to build up their goalie's confidence if not to sharpen their shooting eyes.

What a contrast the Bloozers' game was from the two previous ones: the Mid Knights who played tough and aggressively and Les Rouges who were in perpetual motion. By comparison, the Baby Bloozes seemed to be in slow or no motion, had considerable difficulty getting to the puck and making good plays. Their passes were errant. Worse still, when they had scoring chances, their shots on goal were in the right general direction but more hit the back boards than were directed inside the goal posts or under the crossbar. Andy and the rest of the Old Boys had a very relaxing game. They kind of goofed off and lollygagged through it, scoring on their first three shots and being ahead by eight or nine goals before James and Jock told their team mates to "slack off" and not run the score up ... a rare occasion for the Old Boys.

Games have strange quirks and a lot of luck in them. When people play card games, so much depends on what they are dealt. Even the expert bridge players have difficulty taking tricks when they have hands full of low cards. Crib players need cards that they can make "15s", runs, three or four of a kind and other combinations if they are to win. Poker players cannot get by on bluffing alone. Every now and then they have to have a "full house", a "flush" or other legitimately winning hands. In hockey games, some teams are dealt better players. Well, the night that the Old Boys played the Blue Bloozers was one of those times when our heroes were dealt a winning hand.

Charley and Guy were playing on the same line. Their passes seemed to "have eyes", hitting each other's sticks at just the right time and place. Both were gifted forwards with super skating skills, hard, accurate shots that were usually on the nets and maneuvers that were, at their best, fascinating, if not spellbinding, to behold. Both of them had "hat tricks" before the game was half over and, by association rules, could not score more than that or else they would be penalized for each additional goal. So they slowed down their pace, passed more to poor old Max who was lagging behind more than usual. The "hot shots" even traded positions with Mikey and Big Gerry on defence.

At the other end of the rink, Andy may as well have brought his "geetar" instead of his goal stick. He spent more time by himself than the Maytag repair man. At times, when the action was in the Bloozer's zone, he skated around the net, over into the corners and seemed to be performing one of his musical routines. From time to time, especially after the Old Boys "let up", he got some action but few of the Bloozers had really good chances to score and when they did, old Andy "stoned them". No! he did not sell them drugs!

So the gregarious goalie had an easy time "earning" a shutout.

As the game came closer to ending, the Old Boys stepped up their efforts to preserve the shutout for Andy, mainly because they wanted a free round of beer. The d'men were blocking shots, the forwards were back-checking and keeping the puck out of their own end. The Old Boys did not trust their old penny-pinching netminder and his parsimonious ways. From several past experiences, they knew damned well that Andy would let a weak goal in if he had the chance to do, just so he would not have to buy a round of beer for his team mates. So Andy "earned" a shutout, whether he wanted it or not.

For the Old Boys, it was an ambivalent kind of game. Naturally, they liked to win but not in such a lop-sided way 11 to 0. One-sided games are not much fun for the winner and a lot less fun for the losers. But, for the winners, they had some consolation. Twas a great night for free beer. The sharpshooters, Guy and Charley, scored "hat tricks" and Andy got a shutout. Three rounds of free beer for the boys. Whoop-te-do!!!

About the only "down side", using a financial term for analogy, was suffered by Sam who was hit, inadvertently, from behind and had his stick broken by one of the out-of-control Bloozers. At times, Sad Sam seemed to be like that Joe Schpluk or whatever his name was in Al Capp's Lil' Abner cartoons many years ago. He seemed to be always under a cloud which frequently rained or, in old geezers' terms, pissed on him. Not only did he have damaged shoulders and other body parts but he was injury-prone to boot (whatever "to boot" means). So, there he was in the Bloozers' corner trying to get control of the puck when one of their rather large and awkward d'men barreled into him, crashing poor old Sam to the ice. To add injury to insult, the big old oaf fell on top of him. Some time passed, maybe nanoseconds, while the two players lay on the ice. Both Bloozers and Old Boys, were quite dubious about whether or not Sam had survived the double-barrelled hits by the big Bloozer. After the old Bloozer rolled off, the Old Boys could at least see their team-mate. He kind of moaned, groaned and rolled over on his back, looking very groggy (and not from drinking the stuff) and laid on the ice for a few minutes which really seemed like a long time, even for seniors.

Instinctively, players from both teams gathered around the fallen warrior, asking umpteen questions, few of which made much sense if anybody stopped to think rationally about them. "Are you hurt" was the most frequent dumb query. "Where are you hurt" made some sense, except for the fact that Sam was only semi-conscious and might have said anything in response. Eventually, Doc skated from the players' box to his fallen team mate and asked some intelligent questions like "Are you dizzy", "Can you move your hands and feet" and "Do you feel any numbness in your back?"

After some rather agonizing time for the Old Boys and Bloozers, Sam the sad and hurting one, was helped to his feet, really his skate blades, and half carried off the ice. When he arrived at the players box, he asked where his stick was and was told by Mikey that the "damned thing got broken". Was Sam ever angry. He turned beet purple. He swore, he ranted, raved and damned near went back on the ice after the over-sized Bloozer d'man who had crushed him *and* his hockey stick. To this day, no one is sure why Sam was so mad about his stick being broken. He never bothered to explain his behavior. It was kind of strange, reminding Hank of those famous words by Robert Service, in "*The Cremation of Sam McGee*": "There are strange things done in the midnight sun, by the men who moil for gold." Similarly, there are strange things done on the ice by hockey players or those playing like such.

Post mortem

The lopsided game and Sam's injury put a bit of a dampener on the last part of the game. After the game was over and the opponents' hands had been shook, gently punched or "high-fived", the Old Boys skated gingerly off the ice and into their dressing room. The post-game assessment of the Bloozers' demise and commentary was very much like a wake in that the Old Boys gathered in their room to reflect on their opponents' death and celebrate.

Jean Pierre was sitting on the bench, having a "free" beer and, for the staid old guy, more or less celebrating the game and its results, especially the two hat tricks and the shutout --- the "three freebies". He started to tell a story about some medical report he had heard about on tv. The report was about guys having their penises "broken" and cited a couple of examples. One guy on his honeymoon apparently fell on his "hard one" and it was fractured. Another guy fell out of a tree or off a ladder and broke his cock. Most of the Old Boys were just entered the dressing room and were dubious about the tales being told by J.P. They sounded so painfully incredulous that looks of doubt, puzzlement and wonderment covered the faces of his team mates.

Max (in his usually diplomatic way said): "That 'f'g' B.S., J.P."

Big Gerry (opined): "Sounds like that stuff in those tabloids."

Mikey: (with a look of pain on his face): "Can you imagine how painful that would be...? Hey Doc, could that happen ... really happen ... or is that some kind of crap that the media are using to attract viewers?"

Doc (hesitant to answer medical questions): "Well ... in theory that could happen ... I suppose ... I've never seen a fractured penis ... but have read about some serious injuries. You know that a penis is just muscle, tendons, skin and so forth ... not really a bone ... like it is often referred to ...."

After the brief lull in the room while Doc talked about broken penises, bedlam broke loose. Almost every Old Boy seemed to be talking about the topic, and rather emotionally. Obviously, every one of the old guys could relate to the subject and its rather horrific implications.

Sooner or later, the discussions "petered out". The stories, jokes, banter and other babble turned to various subjects, most of which related to hockey, namely the game against the old, moribund Bloozers.

About an hour later, most of the topics and the Old Boys had been exhausted and were in the process of heading home. It was still early so Sal, Big Gerry, Boom Boom and Charley Hustle thought they would head over to Barney's for a quick one. "A quick one" has a range of meanings for old guys. It could mean one beer (not very likely), one pitcher of beer (more likely) or some other quantity that could be divided by one which meant almost an infinite number of possibilities, far beyond the scope of such a limited narrative.

• •

VIII. Game Four (Go away Willie, we don't need you!)

Superstitions and ominous signs

Before proceeding, some perspective is useful, if not necessary. First of all, the Old Boys had **won three straight games**. In their glorious past, there were seasons when the team had not won three games out of a dozen or 25 percent for the statistically inclined, much less a trio in a row ... like one, two three ... one win right after another. WOW!!! So, in relative terms, and Dr. Einstein proved that everything is relative, the Old Boys were flying high ... enjoying it and even fantasizing ... about an undefeated season. That was when some concerns were raised about breaking their luck and their winning streak. That was when Big Gerry, Sal, Andy and Mike started talking about keeping everything the same so their streak would continue. That was when they decided they did not want to change any of their players, underwear, sox, gear or anything else for fear that their winning streak might be broken.

As you will recall, the Old Boys had won their first three games with a lot of the credit going to their first string puck stopper, Andy. He had played well in the first and third games but his play in goal during the second game against Les Rouges was just short of sensational ... and just a wee bit lucky.

Now, let me tell you if you don't already know or need to be reminded due to the fact that old folks often have difficulty remembering --- hockey players, especially goalies can be or are quite likely to be superstitious. Some don't like making changes when they are winning; they wear the same socks, shorts, shirts, shoes and other items of clothing, eat the same food, go to the can at the same time and whatever else they can do to maintain or simulate the conditions of their previous, victorious games.

So when a team is winning, especially if it is not accustomed to such success, superstitions start to seep into the behavior of individuals, spreading silently and insidiously through the team. Well, the Old Boys were not accustomed to winning, especially three games in a row. When they heard that Willie was slated to play goal in the fourth game, some fairly strong reactions (by old guys' standards) were expressed. Comments were heard like "Why can't he wait until after we lose a game? That will happen soon enough!" Or, "Who the hell does he think he is ... changing our chemistry? And so the strange commentary went, some in jest, some in truth, until and even after Willie strode energetically and enthusiastically into the dressing room.

What compounded the concern of the Old Boys were the ominous signs. Three of the team's "top guns" did not show up for the game ... and the Golden Oldies had a very good team. Yup, the unreliables - Guy, Big Gerry and Larry were not there by game time. Turns out that Big G. was off vacationing in Tahiti or some other exotic place ... where the weather was warm and the women danced with grass skirts and that's all ... or so the rumors go. That night loomed as a bad route for the Old Boys, like going down a long rough road to a beating.

A sense of fatalism seemed to settle into the Old Boys' dressing room. That gloom was heightened as the Old Boys trooped down the dark and dingy hallway and out onto the ice for their pre-game "warm-ups". Fears of losing the game pervaded the team members.

During the Old Boys' warm-up the d'men often passed the pucks out to the shooters and kind of looked over the other team. They liked to get some sense of who was playing for the opposition, how well they were skating, shooting, etc, etc, etc. "Hmm", Hank mused to himself "... seems like some of their hot shots aren't out tonight ... wonder where Dr. Death and Brian are ... and I don't see Jimmy or Franco ... hmmm, maybe they are short, too .... wouldn't that be nice ... would kind of equal out the teams .... maybe we can keep on winning ... even with Willie in goal." Hank started talking to other Old Boys as they skated by, remarking about the absence of the Goldies' hot shots. In response, he heard various affirmative noises, grunts and other sounds suggesting that they were aware of the other teams' turn out and were pleased with it.

Despite the encouraging absences of the Goldies' hot shots, there were more signs that the stars were not ideally aligned in the Old Boys' heavens. No referees had showed up to officiate the game. "Where the hell are Syd and Doug or Hans? Dam it, they know that they are supposed to be 'refing' here tonight", muttered James, the team rep, to anyhow who was close by.

The final superstitious "nail in the coffin" for the Old Boys that night was the fact that Big Gerry wasn't there. One of the forwards had to play defence and that was not a positive sign. "Oh joy," mused Hank annoyedly. "I hate having to play defence with those rookies. ... Sam isn't too bad ... he knows how to play his position ... and James played well last week when we were short on defence". "I don't like the signs" muttered Hank to Mikey who, in his jocular voice replied "Buck up partner, my wife read our tea leaves after dinner tonight ... and I am supposed to be a star tonight." "Oh, my gawd, another hex upon us," snorted Hank.

Time to rumble!

Instead of the game being underway, maybe it should have been described as underhanded. Despite the fact that that most, if not virtually all, of the geezers playing organized shinny are virtuous, a few "bad apples" are still in the barrel. Shortly after the game began, a marginal player by the name of Dick, how appropriate, from the Goldies and Dirk from the Old Boys start a little game of their own, called hooking and tripping. With referees such nonsense would not likely occurred and, for sure, would not have escalated into an on-going contest to determine who could pull off the stupidest stunt of the game.

Like undisciplined children, the unsportsmanlike antics spread. Players on both teams were off-side, sometimes deliberately. Others, especially the more aggressive old buggers got their sticks up as they jostled in front of each other's goal and followed through with "snap" shots that had all the features of "slap" shots. Bumping and pushing of opponents increased in frequency and intensity along the boards. (Remember, old guys' hockey in Joxville had rules and regulations against body-checking and slap-shooting.) Barry took a wicked elbow to the solar plexus that knocked the wind out of him, leaving him sputtering and swearing vociferously.

Then Maxie tripped a speeding Goldie as he whizzed by the slow-moving, almost stationary Old Boy. The tripped Golden Boy didn't appreciate such rude and rough treatment. He got up rather gingerly and cross-checked the league's oldest player from behind. Down went Max so hard that his stick flew up in the air like a helicopter and came down with a clatter against the side boards. "Play" stopped. All of the players gathered around the writhing soon-to-be septuagenarian who was laying face down on the ice, moaning, groaning, muttering and swearing ... profusely and profanely ..."You #@*&f'g sonofabitch, you *&)(+@#%bastard, ..." were just part of the tirade. For the old geezers who knew Max, his swearing, other guttural sounds and the movement in his legs and arms reassured them that he was okay or, at least, still alive. When Max had had his heart attack, he was "deathly still" and quiet. In fact, he was unconscious when he was found him lying on the floor of the dressing room. So, his vulgar verbiage and his body movements on the ice were of some comfort for the worried players gathered around and staring down at the old fallen fellow. Slowly and with the help of two other players, including the Golden Oldie who had flattened him with the cross check, Max staggered to his skates and wobbled off the ice to the players' box where he spent most of the game.

The incident between Max and the Goldie put an appreciable damper on the mood and tempo of the game. The "hot shots" cooled off appreciably. The rest of the old geezers played their regular cautious game and obeyed the ethos, rules and regulations of the game. With the intensity and pace of the game lessened considerably, more goals than usual were scored as the lax play seemed to lessen the concentration of the goalies. Old Boys who rarely scored, like Sam, Sal and Hank, each potted a goal. Doc, Jean Pierre and Charley Hustle add two each. Boom Boom, Mikey, James and, even Max after he had recovered sufficiently to skate, chipped in with one goal each. At last count, the score was more than a dozen each. The last shot on goal was likely to win the game but alas, no such winning goal was scored. The Old Boys and the Golden Oldies ended evenly and with a serious reminder that life is fragile, precious and must not be abused.

When the game ended, a sense of relief came over many of the players. They were thankful that no other player had been injured, on either team. Max's injury was more than enough of a reminder that they were all very vulnerable to being hurt. And it was also a clear reminder that refs were an essential part of the old timers' game, despite what some of the "younger bucks" and other *laissez faire*, "survival of the fittest" players thought about playing without such "officials". Even the after-game handshakes and "high fives" were more gentile and sincere. Virtually every player on both teams, with obvious and genuine concern, asked Max how he felt. Almost to a man, they were sobered by the cross-checking injury to Max, regretted that it had happened and relieved that no serious injuries had resulted ... although they knew that the injured old guy could have serious repercussions even after the game was over, when the dressing room was vacated and they went to their abodes; Max to his apartment by himself. Hank said a silent prayer for his buddy's safe sleep through the night. He and several others asked Max if he wanted to go to "emergency" or stay overnight with them. "Na", said Max in his tough old way ... "I'm fine ... no young "f'r" is going to put me down. I'll be okay ... thanks for asking."

"Overtime"

The somber mood that pervaded the game after Max was cross-checked carried on into the Old Boys' dressing room. With the passing of time, like ten or twelve minutes, careful observation of Max and the return, more or less, of his gregarious demeanor, his team mates relaxed their concerns and inhibitions. Some sense of normality returned about twenty minutes after the game and a brew or two into each of the players. Slowly and discretely, at least for old timers, the chatter, blather and banter was about the game, the dirty play and the abundance of scoring. Somehow, the tied game seemed fitting. It left the Old Boys with a feeling of ambivalence about the game; sad about Max's injury and the dirty play and happy that they had not lost such a lousy game. After the beer was all consumed in the dressing room and the hour was not unduly late, the Old Boys decided that they should have an "overtime" session ... at Barneys.

The truth is that the Old Boys do not play overtime in their league. However, overtime is a word that has various symbolic meanings, like the times that Mikey tells his wife that "they played overtime tonight" ... when he arrives home four or five hours after he left to play a game in an arena that was less than a mile or .625 km away on a clear night in October. Well, Mike's wife, like most gals, can smell a story, especially when their guys return reeking of beer, second-hand smoke and garlic from the chicken wings. What a sensual pleasure that must be for the fair damsels.

Overtime sessions were "played" at the nearest bar, pub or other "watering hole". Typically, the chatter and banter of the dressing room continued non-stop during the overtime sessions. Gathered around several tables pulled together, the talk or sometimes hollering over the din was about the game and sports in general with teammates beside or across the table from one another. From time to time, the conversations became rather serious and personal. After Game Four, Mikey and Hank were sitting beside each other, talking about their children (really young adults.)

Hank: "What are your son's prospects for the college team this year? He sure played well last year."

Mike: "Hard to say. Ya, he had a good year last year but that was last year ... and the new coach has done some recruiting ... tends to play his favorites.... so Jason is on the fourth line right now ..."

Hank: "You're kidding ... fourth line .... thought he might be on the first or second lines after last season ... what's happened?"

Mike: "Well, I don't really know for sure ... I try to have an open mind ... be objective ... but it's hard to be .... you know, it's your son and you want to be supportive ..."

Hank: "Ya, I know, I caused some trouble years ago ... being too supportive of my son ... probably cost him a spot on the triple A midget team."

Mike: "Jason is still on the team ... but we don't know for how long ... the coach cut three veterans .... a goalie and two forwards ... you must remember Kurt Klein, the shifty little centre ... and Billy Berg ... the big winger. They were cut and they were good players ... had been on the team for two years ... hard to say what could happen to Jason ... hope he stays ... he sure loves to play hockey ... don't know what he would do if he doesn't play for the college ... he doesn't want to play industrial league ... too many hackers and choppers."

Hank: "How is he doing with his courses?"

Mike: "He's doing well ... will never be on the Dean's Honor Roll ... but he is doing well ... wants to go into

Management ... he has a good head for accounting and ... (Mike hesitated to consider his words because he didn't want to sound too boastful) ... he has good people skills ... he gets along well with others ... he's worked on construction for the past couple of summers ... knows the aches and pains of labor ... but that was good for him ... toughened him up ... and he has developed some skills ... you know, like dry-walling, some roofing ... those kind of skills ... they're always useful ... especially if you have your own place ... and want to keep it up or improve it ... like Marie always seem to want.

Hank: "Skills are always good to have ... gives a kid better job prospects."

Mike: "Ya, he and some buddies are thinking about starting a small construction or ... maybe a repairs company ... his buddies are all journey men ... plumbers, carpenters ... that kind of work ... Jason could help ... and maybe take care of the management ... but he still has two more years of school ... and a lot can happen in that time..."

Hank: "Like he could get married ... ."

Mike: "Don't think so for a few years ... he's only 21 ... and doesn't seem too serious about any girl, ... yet....but you never know."

Several more old guys sauntered into Barney's. They had just finished their game and were feeling pretty good --- having won handily and knocked back a few brew already. Great combination for a bunch of oldsters still playing a young person's game. But they are kids at heart, even those who had had attacks, angioplasts or by-passes.

From across the table comes a jibe from Willie toward the two defencemen who have been having their serious conversation about Mike's son, kind of oblivious to the others around the table.

Willie: "Hey, you two ... you're looking pretty serious ... what are you scheming?"

Mike: "Bloody sales guys ... they're the ones who are always schemin' ... like lawyers and thinking that the rest of us are doing it ... too."

Hank: "Willie ... did you get Momma's permission to be out with the boys? It's kinda late ... for you isn't it? What about your beauty sleep?."

Willie: "Ya, i phoned her...."

Mike (choking on a mouthful of beer, then splutters): "You what ... got permission ... boy, are you ever pussy-whipped ... yuk!"

Charley: "Come on guys, Willie doesn't get out very often ... be nice to him ... nice to have you join us .... you big fat ugly sieve!"

• •

IX. Game Five (Does the non-losing streak come to an end??)

Before the Game

Lord only knows why some old guys are missed so much when they don't show up for their games. Players like Doc, Guy and Charley Hustle, sorely are missed because they are very good players ... "at both ends of the rink", meaning that they are good goal scorers and, even more importantly to the d'men and the team, they're good back-checkers who know what to do with the puck once they get it on their sticks. Others, like Boom Boom and Big Gerry, are missed because of their presence. Both are large, strong and intimidating to the opposing teams, especially their forwards. Because they handle the puck well and do a lot of rushing and occasionally scoring, they are rather effective defencemen, even if they are converted forwards. Still others, like James, Sam and Max, play regularly and are reliable members of the Old Boy; guys that can be counted on to show up and play well almost every game. Besides, Max is in charge of the beer and other drinks, making him especially important to the Old Boys. And, maybe if the truth were known in its entirety, the Old Boys really do develop a sense of belonging and miss one another if they are not playing ... for whatever reason.

Be all of that as it may, Doc, Guy and Boom Boom were missing for the fifth game of the young season. (Hmmm, old guys playing in a young season ... seems kind of incongruent or inconsistent or both.) From time to time, Doc was "on call", meaning that he had higher priorities, like his professional obligations, than playing old timers' hockey, if that is understandable. For medical doctors, it is understandable. For others, not making old timer hockey the top priority was a matter of some misunderstanding and much puzzlement ... like for Max. "Where the hell is Guy, that little frogaphone," yelled Max. "How can I be expected to lead the "f'g" team in scoring if my playmaker isn't here? ... and Doc's missing too. Cripes, I might as well go home." "Ya, that's fine with us", piped up James "... you brought the beer ... that's all that counts. You can go you miserable little bugger." "Nice talk Jimmy boy ... here I am, your faithful servant ... bringing the beer, retrieving the cans, taking them back for refunds ... buying the beer at the best prices I can negotiate ... and you throw me off like a "f'g" old shoe."

A sudden silence pervades the room as several of the Old Boys remember the last game when Max was flattened by the cross-checking Golden Oldie. Somewhat facetiously James says softly, "Gee sorry Max you miserable little prick ... I didn't mean to hurt your tender feelings" to which Mikey quickly add "no sense, no feelings". "Screw you Mikey", responded Max. "See if I set you up tonight, you motherf'r." Instantly, Mikey replied, "Thanks for nothing Maxie ... as if you ever set me up ... do you know how to pass the bloody puck?" "Hell man, I used to lead the old TO Thistles in scoring ... got as many "f'g" assists as Gretzky ... in one season." "In your dreams Maxie," shot back Mikey "... in your dreams". And so the banter, blather and babble went, back and forth and around the room until the big guy, Gerry strolled into the room looking like a million dollars; all tanned, happy and energetic.

"Well, look who's here ... the happy Hawaiian," chirped Charley. "What are you talking about, my fine feathered friend," replied the returning ball player. "I was nowhere near Hawaii ... that was last year ... you probably don't know Hawaii from Tahiti or Samoa ... do you Chucky Boy?" "Whoa big guy," replied Charley Hustle with a tinge of annoyance in his voice and facial expression. He hated to be called "Chucky" which is exactly the reason that Gerry did it. "Chill out, Chucky", responded Big Gerry, "I'm still in a holiday mood and don't want to get out of it ... if I don't have too ... and right now, I don't have to ... so screw you."

Charley Hustle was not to be deterred in his attack upon the biggest guy on the team. Charley made some snide comments about Big Gerry's bigger gut as the big d'man started taking his clothes off. "Gee", said Charley, "your gut is bigger than your pencil ... at least it sticks out further. Big Gerry, still in a jovial mood responded by saying "You should have seen my big bat at the Seniors' ball tournament. Wow!!! Was I ever hot ... hit about 750 with four dingers ... just cranked those puppies over the fence like rockets ..... and I come back to this kind of treatment ... hardly a fitting welcome for a hero." "Hero, my "f'g" ass", quipped Max. And so the welcome went for Big Gerry despite the fact that every player on the team was pleased that he was back.

Big Gerry wasn't quiet for very long. "Where's the Booomer?," he roared, feigning dismay, disdain and disgust. "Suppose he's off on another vacation ... cripes, he's here one week, gone the next two or three ... and who knows where he is even when he's here ... he's such a rover ... would have been a natural back when seven players were used." "Ya, seven players played the whole game" added James going on to say "Boomer wouldn't last a whole game ... that's why he is on vacation ... or attending some fancy municipal meetings ... or whatever ... who knows?" "Who cares," chirped Max. "All we know is the "f'g" guy is not here and is probably spending taxpayers' dollars wherever he is ... wished I had a soft job like that ... rather than on the end of an idiot stick." Mikey scoffed, "You little bugger, you're lucky you have any stick ... so why don't you get on it and get dressed?" Charley interjected, "Be nice to Maxie ... he's the MVB ... most valuable beerman!" The oldest Old Boy agreed, "Ya, remember that boys ... I'm the MVB"

About that time Hank came into the room. Most of the Old Boys were there, yakking away, getting their gear sorted out, some had been put on as they talked, joked, laughed

... truly a pleasant atmosphere. Who says old guys can't multi-task? Hank walked across the room to sit by his old buddy, Andy. Andy looked a little apprehensive at the approaching d'man.

Hank: "How are you ... flake? Heard you were in the psych ward... Is that true?"

Andy: "F.... off, you dumb d'man."

Charley Hustle: "Now, now boys .... kiss and make up ..."

Andy: "He can kiss my ass ..."

Hank: "That would be better than your face ..."

Big Gerry (sounding kind of annoyed): "Hey you guys, knock it off ... you're disturbing my meditation ..."

Hank: "Just because you look like the Great Buddha doesn't mean you know anything about meditating ... oh, Great Buddha!"

Snorts of laughter, gasping and similar sounds come from the other Old Boys as Mikey comes back into the room from "goin' to the can".

Mike (looking down at his crotch and chuckling): "Hey, what are you guys laughing at? ... did I leave my fly open...?"

Andy: "Ya, and your dick is peeking out..."

Charley: "That's strange ... I can't see it ... and neither can Mikey!"

Big Gerry: "That reminds me of the old story about the fireman .... he went to a whore house .... had a nice chat with the lady of the night, talked about the terms for the evening ... the service ... or whatever.. "

Mike: "Chat ... is that what you're supposed to do with whores? I didn't know that."

Hank: "There's lots you don't know. So shut up and listen to the old pro..."

Big Gerry (continuing his story): "... so after some of the niceties ...

Mike (musing aloud): "... niceties ..."

Gerry (continuing): "Eventually, the fireman and the lady get into it. After some grunting and groaning, thrashing about ... you know the routine ... well, this chick ... all of a sudden says ... 'how are you doin' man?' Well, the fireman is a bit taken back by the question ... and kind of annoyed ... maybe even a little angry ... he stops his thrusting and snarls '... OK! ... why?' .... after a discrete pause ..."

Mike (musing aloud again): "... a discrete pause ... hmmm"

Gerry (continuing): " ... so she says, kind of sarcastically, well ... if you want to put out my fire, you're going to have to roll out some more hose."

Roars of laughter roll around the room as Sad Sam saunters into the room.

Sam: "What did I just miss? ... something about rolling out some hose... what do we have to do? ... flood the rink! ... I remember doing that back in Spring Hills ... when I was a kid .... we were rink rats."

Mike: "You're still a rat ... you little rodent"

Once upon a time, some wise person said that "silence is golden". Maybe that is so in a church or hospital. But, when an old timers' dressing room is quiet, something is seriously amiss. When normally ebullient guys like Andy are quiet, concern rises palpably in or among the team. That must have been what prompted Mike to tease Andy before the game.

Mike: "Hey, flake, you sure seem docile tonight. What's the matter ... didn't make a million bucks today?"

Hank: "Mikey, did I ever tell you how to make a hundred sousand bucks? It's really easy."

Mike: "Ya! Ya! I've heard your dear old mother's favorite story ... oh so many, many times. But I am serious. How much did you make this week ... Mister Capitalist?"

Andy: "If you would just listen Mr. Smart Guy, I would tell you."

Mike: "Ok, I'm all ears..."

Andy: "... more like all big gut ... or big mouth..."

About that time most of the Old Boys were heading out of the dressing room, down the hallway to their players' bench and out onto the ice for their warm-up and game against the Grey Ghosts. The Ghosts were a "regular" bunch of younger guys who were fun to play against. They had no "hot shots" or other overly aggressive guys who hadn't adapted to the old timers' ethos. Most of them did not take the game too seriously, although quite naturally they all wanted to play their best and win. Off the ice, they were a real party team who had all kinds of social activities ... wings at Barney's Pub, tailgate parties in the parking lot, pizza at Mario's, Grey Cup, Christmas, you name the special time and the Ghosts probably had a party for the occasion.

The Game

From the opening face-off, the "Ghosts" swarmed all over the Old Boys. That night, they seemed to be much younger and spryer than the Old Boys; more like a father and son game. Most of the first period was played in the Old Boys' end of the rink. The Ghosts scored first, a "flukey" goal, on a shot by their huge (almost as large as Big Gerry) right winger than deflected off of Mike's skate). Various vulgar utterances were forthcoming from Mike and Andy. Their second goal was not much better. A Ghost d'man scored a "seeing eye" from near the blue line. In fairness to dear old Andy, it was a high screened shot that he never saw. Despite that reality, the loquacious goal tender uttered a stream of curse words that would have embarrassed the most hardened criminal, sailor or salesman.

If it was any consolation to Andy and the other Old Boys (and it wasn't), the Ghosts' third goal was a "beauty"... a three way passing play that clicked like clockwork. A few minutes later, Big Gerry, showing the effects of playing slow pitch in sunny Utah, failed to clear a rebound and a Ghost forward swiped it past the out-of-position and prone Andy. By the end of the first period, the Old Boys were down by a score of 4-0.

Through the second and third periods the Old Boys "stepped up their game" and whittled away at the lead until the game score was even; but in last ten minutes, the Ghosts scored two goals to win 6-4. The "heart breaker" goal came from a penalty shot assessed against Big Gerry, for nobody seemed to know what or why (or else they were not saying). At times, the big guy had a disadvantage. He was so large, so strong and played so energetically, if not aggressively, that "lesser mortals" were knocked, pushed or otherwise moved into various uncomfortable and, oftentimes, horizontal positions. Talk about a "bull in the china shop"!

The Old Boys could have won the game if they had taken advantage of some of their "golden" opportunities. James missed two open nets, like wide open. (More about his cement hands, after the game). By his own estimate, Larry blew "about five good chances" and Mike, Charley Hustle, Sam, Max and nearly all of the other forwards missed quality chances to score, especially against the weakest goalie and defence in the league. As Charley Hustle lamented lamely as they skated off the ice, "Sometimes you can't beg, borrow or steal a goal."

After the Game

Maybe it was the frustration from losing a game they should have won, a full moon or envy about his vacation, sun tan and generally genial disposition, but whatever it was, Big Gerry got "dumped on" after the game ... for only a few minutes. Mikey started yapping about the correlation between their team losing and the re-appearance of Big Gerry. They had not lost in the previous four games. James added "his two cents worth" by stating that there was an "inverse relationship between Gerry playing and the team winning ... same as last year." Charley added to the blather by claiming (untruthfully) that the Old Boys had tried to trade Gerry during the off-season. "Ya, we tried to trade him, even offered to throw in a case of beer but no other team wanted him." After a few minutes of such nattering, the banter about Big Gerry and the loss to the Grey Ghosts waned and other timely topics were being discussed around the room.

Larry, the long time teacher and sometimes philosopher, was relating the loss to some of the dire conditions around the world. Normally a calm, laid back old guy, Larry was really "steamed" about the invasion of Iraq by the Americans and their phony "coalition of the willing". He was fuming as he said, "Sure Saddam Hussein is a dictator and probably a brutal one at that. But then so Mugabe in Zimbabwe and most of the leaders throughout Africa, the presidents of most of the former Soviet Union republics ... and China ... Burma or whatever they call it these days ... and on and on. What did the blankety blank Americans do about those bloody dictators?" Before anyone could say anything, Larry continued expressing his views, "Nothing! that's what the bloody Americans did ... nothing! There's only one reason why those bastards invaded and are occupying Iraq ... OIL," he shouted as he stood up abruptly and shaking his fist to emphasize his point of view. "Hell, Bush and Cheney are more evil than Hussein ... they have more blood on their hands than he does ... and the devastation of a country, its history ... and culture, its people and their future. Why don't the Americans impeach those bastards ... that Cheney and his puppet Bush Jr.?", asked the little guy with the sharp mind and Christian ethics as he headed off for the shower room, muttering angrily as he went ... "Thou shalt not kill!!!!"

Larry's views about the United States, stimulated some other conversations about conditions in that country. Big Gerry, just back from "down south" was talking about "the killings by the sniper around Washington, DC. The big old guy mentioned that about 13 people had been shot in Maryland and Virginia, apparently by some expert sniper ... reportedly trained by the U.S. military ... and the madman was threatening to kill little children because he wanted money." Gerry opined that "the chances of finding the killer were increasing because he was getting so brazen that he was bound to be caught ... like he had a death wish ... really crazy." Somebody asked: What would we do if such killings happened in Joxville? That halted the discussion momentarily as some of the Old Boys seriously pondered that scenario.

Mike: "Man, that's really hard to imagine ... for me. We seem so civilized ... few guns ... but then there's always the possibility of some crazy doin' a stunt like that ... like that kid in Sugartown ... a few years ago."

Hank: "Guess I would drive the kids to school in the van ... right up to the curb ... let them out the side door and have them run to the nearest door ... maybe even run with them. Heidi would keep the kids home until she was 500% certain that it was safe for them to go back to their classes ... and then she would wait a while."

Mike: "I don't know about using that van ... you're so high up --- you would be 'good pickin's' for a sniper ... better to use the car so you're lower in the traffic."

Max: "I wouldn't change anything I do ... that bastard wouldn't get me ...I'm such a old 'f''r'. Why would he want to shoot some old bastard like me?"

Charley: "Are you insane ... crazy guys will kill anybody ... look at those Chechnians or whatever you call them ... killing all those innocent school children in Russia ... they're insane."

James: "Ya, they must be insane or deeply disturbed by injustices or other harsh conditions ... poverty ... discrimination ... repression. Lord only knows what some of those people have suffered through before they explode ... in such terrible travesties..."

Charley: "Guess they just get to the point where they're so desperate and fanatical ... but to kill innocent children ... that's sheer madness!."

The intensity of the emotion and discussion of the brutal Iraq attack and the massacre in Russia seemed to drain much the vitality remaining after the Old Boys' game against the Ghosts. A calmness settled over the room as the old fellows mulled their thoughts about the crises and miseries around the world. The increasing price of gas, petrol to the Brits, was another annoyance.

Mike (being uncharacteristically somber): "Seriously .... what would you do about going to work ... or shopping ... of getting gas ... when the price is going up so much?"

Charley Hustle (also uncharacteristically somber): "I go to work early in the morning, so I'd be okay but my wife goes later ... she might be in trouble ... would have to make other arrangements ... like ..."

Big Gerry (characteristically flippant) "What the hell does going to work early in the morning have to do with the price of gas?"

Dirk (sarcastically); "Well... Charley old boy, you've said you wanted to get rid of her ... might be a good chance ... low cost ... low pain..."

James: "Cripes you guys are confusing me. What the hell are you talking about ... high price of gas ... getting rid of your wife ..."

Andy (angrily): "Shut up, you nerd ... this is a serious matter"

Hank: "I'd buy gas really late at night ... after midnight .."

James: "Oh, now I understand, you fuzzy-brained guys are back talking about the sniper around Washington ... boy, you sure lost me along the way."

Big Gerry: "Jimmy boy, you've been lost for a long time. Anytime you take an engineer away from his slide rule ... he's sure to be lost."

James: "You dummy ... I haven't used a slide rule in years!"

Gerry: "Ya, and you see what happens ... you are lost ... and confused... better find your slide rule ... and use it, man!"

Andy (wanting to bring the discussion back to the sniper ... for some reason or other.): "But that guy shoots people during the night ... he killed at least one at a service station ... while the guy was pouring gas into his car."

Mike (musing out loud): "Must have had a night scope on his rifle."

Charley: "And knows how to use it .... must be highly trained ... probably ex-military .... or maybe still in the military ... lots of military personnel around Washington.."

Hank (still thinking out loud about the earlier questions): "We would buy our groceries at a store with a big parking lot ... far away from the freeways ... he seems to be sniping from places close to freeways ... so he can make his escape"

The serious conversation continued for an unusually long time; maybe ten or twelve minutes as the Old Boys pondered the matter, especially within the context of their own daily living. Joxville was such a peaceful and civilized community it was hard to imagine such a tragic event. When Andy said it wouldn't happen around Joxville, the old geezers challenged the goalie's complacency.

Mike: "Who knows where the next madman is ... with all the guns around, especially in the U.S. ... and they bring up here."

Hank: "... Americans and their bloody guns ... their Constitution needs to be changed ... it's 200 years out of date ... was OK for the militia to bear arms back then ... when blunderbusses were used ... against bandits ... and wild animals ... but today ... with AK47s ... with scopes and clips and God knows what kind of screwed-up guys have them!

James: "Ya, those NRA clowns say it's not the guns that kill. Hell, those are weapons of mass destruction ... more Americans have been killed by guns in the U.S. than in all the wars they've been in."

Various snorts, guffaws and other sounds of disgust erupt throughout the dressing room.

Larry (seething as he spoke): "Ban all those bloody guns ... starting with hand guns ... time to become a civil society down there ...!"

Andy: "How many could such a crazy guy kill with a knife ... or a baseball bat ... or some other weapon before he'd get caught ... maybe a few but not 13 ... who knows how many he will kill before they get him!"

Mike: "I hope they string him up by the balls and let him hang there ..."

Max: "They should behead the 'f'r' in the city square!"

James (appearing to be calm): "Whoa ..... you guys sound as crazy as the sniper ... aren't we supposed to be civilized?"

Larry (in his moderate voice): "Yes, we sure are ... but are we?"

Andy (angrily): "Screw that shit ... if my kids get shot ... or my wife ... I want the guy's balls ...how can you be nice to a killer like that?"

James: "It's hard ... but we do have justice ... and a legal system ... you know ... the due process of law."

Mike (clearly annoyed): "Ya right, but it's all screwed up ... especially in the States ... letting so many people have guns like that. What are guns for? ... killing! ... killing! ... killing! ... killing! that's what they are for ... get rid of them....'

Hank: "And the Bible says thou shalt not kill .... one of the Commandments."

The serious discussion went on for a while. Clearly, the Old Boys were not happy after their fifth game. Maybe it was the on-going negative "news" of the media, maybe it was losing their first game of the season or maybe it was a full moon or some astrological phenomenon. About the only upbeat comments had to do with the different brand of beer that Max had brought.

Sam: "Good beer, Maxie ... about time we had something other than that dog piss that you've been bringing."

Max: "Go to hell ... that Old Pilsner is cheap ... we need some f..g money for the party fund ... ."

Andy: "Quit griping, Sam ... or you can bring the beer ... each game."

Sam: "I'm not griping. I was just complimenting Maxie about the good beer he brought tonight. What's wrong with that? Besides, I'm the back up beer man. So I've been there, done that ... have you ever been the beer man ... Andy?"

Andy: "Look at the gear I have to bring ... dummy. Do you think I could bring the beer ... too? smarten up, doufus!"

Thus endeth the snippets from the Old Boys' games, at least in their regular league. More action is included in following parts of this tome, mainly in the chapter following: *On the Tournament Trail* or some such title having to do with tournaments. OK?!?

X. On the Tournament Trail

Time is of the essence

Somewhere along the highways and byways of life, old guys and gals realize that their journeys are coming to an end. Few, if any, know when, or where, or how, their trip will end ... but they know and feel that they are coming down the "home stretch". So, they must skate, dance and get around as much as they can ... while they are able. Time is of the essence!

In that vein, one lovely lady has been heard to say poetically;

> Come on old boy,
> Time for more joy.
> Let's hit the road,
> While we can carry our load.

What attracts old guys and gals to tournaments? What motivates them to get off their sedentary back sides, go to all of the effort, time and expense of going to some place or other for several days of displacement and disruption of their laid back, easy as you go, pleasant life-styles?

For a whole lot of reasons, tournaments are special times for shinny-playing old folks. Some of the old guys and gals are retired, have an abundance of "free time", enough money to enjoy that time and, as the poem infers, the realization that their time is "running out". So they may as well enjoy life as much as they can, while they can.

And, as the trite old saying goes, "variety is the spice of life". Old geezers' tournaments provide "spicy" opportunities to get away from the routine of every day living, some of which is damned mundane and boring, especially for folks who have enjoyed active, meaningful lives. Going to other places, even down the road 40 or 50 miles (or metric equivalent), under the guise of "playing hockey" really appeals to poppa and, especially to momma ("shop 'til you drop" time). They relish the joys of travel ... seeing new or even old, familiar sights, eating a greater variety of foods, drinking different brands of beer, pigging out at banquets, "barbies" or other fetes, going to dances (of various tempos and decibels), enjoying the "entertainers" (professional and otherwise) and just plain, down-to-earth sharing of good old-styled, genuine camaraderie ... with new and old-time acquaintances. And then throw in the fun of some recreational games of shinny, pool, cribbage, whatever.

The gals like going to tournaments because they don't have to make meals, keep the house clean and can go shopping with reckless abandon. Most of them seem to enjoy the games, if not for watching them as much as having a good chat with their female friends. And the odd gal is there to comfort her "warrior" after he suffers from various physical and socio-psychological injuries ... such as losing to long-time rivals. It's amazing how the gentle gender's tenderness is balm for the old warriors' wounds.

Special Places

Some of the old fellas play in tourneys of one sport or other, throughout the year; well, almost the whole twelve months. Almost any month, you can find a golf, slow pitch ball, cribbage, cricket, tidily winks, lawn bowling, horse shoes or shinny tournament somewhere in the world, if not North America. Imagine senior's shinny being played in such far off and exotic locales as Spain, Australia, Japan, Scotland, South Africa, Russia or Cucamonga (if there is such a place). More likely, hockey contests are held in places like Balzac, Banff, Boston, Chibougamau, Flin Flon,

Gander, Goose Bay, Minsk, Moose Jaw, Oslo, Plaster Rock, Red Deer, Stockholm or Thunder Bay.

Tournaments, by whatever label they are named, range from small, e.g., four team week-end events, to week-long tourneys with many teams. The small events are usually in nearby towns or cities, involving three or four games, lots of beer drinking, some great food, often "home-cooked", plenty of laughs and just simply having a good time with little cost. Larger contests, like the "Snoopy" in sunny Santa Rosa, require significant "cash", time and travel --- hundreds to thousands of miles (and dollars), arranging travel, meals, credit or bank loans and then having a good time doing it --- epitomized by the fun-loving, super-gracious team from Japan which has participated annually for decades and are happy to score a goal and, maybe, some year might win a game. "Hope springs eternal in the human breast."

That, in a nutshell, is generally what makes shinny tournaments appealing. Each tourney has its own special attractions. In the autumn, Fruitland put on a small, eight team tourney and international pool competition in a beautiful valley at a time when the apples, pears, pumpkins, potatoes, other fruits and veggies were ripe and ready for consumption. The valley was covered with the glorious colors of fall - yellows, golds, rusts, crimsons of the foliage. And the unique, natural fragrances of autumn were in the air. A few weeks later came the Mountainview event which featured pig roasting, great food, beer, dancing and other forms of entertainment, highlighting the Hanson brothers. Joxville had its own annual tournament in early November, about the time of the first winter blizzard. Oceanview's contests are located in a charming old city on the Pacific, with its warm, balmy weather and herald the advent of spring, with its warmer weather, flowers and other beauties of nature. And then, believe it or not Mr. Ripley, in mid-summer the most special event of them all was staged - the Snoopy Tournament in Santa Rosa, California. Who would ever have thought or dreamed of playing hockey in California during July? What made it so special was not only the games and related activities but the great location and the pleasures of getting there --- along the rugged, picturesque Pacific coast and its quaint coastal towns, especially Mendocino with its many wooden water towers and annual musical festival. Naturally, the time for fun --- to *play*, drink beer, reminisce and tell stories, have lots of laughs, renew and make acquaintances, go shopping with "the wife", play a round or two of golf, or just lay around in the sun and "goof off" were treasured fun times for scores of ageing shinny players who travelled to the Mecca of old guys' hockey.

Snoopy's Senior World Hockey Tournament

Some history and other profound insights

One of the oldest, largest and most "prestigious" oldsters' shinny tourneys in North America, if not the world, has been "the Snoopy". It is usually held during the third week of July in Santa Rosa, California. Charles Schulz, the revered originator and prime sponsor of the event, was a very avid hockey player and fan. He was born in 1922 and raised in the shinny playing state of Minnesota. As the creator of Peanuts and its gang of cartoon kids, like good old Charley Brown, Lucy, Sally, Peppermint Patty, Pig Pen, Linus and the beagle dog Snoopy, Mr. Schulz, "Sparky" as he liked to be called, moved to California. In 1975, he started the tournament with three divisions and 12 teams. He was also a very strong supporter of his daughter's figure skating talents. That support was one reason he built the Redwood Empire Ice Arena, described in the tournament program as "The Most Beautiful Ice Arena in the World"; an exaggeration in the true American way. All of the games were played in that attractive arena. It was the only ice arena in town.

In tourism terms, Santa Rosa was a great location. Years ago it was an easy 90 minute drive along highway 101 to that great city by the bay; where that crooner Tony Bennett left his heart. Despite the many and various attractions of 'Frisco, one could choose to go in other directions from

Saint Rose. The wine-growing valleys of Napa and Sonoma are an hour or so to the east. About an hour to the west is the Pacific Ocean via a beautiful, mostly tree-lined route along the Russian River. For golfers, the area is a haven of golf courses, with something like 50 within 25 miles or 25 within 50 miles --- whatever --- more than most people could play in a week or three.

Santa Rosa is truly a lovely location, although not necessarily for a hockey tournament. It's a great place for horticulture ... which has nothing to do with prostitutes. Luther Burbank did much of his scientific work there and developed all kinds of new plants, including new species of Adam and Eve's old favorite ... the apple. It's a great place for sports, culture, culinary and other activities. But in July, the weather is just a little warm for *ice* hockey. Imagine the thermometer "going down" to 60 or so degrees Fahrenheit (and that's above zero) during the night and then, as if programmed, the morning fog dissipates about 10 am. Then *voila,* blue sky, sunshine and temperatures in the 80s . Well, that's the shinny playing weather in St. Rosa --- boring but beautiful and very appealing to crotchety old pucksters from many places in North America and other parts of the world.

During recent decades, the event had an unique pattern. As the venerable Sparky, the "mover and shaker" behind the tournament, aged five more years, another age-based category was added. He was truly an amazing man --- never seemed to age, almost always had a pleasant smile and like demeanor, except when he was getting ready for a game. (More about that later.) Ultimately, the age categories went up to 75 years+ before Sparky passed along to hockey heaven.

Not only did the number of teams increase but so did the creativity of their names. Some of the team names were quite creative, rather appropriate for a tournament sponsored by one of the world's leading cartoonists. Many of the names had spins on age, especially old or olde. There were the North Shore Old Goats, Brooks Old Cocks, Ottawa Olde Tymers, Kirkland Lake Goldtimers and Sydney

Olde Buoys. Some of the more catchy team names were the Walla Walla Warriors, Boston Moby Dicks, Edmonton Rusty Nuts, London Huff and Puff, Delta Sundowners and the Out to Lunch Bunch. Calgary had several interesting team names, including the Old Buffalos, Fading Stars and Spanish Flyers. Who says old guys are not creative?

One team that had an especially compelling name was from Sparky's home state, the Minnesota Madness. Now there's a team that seems to have an appropriate name --- madness. When you think about playing ice hockey in the midsummer, there must be a touch of insanity. When you consider the potential dangers in shinny game with old guys ageing up into their eighties, it really is madness for those less-than-totally-well-coordinated and out of shape old fellows to be playing such a game. Madness, thy name is old guys' hockey as well as the name of one such team.

Preparing for the pilgrimage

For many old timer shinny players, going to the Snoopy Tournament was like going to the hockey Mecca or some other sacred place. Some might consider it to be a pilgrimage, a journey taken for religious reasons, religious meaning that the devotees of the Snoopy Tournament commit to a form of faith in and worship of the event. Many old guys try for years to play in the tournament. Some teams suffer group psychoses and even neuroses in various forms, like frequent muttering and chattering about wanting to play in "the Snoopy", having twitches each and every time the tournament is mentioned. Some old guys are downright pathetic in their desire to play there. Not every team that applies to play is granted that privilege. In fact, many teams apply and only a few are chosen. For years, rumors persisted that only 20-25 percent of the teams applying were accepted. Who says there isn't a demand to play old guys' shinny, even in the California heat of July???

Even before old Hank and his new-found buddies (but not necessarily from Newfoundland and Labrador) donned their moldy old gear, they had to make commitments to the tournament, the team and the patron saint of hockey, St. Luck, like it rhymes with puck and is close to Luke. The first commitment was to mortgage the house so that money was available for entrance fees, travel costs, food, booze, shopping for the dear old gal and her "bargains", golf, entertainment, etc, etc, etc. Ah, the joys of the consumer society and credit!!! The federal gummits' budget likely has fewer line items than some couple's budget for "the Snoopy".

Seriously speaking, Snoopy tournaments cost the old guys and gals some "real bread" as deputy assistant coach, general manager and gate opener Colin liked to say. The $60, $70 or more bucks for each player's entry fee is only the "teeny tip of the iceberg", although the impact is not as dramatic as it was with those folks on the Titanic. About $3,000-$4,000 later, you get the full impact of the journey. Oh well, it's only money and "you can't take it with you", as Dad used to say which is not necessarily so but it does make some sense and provides balm for the spending wounds. And, what the hell, you might as well enjoy "it" while you have your health is another way of thinking about the cash crisis created by going to "the Snoopy". Morally (?!) speaking, it is an indulgence of the affluent. But then most moralists do not play old timer hockey. They are too busy out doing good deeds for those who need help. Putting that dash of cold water aside, we return to the main stream of this scribbling.

Thus, it was one year in late May that Hank and various old timers from here and there went to "training camp" - with pleasant anticipation, some serious perspiration and much enthusiasm. Doesn't that term "training camp" sound kind of ridiculous ... what for beer drinking and story telling??? So anyhow, Hank was off to Cowtown to practice with the M*old*y Mavericks. Like many tournament teams, the Moldies were a collection of players from various teams and, for this tournament, from different locations. As it turned out, Hank was playing defence with an old plumber from Calona, a town where some pretty decent (not necessarily fine) wine was vinted. To strengthen their offense, the Moldys added a couple of "snipers" from Olds (what an appropriate source for senior shinny players!).

Hence, from early June, practices were held in a rather concerted effort to "shape up" the oldy Moldys for a respectable, if not winning, effort at "the Snoopy". Nobody likes to be embarrassed, including the old pucksters. By the time the end of June rolled around, the Moldys were feeling pretty good about their team and were enthused about heading to Santa Rosa. Hank even heard one wanna be Caruso "singing" ---

> Hi ho, hi ho,
> it's off to Santa Rosa we go
> with plenty of money and gear,
> some trepidation and some fear,
> hi ho, hi ho,
> it's off to Santa Rosa we go.

Hank fled the room, lest his ears be further damaged and he lost his lunch.

Old Timers' Nirvana

For years, Sparky and his gracious wife, Jeannie, hosted a welcoming soiree during the Sunday evening prior to the week's games and social activities. It was a time for greeting and eating, imbibing and confiding. A sensational spread of fresh fruits, cheeses, crackers, chips, dips and free drinks was set out for the great unwashed. Sparky said a few words of welcome, smiled and then went about making the old folks feel welcome ... the most eminent host.

On Monday evening, before the feature game of the week, the tournament's official opening was held, complete with honor guard, local dignitaries and the genial host, who said a few words of welcome, smiled, waved and sat down. After some banal rhetoric by "officials", the party left and the teams "got at 'er", as one old sod buster from Saskatchewan would say - too often.

Tuesdays and Thursdays were for playing games and "doin' your own thing" - a popular saying of the times. Well, there was lots to do and the old guys, gals, families and friends did their best to "get 'er done", as the same semi-senile Saskatchewan sodbuster liked to say - frequently.

On Wednesday night, the Bar-B-Q, with plenty to eat and drink, was held in a field across the street from the "Ice Arena". Music by a live and lively band inevitably drew some of the mommas with their reluctant, crotchety poppas to the small dance floor and into the surrounding field.

For many of the folks, especially the gals who were keen to "dress up", the social highlight of the "Snoopy" was held on Friday evening at the beautiful Burbank Center. The evening featured top entertainers, like the Smothers Brothers, a great assortment of snacks and drinks and dancing with music by a real live band that did *not* blast the patrons out of the building or even damage their hearing. *Tres beau!!!*

An awkward encounter

Not all was sweetness and light in Snoopy's shinny utopia. On one unusual occasion, Hank experienced Sparky's intensity for the *game* when the latter was 70-odd years old. The situation unfolded as follows. Hank's son-in-law had a brother who was an emerging cartoonist. Since Hank had had a book of Peanuts cartoons previously autographed by Sparky, he thought that the up-and-coming cartoonist might like one also. So, Hank bought a book of Peanuts cartoons and tried to locate the illustrious Mr. Schulz to autograph the book. Well, as fate, activities or whatever would have it, Hank did not encounter the famous cartoonist at a time when he had the book with him.

As the tournament week came all too rapidly to a close, a concerned Hank made a concerted effort to find his favorite cartoonist and get the book of cartoons autographed by him. In a "last ditch" effort (sounds melodramatic doesn't it), Hank went to Sparky's last game of the tournament. He waited patiently by the players' benches for the cartoonist/

player to appear. As luck would have it, the first player to skate to the benches was Charles Schulz. What a relief Hank felt. A few minutes after Sparky was seated on his team's bench, all by himself, Hank approached him. After briefly and courteously re-introducing himself and explaining about the budding cartoonist, Hank asked Sparky if he would autograph the Peanuts book. Whoa, what a surprise Hank got!!! Sparky really sparked; he might have short-circuited. Emphatically, he told Hank that he was getting ready for a hockey game and he did not want to be bothered with autographing books ... in effect, to go away. Hank, who was not easily dissuaded, apologized and retreated, disconsolately. He never did get the book autographed. And that was the last impression he had of Charles Schulz, unfortunately. Sparky passed away later that year.

Fortunately, the Snoopy Tournament is much more than a single, unfortunate incident. The event is more than one person, however large or small their roles and responsibilities. It was and continues to be a week of great fun --- usually a vacation time when hundreds of fine folks got together to renew old or make new acquaintances, enjoy the very special camaraderie of old guys' shinny, drink beer, tell stories, go to 'Frisco, see the sights and a ball game, eat seafood at Fisherman's Wharf, walk through Chinatown or around Nob Hill, visit a few wineries in the Napa valley, play golf, go to the Pacific Coast, get sun burned, drink too much, eat too much and, oh yes, play three games of shinny in the "world's most beautiful ice arena". Thank you Sparky!!!

Harvest Hockey Jamboree

Its unique modus operandi

(such an erudite-sounding term)

In comparison to the Snoopy Tournament and by most old timers' measures of time, this Jamboree is young. It was started in 1996 when two fine old, irrepressible hockey players contacted a retired but certainly not tired school teacher, administrator and hockey aficionado by the name of Mac Dodds in the Okanagan of British Columbia. Believe it or not, the two old timers were looking for a tournament to fill a gap in their schedule between Appleton and somewhere else in western Canada. Who knows where these nomads roam to play hockey games? Anyhow, Mac had plenty of time, talent and eager motivation to develop another, albeit quite different, hockey tournament.

For most old pucksters, the Senior Oldtimers' (seems redundant) Harvest Hockey Jamboree is an unique event. What makes it so unusual is the fact that only individuals are allowed to enter. No teams are entered although teams play in the Jamboree. Confused?! Don't feel like the Lone Ranger. For the first time participant, team formation seems to be a real confusing puzzlement, especially if you're an old fellow who is accustomed to teams, routines, traditions and familiar arrangements. For some old guys, changes can be discombobulating. But keep the faith, there is hope and a process for discombobulatees. It was based on old road hockey principles and ways.

Individual players are assigned a team according to age, ability and position. Like most shinny activities, ranging from road hockey to the old guys' games, players range in capabilities. At the Jamboree, such variances are, in part, accommodated for by three divisions: the Legends ("roughly ages 70 -84", although one goalie with two hip replacements was 85 and was truly a hockey legend); the Classic division ("roughly ages 64-69"); and the Rookies ("roughly ages 55-63"). "Roughly" is a fudge word that allows the guy in charge to make "adjustments" to the teams, like a "hot shot" 70 year old playing with the Classics or, by contrast, a tired old guy who is recovering from a heart attack, a cancer operation, joint(s) replacement or some other combination of such limiting conditions being allowed to play in an older division; such a sense of fairness. If only the world was so sensitive, fair, just, equitable and downright decent! What civil societies we would have!!

What twigs one's curiosity, especially for the neophyte or "rookie" player, is the clairvoyance, networking intelligence, abracadabra or other magic used in assigning players to teams when the players are there for the very first time. Somehow it is done and rather fairly or so it seemed to Hank when he played in the Jamboree for the first time. The results of his team's three games with the others in the division were 3-4 (a loss), 2-1 and 3-1. In the other two divisions, scores were similarly close. Information, intelligence and good luck, rather than magic, are keys to forming teams that are comparable in competitive capabilities. Mac was a master at creating such teams.

At this point, a word or three about Mac's philosophy of *competition* might be insightful. The creator of the Jamboree wanted the event to "take the edge off team competition". That principle was the basic reason for allowing only individuals to enter. As long-time players in hockey or other team sports realize, team rivalries develop for various reasons over time. If teams are not allowed to enter and the individual players are mixed up among the teams from year to year, as well as being mixed up in the normal "swim of life", the chances of overly zealous, competitive games are minimized. In a similar effort to minimize overly competitive or aggressive "play", one nearby town was preparing for a tournament in which all of the players would be on different teams for *each* of their games. Talk about a bunch of mixed up old timers! Such a tournament should really do the trick.

Well, Mac D. and his buddies had their ways and means of sorting out and organizing the numerous and various players, probably not unlike a sheep dog rounding up the flock and making sure that they headed in the right direction ... to the arena rather than to a pen. That process of herding the sheep, oops sorry, the old coots started with an introductory dinner during the evening prior to the start of the games. The players were sorted out, at least in their own feeble minds, by receiving a dinner ticket with a table number, from one to thirteen (the total number of teams formed for the Jamboree), on it. Believe it or not Mr. Ripley and not by coincidence, that table number was the same as the team number for the players at the table. What a neat, efficient and effective way for an old guy to meet his new team mates and get their team organized in even more detail, like forming forward lines, defence pairings, getting sweaters and socks and finding out the games schedule. There is just nothing like good grub and boozes to make old guys passive enough to be herded.

Wow!!! What a wonderful schedule. No midnight or 6 am games like one suffers through occasionally at other tournaments. Not only are the games at a civilized hour, like 9, 10 or 11 am but they are played in an impressive new arena with excellent lighting, dressing rooms large enough for 15 to 20 bulky, awkward old players, all with bags of gear, hockey sticks as well as the garbage cans, beer bags and miscellaneous items that clutter a room and take up space. By damn, there's even enough room left over for a dance ... and a shower room with four showers, all of which work, including enough hot water to get clean. (No numbing cold showers like those straight from very deep wells in Belarus.) Even the players' bench was spacious. Players were not sitting or standing on one another, getting in each other's way or in a second row. This is hockey heaven ... for most of the old guys.

Just like a barrel of apples may have a rotten one or two, so do old timers' tournaments. According to Mac, a few years ago, there was a goalie from Spokane who refused to play for the team to which he was assigned. When Mac talked to the goalie, he offered no reason but was quite adamant about wanting to play for another team, sort of like a spoiled child in pre-school. So, good old Mac changed the discontent goalie with the one on the team that he wanted to play for, apparently. Unfortunately, the malcontent was more screwed up in the head than the typical flakey puck stopper because he arrived a week late for the tournament ... then audaciously telephoned Mac and demanded that his entry fee be returned to him. Paraphrasing the unflappable Mr. Dodds, his message to the disturbed goalie was "you're out of luck" ... no refund. Others might not have been so compassionate or discrete in their choice of words. Several phrases come to mind, none of which very nice ... au contraire, mon ami.

Competitive tactics ... really!

Only a fool or life long spectator would believe that old timers or any other team games are not played competitively. Who likes to lose? What fun is that? In the Jamboree, team 8 lost its first game four goals to three. After that game, the dressing room was kind of quiet and somber, even a little moody and morose. One day and a game later, the dressing room with the same players in it, resounded with levity bordering on the raucous, at least by old coots' standards. What was the difference? In one word: winning. By scoring two goals to one against their opponents (#6), the team considered to be the best and favored to win the division, was very satisfying and "fun". Like most mere mortals, old timers like to win.

Did that win just happen? Hell no! In managerial terms, Team #8 did some very serious intelligence and information gathering, critical analysis, tactical decision making, astute planning and brilliant executing (a rather dastardly sounding word but remember this epistle is written tongue in cheek). Team #6 was scouted during its first game which it won rather handily 7–3. After some rigorous assessments (by old guys' standards), two key conclusions were reached: team #6 relied on two very good forwards, i.e., #7 and #13, who played on the same line; and team #6 had a relatively weak defence. It did not take rocket scientists for Team #8 to develop three vital tactics: get into the faces" (and spaces) of #7 and #13; shoot the puck into the other team's end of the rink; and fore-check like crazy, well, at least, like hound dogs after a rabbit. Player #13 scored the only goal for Team #6 while the "in your face", aggressive fore-checking and scrambling play of Team #8 produced two ugly goals. But ugly goals count just as much as "pretty" ones. Besides what does beauty have to do with old geezers playing ice shinny?

A mix of experiences

As Hank sat around the Jamboree dressing rooms "shooting the breeze" with other old guys he heard several stories of challenges met and overcome by ageing men and women from all walks of life. He heard a detailed account of the 85 year old goalie named Jimmy who was still playing with two, yes 2, hip replacements. The next day, he saw Sir James play --- such an amazing man. Later that evening Hank met him, had a beer or three with him and his "buds", and enjoyed a couple hours of conversation, truly a meaningful experience. Such a man is really quite extraordinary. More "ordinary" guys have one hip replacement, a knee or two reconstructed, shoulder, elbow and various other operations, including heart pacemakers, stents (or stints?), angioplasty or the odd transplant, not to mention a long list of injuries.

One of the joys of going to tournaments is common to recreational travel --- the opportunities to experience new and different eating places. Just going to Kelly O'Bryan's neighborhood restaurant, actually more like an Irish pub, is an upbeat treat. You walk into a medium-sized room and the atmosphere hits you --- dark paneled walls, humorous Guinness and Kilkenny posters, various Irish artifacts, lilting Celtic music and smiling young waiters and waitresses in kilts and Guinness shirts. Maybe that is not some people's "cup of tea" but it sure was for Hank. Just reading the menu was fun and even inspirational because of such old Irish sayings as:

> "May you be in Heaven half hour before the Devil knows you're dead;"
>
> "Wherever you go and whatever you do, may the luck of the Irish be there with you;"
>
> "Irish Toasts: Here's to being single ... drinking doubles ... and seeing triple!;"

"Here's to our wives and girlfriends: may they never meet;"

"May you live as long as you want; and never want as long as you live;" and

"As you slide down the banister of life, may the splinters never point in the wrong direction."

For Hank, the menu included some downright enjoyable reading, like "Brain Teasers", "Under the Kilt", "Irish Laws", including the creation of the L.A.D.D. (Leprechauns Against Drunk Driving). An Irishman's Philosophy of Life" was insightful even wise, to wit:

"In life there are only two things to worry about, either you are well, or you are sick. If you are well, there is nothing to worry about, but if you are sick, you have two things to work about; either you will live or you will die. If you live, there is nothing to worry about, if you die, you have two things to worry about, either you will go to heaven or go to hell. If you go to heaven, there is nothing to worry about, but if you go to hell, you'll be so busy shaking hands with your friends, you won't have time to worry."

Another endearing characteristic of oldsters is the ability to renew and make new friendships. They meet others, assimilate and almost instantaneously develop harmonious relations, if not enduring friendships. Some old guys forget their own wedding anniversary, birthdays of spouses and children or other events of importance but they will rarely forget the names and other minute details of guys they played hockey with or against 33 years ago (give or take a few) in Podunk, Slippery Rock or anywhere else. Their networking is incredible. Some guy from Shediac, New Brunswick played in a Quebec Cite tournament in 1979 and knew Joe Blow from Vancouver who was playing for the Ottawa Olde Senators.

Being forgetful or having selective retention is a characteristic of all human beings of all ages; children, especially teenagers and old timers. Everybody knows a funny story or maybe not-so-funny story, like locking one's keys in the car and not having a spare one. While getting dressed for the second game against Team #6 and its two hotshots (remember #7 and #13), one of Hank's team mates, Lanny, was looking around for his elbow pad. He was digging around in his large bag, looking under Hank's bag, under the bench, looking bewildered and mumbling aloud about "where the hell is my other elbow pad?" ... until Hank looked at him quizzically and suggested that old Lan look on his arm. Incredulously, there it was ... right where it belonged ... on his elbow ... sort of like the absent-minded professor who cannot find her glasses until she realizes that they are propped up in her hair.

Lanny's forgetfulness did not stop with not being able to find his elbow pad and being the brunt of Hank's prank. Lanny had to be reminded four or five times by several of this team mates about what time their third game was to be played. Since the first two games had started at 11 am, Lanny somehow thought(?) that their team's third game would start at the same time. Hank figured that it was better for Lanny to be an hour and a half early. Only a few of the players were surprised when Lanny told them, the next day, that he came to the arena at 11 am "to watch some of his buddies play in the earlier game" and not because he had forgotten the time of his team's game.

The humorous behavior of Lanny and other old timers' naturally leads to a stream of funny stories and jokes, like the one told by an old guy from the "audience" at the Wednesday night dinner and get together held in the Army, Navy and Air Force (ANAF) hall. Well, it seems that the jokester was "puzzled by the women in Okanagan ... seems that they really, really liked a certain brand of chocolate bar because the previous night he had been trying to go to sleep ... and he kept hearing a woman in the next room saying, rather emotionally, 'Ooh Henry, Ooooh Henry, Ooooooh Henryyyyyyyyy'".

The laughter following that story encouraged the jokester to tell several more stories. The only one that Hank could remember was one about a golf pro who had been instructing some of the gentle gender on how to improve their golf game. Seems that one of the ladies was out playing a round with some friends. After the first hole, she was stung by a bee and hurried back to the club house, seeking solace and first aid from the pro. He asked her where she had been stung. She replied that it was between the first and second holes and asked, with some urgency, what she could do to keep from being stung there again. Looking a little uncertain and very uncomfortable the pro suggested that she "Try closing your stance."

Conversations

As mentioned a few paragraphs previously, networking has a lot to do with the camaraderie that develops among the players on teams who have never met one another before. Conversations just naturally happen. Often such gabs are started by one old guy knowing somebody from another geezer's hometown, places where their paths have crossed or had some common experience. During the evening before the games began, Hank had just sat down for the "get-acquainted" dinner when a player named Harry wanted to know if Hank knew Ken from Joxville. Sure Hank knew Ken. They had just played against each other the previous Tuesday night. Well, it turns out that Harry and Ken had been involved for years in a provincial eye bank - yes, an eye bank - not a commercial bank, credit union or other financial institution -but an eye bank. Turned out that Ken had had a cornea transplant a few years previously, quite unknown to Hank who thought he knew Ken quite well and liked to "look people in the eye".

From the topic of eye banks the conversation evolved into education, politics, family and hockey. Harry and Hank had gone to graduate schools along the west coast of the United States. So, they compared their graduate programs, football teams and universities during the late '60s. They agreed that the USA had not learned much from the Viet

Nam war because, more recently, it had invaded and were in the process of devastating Iraq. "America" was not likely to get out until another president or two had been elected, thousands of more lives would be lost and billions of dollars wasted in a deceptive effort to secure oil supply for the overly self indulgent Americans. How disgusting were the politics of lies and deception for the purpose of developing militarily, a reliable source of black gold upon which the wasteful consumption of the "developed" countries relied. Realizing that their blood pressures were rising, maybe to an unhealthy level, Harry and Hank changed the subject to hockey, where they had played, including the various tournaments and guys they might know. So the gabfest went on pleasantly, even joyously, until it was time to eat. It's amazing how a good-sized banquet hall, filled with women and men, can become so quiet once the food is served.

Following the first game, another good gab session got gotting between Hank and a team mate named Manny. Like Harry, Manny read that Hank was from Joxville and wondered if he might know Ronny, Roddy and Billy. (Have you ever wondered why so many shinny players' names end with "y"?) Manny seemed to have an *ee* fixation for names - Ronny, Roddy, Billy and others. Well anyhow, the chinwag started out with an exchange of observations and thoughts about mutual acquaintances and went on for an hour or more and a few brew. Hank and Ronny had gone to the New York Ranger amateur camp away back in 1955 --- over a half century ago. Wow!!! how time flies - must be having fun. So Hank told Manny about the overnight, "milk run" train ride that he and his buddy Ronny took from central Alberta to Saskatoon ... and the twice-daily hockey drills and torturous practices that were surely meant to kill man or beast ... and then the long walk from the arena back to the hotel up a hill comparable to Mount Everest carrying their bags of gear ... then collapsing onto the bed for some life-preserving sleep ... then having something to eat before collapsing in bed for the night.

While the great majority of old guys' and gals' conversations are pleasant and "light-hearted", if not "light-headed", the occasional one can be serious. Such was the chat that Hank and his defence partner, Albert had following the second game of the Jamboree. Albert was still suffering from a recent shoulder operation that limited his ability to handle his (hockey) stick. As well as being a very good hockey player, he was a gutsy guy. A few months earlier he had had a serious prostate, often wrongly pronounced prostrate, operation. Hank was interested in that operation because a few days earlier he had had a colonoscopy and, during a phone conversation the previous evening with his wife, Heidi told him that the doctor had found a polyp in his intestine. "Oh joy", had been Hank's facetious response to the news. So, Hank wanted to find out as much as he could about polyps and colon cancer.

Hank: Albert, you've had some experience with colonoscopies and whatever comes with it. Tell me about polyps. What the hell are they?

Albert: I'm no doctor but my understanding is that they are some kind of growth in the intestine that could be ... some times are cancerous ... and sometimes they are benign.

At this time Jerry, who was sitting on the other side of Albert, jumped (figuratively) into the conversation.

Jerry: Ah, polyps are nothing to worry about. I had a couple of them in my gut last year and they turned out to be benign.

Albert: Whoa, wait a minute buckoo ... don't be so casual about them. They can be cancerous and cancer can kill ... dead.

Hank: Hey guys!!!! Tell me more about the science ... like what size are the polyps and what happens when the doc cuts them out. What happens to the intestine? Does it have a hole ... a cut ... some kind of gap in it? Or does the doc use lasers and zap the bad part out?

Albert: I don't know how they do it but they take out the polyp and no apparent damage is done. Then they send it away to have it assessed for cancer. If it is cancerous then the fun begins ... seriously, the doctors have you come in pronto for some further tests and start you on your way to surgery. That surgery can be hell ....

Jerry: (interrupting) Ya, I play ball with a guy, an old banker, who has had two or three operations on his large intestine ... every time, they take another chunk of his bowels out. Poor bugger looks like death warmed over for the next six months or so. He had to quit playing ball because of his bowel cancer.

Hank: Ya, that reminds me of Ryan, one of our old timers ... back home. Years ago ... maybe 10 or more, I heard that he had had some kind of serious operation ... so I visited him in the hospital. He looked bloody awful ... just laying that bed ... kind of grey and all wired up with tubes coming out of his body like a plate of spaghetti ... Oh Lord, he looked awful ... and probably felt a lot worse. So he was telling me about this operation and having some of his large intestine taken out ... and how he was going to have a bag attached to his gut so he could crap in it. What a crappy story that was ... it was disgusting and you know, it turned me off from being concerned about such problems ... probably dumb, eh?

Jerry: Sure as hell is dumb! You've got to keep checking up on yourself. Don't expect the doctors or anyone else to do it for you....

Albert: You're right. A guy has to be checking on his health all of the time ... especially when you get to be our age, even younger if you are smart enough to do it.

So the conversation went on about various health problems the three old puck chasers and others in the room had experienced, especially in recent years. After a while, they became weary of the discussion and changed the subject, ultimately back to hockey and a leaflet that some old guy had given to Jerry as he walked through the arena earlier. It was an announcement and registration form for a "Skills Camp" .... for Adult Recreational Hockey Players during the coming month - that apparently catered to old pucksters. Just the term "skills camp" made the three old guys laugh ... skills ... training ... in old timers' hockey! Somebody is out of their mind ... they're dreaming in technicolor. They've got to be kidding!", exclaimed Albert.

Then the three players got going on the amount of ice time - 90 minutes of instruction daily. "Cripes", exclaimed Hank, "after 90 minutes, I would need resuscitation, recreational hockey." They joked about the prospects of heart attacks, various and sundry other injuries, especially when they read that 30 minutes of *power skating* was scheduled. That prompted the threesome to get into a conversation about "doing stops and starts" back in junior and college hockey days. "No thank you", said Jerry. "I had enough of those skating drills to do me forever ... and a long time after that."

Fruitland's tourney ... and Jock's international pool championship

Every autumn, Fruitland hosted a great old boys' shinny tournament. The picturesque little town was located on a gentle hillside, overlooking a verdant valley, with several non-polluted, fresh-water lakes, great fishing, four or five challenging golf courses nearby (find one that is not challenging, even if it is a pitch and putt or a mini-golf course). Driving to the week-end event from Joxville took about six hours on a pleasant day, about half of it through the Rocky Mountains. If the weather was windy, rainy or, worst of all, snowing then the trip took appreciably longer. Sooner or later, with determination and perseverance, the Old Boys would arrive at La Hacienda Hotel and Spa. As soon as they arrived they inquired about the room Gentleman Jock and his wife were in, because that was where the party was, or soon would be!!!!

Besides its location, several other features of the town and tournament made going to Fruitland enjoyable. It was a small tournament. Only 8 teams were accepted and they were fairly evenly matched. Occasionally, a hot shot team would get in, womp the other teams and then not be invited back the next year(s). The town was small and easy to get around in - no hassle of the big city with its endless traffic, congestion and air pollution. Nope!!! just short, pleasant drives or walks in clear, fresh air - very invigorating ... revitalizing.

One of the highlights of the week-end was the very prestigious sounding Jock MacKay International Pool Championship, named after everybody's favorite gentleman. The pool tourney was held during the Saturday afternoon of the hockey tournament week-end. The "championship" did not start out as such an illustrious event. Like many great events it started small and like Topsy, just grew. After a few years of such growth and increasing fame (or infamy), Hank and a younger old guy named Mac (no relation to Jock) decided, as the reigning champions, that they would buy an awesome trophy, have the mug suitably engraved and put it up for annual competition at Roy's Saloon and Pool Hall just across the Excited States border at a non-descript place that really had no official hamlet, village, town or other status of geo-political incorporation. All it was really was a local "watering hole" with a pool table.

During those bright, warm wonderful Saturday afternoons, Roy's emporium of dereliction took on a new life. That's when pairs of pool players would challenge for the trophy. Teams included the gals, either with their guy, some other guy or another gal. Similarly, guys would pair up for the keen competition. What made it so interesting and really funny was the *ad hoc* way it happened through the afternoon. In true old timer form, the "event" was unorganized, spontaneous and highly hilarious. The first two teams to arrive at Roy's would start playing. The winner would then be challenged by another team. Each game's winner would be challenged. Challenges seemed to go on endlessly. Then, late in the afternoon, the effects of too much beer and fatigue reached the level that the consensus best two teams would play off for Gentleman Jock's International Pool Championship trophy.

Bets were placed, rounds of beer were ordered, beef jerky or garlic sausage was being chewed, cigarettes or the odd cigar was being puffed on and the grand finale would begin and played with the skill and ferocity of Roman gladiators - without any blows being struck. Fierce competitors stopped gluggin' their beer and became focused - as focused as inebriated old men and women could get. Tactical consultations were whispered between the pool partners. Deliberate, expert shots were tried and sometimes made - much to the great surprise and joy of the shooter. "Dirty pool" tricks, like "hooking" or "snookering", were used as defensive maneuvers. Muttering, occasional swearing and flashes of rage came from the intensely competing pool players. Sometimes, the final game took an hour, more or less. (Good old boy Roy only charged the players by the game, not by the time it took to play the game. He made his money from all of the booze and junk food that the players and spectators consumed. So he didn't care how long it took for the game to be played.) Ultimately, a team emerged victorious and jubilant, like they had just won the Stanley Cup, the World Series or the World Cup of Soccer. Joy has few bounds when you're a winner, even if it was a little-known pool tourney in a non-descript bar room in an unknown locale. But the trophy was impressive and gave the ultimate joy to the winners – team bragging rights for an entire year!!!!

Moreover, the great joys of the Fruitland shinny gathering were not limited to the pool tourney. Usually, the old guys had three good games of hockey, more great food than the average Canadian cow could eat in a day, lots of beer, story after story and wave after wave of laughter. Quoting that uncouth and unworldly philosopher Max, "It doesn't get much better than this, boys" ... about the only sentence he ever expressed without using the "f" word, either as a verb, adverb, adjective, noun, pronoun, subject, predicate or whatever in the English language.

Unfortunately and regrettably, not all was joyous in Fruitland and some of the other towns where fine old timer hockey tournaments used to be played. Naturally and unfortunately, the older old timers got older and the younger old timers who were so full of interest, "piss and vinegar" (whatever that means), did not have the same kind of energy, motivation, commitment and capability to carry on the annual tournament. So, coincidentally, in the same year that George W. Shrub was elected President of the Excited States for the first time, the Fruitland Hockey Tournament was cancelled. C'est la vie or, in the Bush/ Cheney mindset, c'est la guerre.

Mountainview's Momentous Shinny Shindig

Talk about "good old boys". The three Hanson brothers and their buddies in southwest Cowtown were some of the best. For a couple decades or more, those "good old boys" put on a tournament that was "top drawer" or first rate. Like the Fruitland Tournament, it was small in numbers but huge in quality. First of all, the Hanson arranged special room rates at local motels and hotels for their out-of-town guests. Those brothers treated every out-of-towner like they were a favored member of the family. By golly, it sure made the guys and gals feel good to be treated like that. Secondly, the game schedule was set up with justice and some clear forethought. Teams from the farthest distance had the latest first game and the earliest last game thus taking into consideration the miles or metric equivalent and time they had to drive. Who says old timers are not considerate and caring about their fellow humans??? Thirdly, the games were held in the arena adjoining the hall where the social activities were held. After the rigorous games of shinny, a short walk to the beer and grub supply was always welcome.

Notwithstanding the fine attributes mentioned above, the event's *pieces de resistance* were the roasted pigs on the spits served at the Saturday evening *fete* - an occasion during which the critters, whole roasted, were paraded by suitably attired, fat old guys into the dining hall on large slabs of wood, really 4' by 8' sheets of plywood, decorated and embellished, including Adam and Eve's apples in their beastly mouths. The accompanying festive pomp and ceremony might have made Henry VIII lose his own head - with envy. In later years, as the Chandler boys and their buddies aged and maybe more aware of carcinogens from the smoking pits in which the pigs were cooked, the "pigs" became various creations, shaped and stuffed like animals and still carried pompously into and around the dining area on slabs of wood. Those roasts of pork never slipped in quality ... or quantity.

By most old timers' standards, the Mountainview event was a "real winner". However it seems that there was an element of sadism in scheduling several hours of dancing after the old guys had played a game or two, drank and ate too much and were hardly fit enough to sit up and keep their eyes open, much less prance around a dance floor. While the women were ready to boogey; their men were in some state of suspended animation. For reasons clearly understandable to the guys, they were not as keen to dance as their gals were ready to "rock and roll". But being the good sports that they were typically, the old guys and their gals would go out onto the dance floor and shuffle around for a while before they shuffled off to their hotels ... and a good sound sleep.

Ocean City Tournament

Each spring, since Captain Cook was a kid, Ocean City has hosted an old timers' hockey tournament. Factually speaking, the tournament started in 1975, coincidentally the same year that Sparky started his Snoopy get-together down south of the redwoods in western California. By contrast to the "Californianess" of that tournament, Ocean City is a place steeped in the history and culture of jolly olde

England. There, on the Pacific Ocean with the freshness and beauty of the springtime, the Old Boys and a couple dozen other teams gather to play shinny each spring. Many of the gals accompany their "aging warriors". The gentle gender added lots of chit-chat and vitality to the affair, that is, the hockey-related activities. What other affairs happen are beyond the scope, if not the imagination, of this scribe.

Getting "organized"

One of the "stumbling blocks" with the Old Boys' tournament teams is the fact that the group that is originally "put together" is rarely the team that actually plays in the tournament. No, it is not due to any deception or some devious skullduggery, overly rigorous training program or evaluation process that depletes the ranks. Rather, it's the dynamic vagaries and ever-changing circumstances of life for old folks. Usually, some players are injured or less inclined to play between sign-up time in December and the tournament in late March. Hence, replacements need to be found, hopefully more alive than dead. Believe it or not, finding capable (meaning that the old guy can skate, hold a hockey stick and chew gum) replacements is not so easy.

Then there is the guy who commits to playing in December and then decides in early March that he wants to spend another week or two in some warmer southern climes. Besides, Momma's content and the Old Man is too lazy or "laid back" to pack up and head north. The third cop-out category is the one which basically boils down to loss of motivation or memory. Or maybe the budget is a little tight, some health problem popped up, one or more of the "kids" needs help or any number of other situations that make going to the tournament "impossible". Other old guys just plainly and simply forget. So, the team rep, coordinator or whatever his label gets on the phone or the internet and tries to recruit enough replacement players to "ice a team".

So it came to pass that in the Spring of '04, Hank signed up to play for the Old Boys' tournament team. Most of the players were familiar to Hank. But there were a few foreign names on the list. He asked a couple of his team mates, Lenny and Ian, about the "unknown quantities". First of all he had to learn and remember their names --- quite a challenge for old guys. Next, it kind of helped if he knew what position they played. Most important of all was finding out who were the "go-to guys" --- who handled the puck well and could SCORE. According to the "intelligence" that Hank acquired quickly, a center by the name of Ray (a "ringer" from Queen City) and Mac, a right winger, were the "go to guys".

Well, among the teammates, there was a misfit, Dr. Dud, for Dudley Dolittle, M.D. First some perspective is needed. Every year, for every tournament, the teams were different. Most of the players were decent, reasonably able old coots who have pervaded old timers' hockey for eons. Occasionally, very rarely, there is an exception, like Dr. Dolittle (a nickname for an aging medic who never was able to play hockey very well and was a risk to his own life as well as the lives of others anywhere near the guy when he was on the ice. Yet, he insisted on taking a spot on the team --- the #$*+><*~#@*&> arrogant egomaniac!!!!) Dr. Dolittle, whose real name was Dudley Orville Little, was very definitely the very worst "player" to "strap on a pair of blades" since that guy Methuselah was a child. Not only was the guy not physically able to skate, handle a hockey stick or himself but he had an arrogant attitude which defied good sense. According to a few of his buddies, Dr. D. wanted to play in the tournament so he could receive a plaque recognizing his age (73 years).

In Hank's 60+ years of hockey experiences, the "good doctor" was, without a word of a lie or exaggeration, the worst, absolutely and comparatively, adult to put on hockey gear, much less even suggest that he could play the game. Start with the basics: he had difficulty standing up on his skates. He skated on his ankles. He could hardly move - seldom more than a few inches at a time. His stick was used mainly to steady himself, like a crutch, to lean on or to get in the way of other players, usually his own teammates. If he did get the puck on his stick, he could not shoot it. Having him on the ice was like being penalized and playing short-handed. Yet, he had the gross audacity to want, even insist, on playing in the Ocean City tourney. As that trite but true old saying goes, "there's no fool like an old fool". And his nice-guy buddies did not have the heart or guts to tell Dr. D. that he was a huge detriment to the team or words to that effect. Such was the situation faced by members of the team as they tried to think of ways to dissuade Dr. D. from his folly.

Early in the first practice prior to the tournament, Hank had a "heaven sent" opportunity to discourage the doctor from playing. They were sitting in the players' box waiting for their turn to go out on the ice and play. The short conversation went something like:

Dr. Dolittle: " Hank, you're a pretty good player ... what do you suggest that I do to play better?

Hank (panting from his last shift on the ice): "Hmmmm, he mused pensively trying to think of the best words possible to convey truth to Dr. D. "Well", Hank said very hesitantly, still trying to "catch his breath" and get the right words to respond with, "Why not be our coach ... or our manager ... ? (reluctantly not suggesting that the doctor could be the stick/water boy or door opener for the team.)

Dr. Dud (visibly stunned, then with his face growing rather red, snorted, like an ill-trained farm animal, then said, like the Great Gildersleeve of long ago radio programming): Hurrumph!!!!

After a few more very uncomfortable minutes passed, that seemed like an eternity to Hank, Dr. D. got up awkwardly, stumbled out of the cozy little players' box and staggered to the team's dressing room, not to return for the rest of the practice or the other practices before the team left for Ocean City.

Ah, the joys of spring ... in Ocean City!!

For most people, arriving in most other cities is no big deal. But, arriving in Ocean City from the lingering, even punishing winter of the Prairies, during late March is heavenly. What smacks the old folks fleeing from winter in the hinterlands is the absence of snow, the presence of warmth and the heavy fragrance of flowering trees and plants that are green and vital, rather than grey and deathly in appearance. Such climatological differences sure hit the prairie people as soon as the plane door opens and in rushes the warm, wet air (even if it is laden with the odor of jet fumes). Once away from the plane, the wafts of truly Spring air bring its flowery fragrances and the burning question: "What the hell do I do with all of the winter clothes I have on?"

From the airport to the hotel, the roadway wends through magnificent stands of evergreen and flowering trees. Ah, there's Bly's Lake, a glorified slough named for some guy named Bly and nobody seems to know why. But it's a beautiful pond, especially with a few sail boats on it and the sun shimmering across its surface. As the miles or metric equivalent whiz by, the passing scenery is so alive with the growth and colors of the season. Almost all too soon, the jaunt to the hotel is over. The car is parked, luggage is unloaded and Hank saunters casually into the lobby.

Hi! How're ya doing?

Almost any time an old puckster walks into a tournament lodging place, he will see other old timers from various teams standing around or sitting in the bar having a beer and shooting the breeze. Old timers are like a fraternity. They are always a "brother" whether or not they know the other old guys. Almost inevitably some body engages you in conversation or invites you to "have one with the boys". If you express reluctance, various persuasive ploys and comments result - like "what the hell, your old lady's not here" or "don't be a poop" or "what are you trying to do .... get into shape?" Almost as inevitably, the new arrival would stop and had a brew or two; renewing acquaintances with some of the "boys" (as silly as referring to older women as "girls") and meeting some new old timers (or old new timers). Sooner or later, fatigue sets in and the old timers tell one last joke, glug back what's left in their glass, bid adieu to the others and head for their rooms and a good night's sleep. "Tomorrow is another day ..... I hope" one or other would mutter as he sauntered off toward his room.

"Ya, tomorrow is another day", comes a reply. Who do we play? ... where? ... when?, "come the questions from a couple of the old cronies still at the bar. "Let's see," said Ray looking at his tournament schedule "... Parksville Panters, Setting Sons, Silver Streaks, Fractured Fathers! ... who says old fellas aren't poetic? .... look at the alliteration in those names .... the historical references ... Old Buffalos, Miners, Elder Skatesmen ... and humor ..... Fractured Fathers, Slow Pokes, Raggedy Assed, Retreads, Huff 'n Puff. Such creativity .... too bad the rest of the world can't enjoy it ... it's just being wasted on us seniors."

One of the old, old guys who always seemed to be at the tournaments was the venerable Mario, all vital eighty-odd years of him. In recent years, Mario had been "promoted" to "coach" of the Seaside Senators. In fact, he opened the players' bench gate for the defencemen. But that reality was insignificant relative to what else he brought to the tourney and to the team ... be he in its dressing room, during the game or at other times. Mario was an unique man --- usually quiet, smiling and very soft-spoken when he did make an utterance. His smile, knowing looks and calm demeanor spoke volumes, at least to Lenny, Hank and other players who had known the charming "wop" (his self descriptive word) for some years. (More about this wonderful old timer and his stories in the Special Times following in the next chapter.)

A few highlights ... and some screw-ups

Thinking about past experiences at the Ocean City tourney brought back a flood of wonderful memories into Hank's porous mind. He recalled the first team he played with;

the NeverSweats. Larry, an ex-N.H.L.er and he played together on defence. Larry's hockey career had been based on his scoring prowess. By contrast, Hank was a defensive defenceman. He often blocked shots of the opposing players. On a rare occasion, he would get a breakaway for his efforts. Getting a breakaway for Hank was usually an exercise in futility and frustration, mainly because of the concrete in his gloves.

Be that as it may, and as dumb as it was for old guys, Hank kept on blocking shots. Well, the NeverSweats were playing the Golden Oldies from a place called Swift Current. After Hank blocked an opposing player's shot near his team's blue line, the puck bounced off his shin pads and straight ahead of him toward the other team's goal. Hank took off after the little black disk in hot, really lukewarm, pursuit ... sort of like the first goal he ever scored eons before in bantam hockey. The lumbering (and laboring) d'man was skating mightily and stick-handling beautifully (remember tongue in cheek) with the puck when out of nowhere came a stick from behind that went between his legs and was followed by a quick twist. Imagine ... picture if you can ... a large, padded old man spinning out of control above the ice, upon which he landed unceremoniously a couple of nanoseconds later. The Shark from "Speedy Creek" had struck from behind and spilled Hank on his ample old derriere. About the only consolation was that the Shark received a two minute penalty during which time the NeverSweats scored a goal, something Hank would not likely have done with his breakaway.

With the odd exception, old timers "by and large" (whatever that means) are really good-hearted, considerate fellows. They have "all been through the mill", as the old saying goes. They have had lots of life experiences, some of which are not very pleasant. In fact, some of the experiences were down right miserable or worse. Playing with the NeverSweats in the Ocean City Tournament, circa 1990, provided a glistening, like sweaty, example.

A good old boy named Donny was in the middle of an acrimonious divorce. He was suffering "big time" from the wretched legal process, compounded by the involvement of adversarial lawyers, money ("the root of all evil"), wife, children and others. Donny was playing in Ocean City to escape the misery of his life on the other side of the Rockies. Other Ne'erSweatie players were doing their best to make his escape as enjoyable as possible. Donny played hard, skated up and down his wing diligently, fore-checking, back-checking and scoring the odd goal. Although not sensational, he was a solid, reliable player. So, when he was named by the NeverSweats to be the team's "rep" on the tournament All Star team, Donny just about exploded with joy and other emotions that will be left to one's imagination. Clearly, Larry was the best player on the NeverSweats and, in terms of talent and performance, belonged on the All Star team. But he was a magnanimous, self-confident old fella who relished the opportunities to make others look and feel good. So, all factors considered, including human ones, and without a shadow of a doubt, Donny was the best choice for the "dream team". The looks of joy on his face as well as those of his team mates spoke silent volumes. Clearly, he was the unanimous choice. You're a good man Larry!!!

Lots of other human experiences merit mention. Only a few will be revealed. Many of the real, real old timers play the game with some kind of physical handicap. Maybe it's a wonky heart, a hip or knee replacement, concussion, the consequences of a cancer or other operation. In Hank's many eons of playing hockey, he could only remember playing in one tournament against an "one–armed bandit". That term usually refers to slot machines. But, by golly, in their first Ocean City Tournament, the NeverSweats encountered one of those "bandits". In the context of the hockey, the term was used, with all due respect, to identify one very clever, crafty and talented player who only had one arm. The other had been removed during an accident many years ago. Losing an arm did not keep this fine athlete from playing the game he loved.

"The bandit" was well-built, in good shape (relatively speaking), a strong skater and maneuvered extremely well. He was the star player of the Olde Grumps from Meadow Lake. In a game against the Neversweats, he proved himself many times over, especially when he slipped around from behind the Ne'rSweats' goal, lifted Hank's stick, stole the puck and popped it into the net while the goalie and others looked on in amazement. The "bandit" had done his dastardly deed so deftly it would have been an amazing feat even for any player with two arms and hands. To this day, when the old boys reminisce about the Ocean City tourney, the name and feats of the "one armed bandit" are often recalled and discussed with the same respect and admiration as you might experience when talking about "the Great One", "Magnificent Mario" or the "Golden Jet".

Joxville's own bash and hash

For the past 27 years or so, give or take a few, the Joxville Oldtimers' Ass'n has put on a glorified shinny tournament. It's held early in November, about the time the first blizzard hits. (Seem to be repeating myself. Darn! Oh well, repetition aids retention or so teachers are taught .... but I digress ... again.)

Like most every thing else worthwhile in the world, the tourney started small. Like Topsy, it just grew. (That's been said before but it's so appropriate here ... déjà vu all over again, like Yogi says.) In recent years, the tourney has become "good-sized", with 40 teams, more or less, and usually 10 divisions. Unlike the Snoopy tournament which has creative names for its divisions - like Charlie Brown, Peppermint Patty and Molly Volley, Joxville goes with the alphabet, in its simplest form, like A, B, C, D (you get the picture) for its divisions. Each division has a four team "round robin" and a championship game, the winner of which gets ego boosts and nothing more - no trophies, plaques, medals, belt buckles, mugs or even pins - just plain and simple "bragging rights" which get pretty boring after hearing it more than once.

For the year in this story, Hank's team was in the oldest ... and the slowest ... and the least talented - "H" (like Hades) division --- the bottom rung on the ladder. For those who are arithmetically-adept, the "H" division is the eighth letter in the alphabet. With each division having four teams, then only 32, of the 40 teams entered, are accounted for. Right?! Yes, but the Joxville "brain trust" does have some creativity. For age and skill categories with more than four teams, there are double alphas, like BB, EE and FF or two "H" teams --- kind of confusing but then that is part of the challenge for senior folks; to overcome confusion. Anyhow, it's not really important so long as the players are in age divisions where they belong, if they belong at all --- which brings us to a strange way to create tournament teams.

"Sign-up teams"

I've been going to mention this aberration of the Old Boys' agglomerations for tournament competitions but seem to keep forgetting. To "appreciate" such teams requires perspective and insight, if not wisdom.

The participative nature of old timers' hockey is "beautiful" and is manifested mainly by its openness and transparency, two conditions that all political and corporate reformers advocate but their archaic institutions so seriously lack. Such authoritarian, hierarchical structures of (in)humanity could take some valuable lessons from old timer hockey organizations, like the Old Boys' Association in Joxville. But that's beside the point ... whatever that may be.

For most of the tourneys in which the Old Boys play, they enter "sign up" teams. In every day language that means that active Association members, in good standing (on skates), who were able to write or print their names and pay a deposit for the event, could play for that team, usually.

What is the karma? The short answer is: confusion, lack of coordination, ineptitude and other chaotic, yet not unusual, Old Boys' conditions. Every Old Boys' team has different players for every old timers' tournament in which they participate. Yes, hockey is a team sport. Yes, it really helps if the players usually play together on the same team. But no, Joxville does not pick their tourney teams that way which contributes to the karma and losing a very high percentage of their games. Losing is not fun, no matter how you spin it.

So the sign up teams are formed, with one big strike against them. Then there is the second strike of being so democratic that the guys who sign up are the guys who are on the team even if they are !@#$%^&*()_+?><?!X "players" - like Dr. D.O. Little, Cement Hands and Big Mouth (not their real names but used to protect the "innocent", including this scribe).

A week or two before the tournament, the Old Boys start searching for the team rosters. Almost inevitably, the muttering starts as they look at the line-ups - no, not police line-ups, the tournament team rosters. Max and Hank are looking at the rosters and muttering.

Max: "F....!, we've got Big Mouth on our team.... we won't need the Colonel to coach us. We have Big Mouth to tell everybody what to do ... and what not to do. F....!!!"

Hank: "Ya, and we have five defencemen ... I really hate five d ... have so many different combinations that you never know what the other guy is doing ... where he is ... or where I should be ... son of a bitch ... it would be better with one less ... or even one more ... especially when we are playing so many games this week."

Max: "Ya, we practice on Tuesday, play Old Boys' games on Wednesday and Thursday ... then tournament games on Friday, Saturday ... and if we win those, play in the finals on Sunday morning ... let's see ... that's one, two, three, four, five .... and maybe six or seven games in six days ... hell, even the kids ... or the pros don't play that many games in a week ... and we're the oldest ... of the old guys!"

Hank: "Shoot, I'm not going to play all of them ... going to miss our game Thursday night against the Rouges ... knees can't take it ..... neither can the rest of me."

"Practice" game, scrimmage, getting sorted out, whatever

During "tournament week", along comes Tuesday night and the practice game. Yes, only one practice game of sign-up players for the biggest event of the year for most of them. As Larry, always the teacher, said, "... at least we can learn each others' names ... maybe!" So who troops in through the door to the dressing room? Bernie is there when Hank arrives. So is Tom. Tom and Bernie (not Jerry) are coordinating the team ... like herding cats!!! In hushed voices, they are talking together in the corner of the room, trying to figure out who would play best with whom ... forming forward lines and defence pairings. "Ah Hank," Bernie says, "maybe you can help us. Who do you want to play "d" with?" Hank, being one of the older "seniors", drops his bag of gear and sticks on the floor and starts stroking his whiskered chin.

Hank: "Who's playing defence?", he asks.

Bernie: "There's Jimmy, Nellie, Gordy, Eddy and you".

Hank (scrunched up his face quizzically and responded): "What difference does it make with five d'men, there's going to be at least three or four different combinations during the game .... knowing old timers, they will forget who they're supposed to play with during the game .... five d'men causes confusion .... more so than is normal, whatever normal is, for old timers."

Bernie:"Ya, ya, you're probably right! But that doesn't answer the question!"

Hank (having thought some more about the question said): "If I had my choice, it would be Eddy ... we've played together ... we know each other's style ... or whatever you call it ...habits maybe. We play pretty well together ... I think ... but you guys are in charge ... do what you think is best. That will be fine with me. OK?"

Tommy: "Ya, that's fine ... I guess. You damn d'men are always a problem".

Hank, (never one to ignore a jibe at defencemen retorted): "You bloody forwards ... always attacking the heart and soul of your team .... instead of the opposition. You're all screwed up! Tres dommage!!!" Tommy (with feigned indignation): "Don't swear at me!"

Bernie: (of French-Canadian ancestry) "Ah, you dumb Anglo, he was being empathetic with you and all of your trials and tribulations ... all of the challenges in managing this Old Boys' team ... in a nationally televised tournament (remember tongue in cheek!). C'est un grand problem, n'est pas ... mon ami but we can handle it ... oui ... non?".

Hank: "You guys will sort it out ... all's well that ends well ... that means winning! Right!"

As is well known in shinny lore but not documented, old timers do not score many hat tricks. So, when one is "notched", the other players are ready to celebrate or, at least, have a free drink at the expense of the "sniper". The goal scorer's team mates are like a pack of jackals who smell blood; they're relentless in their attack until the "hat tricker" (if there is such a term in the hockey dictionary) puts his money out for the free round. The "jackals" were at their blood-thirsty worst after Flying Freddie scored three during a *practice* game for the annual Joxville tourney. When "buying a round" is consensually or democratically determined, there's no way of escaping that obligation. It's recorded in the minds and hearts of the other players until it is fulfilled fully. Despite his vehement protestations that "it was only a practice game", the peer pressure was overwhelming on Freddie to buy for the boys. Being the good guy that he was, is and evermore shall be, he bought a round for the boys. And the expressions of appreciation must have been worth the $20 paid because Freddie was smiling as he left the dressing room and headed home. But then, maybe he was thinking of his luck there!

Eat, drink, make merry, other incidental activities

By most generally accepted and objective standards, Joxville put on a good tournament. It must be. It has been held for more than a quarter century. More than 500 players, their wives, girl friends, partners, family members, various and sundry others descend upon the town for a week-end of glorified shinny, beer-drinking, gorging, beer-drinking, reminiscing, beer-drinking, gorging, playing various games and just plain having a good time.

The good times start on Friday. All the teams play their first game sometime that evening in one of several arenas scattered around the city. For those interested in minutia, six arenas are used for five hours each day/night to accommodate those games. Then the real fun begins. Players find their way to Anderson Arena, sentimentally referred to as the "Ice Palace" - where the free food and bottomless $5 mug of beer (or various other drinks) abound.

"Action central" - the kitchen- is located in the bowels of the arena. Sounds kind of disgusting, doesn't it? That's where Billy (commonly called "Billy Bob" because he comes from southern Saskatchewan), Lee, Dougie, their wives and others cooked up the beef 'n beans. Lest cynics or ignoramuses assume that these cooks merely opened some cans of beans, dumped them in a big pot or two, heated and stirred the contents and then put them on rickety old tables for serving the hungry hunks who gathered for sustenance, please be advised that such was just not so. Lore has it that the pork and bean recipe was ancestral and handed down from generation to generation until it had reached, was treasured and used by the current family of "bean cookers", not to be confused with "bean counters" - that's accountants you know.

Along with copious quantities of brew, the three "chefs" started cooking those beans, chunks of ham, sauces and other secret ingredients three days before the tournament. And they used only the finest white navy beans (no biases or discrimination intended) available in Joxville. They soaked those beans for at least a day. Then the extraordinary creativity and innovative ways of the old guys and gals took over - with considerable ritual, like opening a new jug of rum. Strict security pervaded the kitchen. Few people knew the "recipe" or what was thrown into the pot besides the beans, ham, spices, water and "miscellaneous". For those old Lil Abner fans of years long gone by, making the pork 'n beans was sort of like the "kickaboo joy juice" those primitive old hillbilly boys, Smokey Joe and Polecat, used to make. Rumors abound about what goes into the pot. But, to date, no dead cats, bats or moonshine have been reported. No one has ever died or even knowingly been smitten with ptomaine poisoning. Any sickness was usually attributed to too much booze or exhaustion from playing too hard!!! And it's amazing how many helpings those players and their lady friends, not to mention what the odd teenager, consumed. But the "bottom line" is that those beans were delicious to eat, difficult to digest and bloody awful to smell the next day.

Saturday was the big day of seniors' shinny. All 50 odd teams played two games starting at 7 in the morning which was very early for the very heavy drinkers ("soaks"). And you could see it or at least sense it. The really old drunks could hardly focus their eyes, keep from mumbling and desperately tried to move in some semblance of coordination, on and off the ice. They wobbled more than usual. Some staggered into and out of their dressing room, down the walkway and into the players' box. There they sat with a sense of relief from having gotten that far and from the cooler temperature and air that an arena brings to a booze fever, nausea, a headache and the other aches and pains that permeate their battered and bruised old bodies.

With a sharp blast from the ref's whistle, the games began. "Can't they put a muffler on that thing," grumbled one over-indulgent old coot. That started a stream of banter, much of which was derogatory toward the grumbler, his drinking habits, ancestry and various and sundry other irrelevant matters -that didn't really matter at all. But the blather served as a stimulant for the other players and their moribund minds and bodies. Some of the old geezers were feeling quite sanctimonious because they had not over-imbibed , likely because they did not have the strength or energy to go to Anderson Arena for the beef, beans and beer or "Momma" was along to keep "Poppa" in line.

An amazing transformation occurs once the game begins. Players who had looked like "death warmed over", totally "chilled out" or appeared hardly able to stand, much less skate loaded down with pounds or kilos of equipment, were flitting up and down the ice sort of like Guy Lafleur or Paul Kariya (in slow motion). They had come to play; out on the ice giving their all or what was left of it. Up and down the ice they went. Rarely, very rarely, maybe even never, was a penalty called during a tournament game. Likely, it was because each team really wanted to win and no player wanted to let his team down by taking a penalty, having his team scored upon and being reminded of his sin for months afterwards. Maybe it was because the old timer ethic prevailed over other inclinations. Maybe it was because the tournament had rather young referees who were used to brutal mayhem when they played.

Actually, games were quite "clean" by historical hockey standards. Very few players were hit by players on opposing teams. Occasionally, the worst kind of body contact occurs. That's when two players on the same team collide, like when little Mike Wong and big Barry Becker, both with the heads down, skated into each other near center ice during the practice game between the Cowtown Brew Boys and the Joxville Sunsetters. Talk about the irresistible force meeting the immoveable object. In fairly good shape for an old timer and weighing about 160 pounds with his gear on, Mikey usually skates 100 miles (or more likely 1000 feet) an hour. He is in perpetual motion, zigging and zagging, stopping and starting, skating full out. Other players get tired just watching Mikey skate. Then there is Barry, all 260 plus pounds of him moving like an ocean-going ship --- going straight ahead. Such collisions were "no fault" accidents, despite the injuries incurred. Needless to say, Mike got the worst of the collision. In fact, he was down on the ice for several minutes, staggered off the ice and did not return.

Any account of the Joxville seniors' shinny competitions would be incomplete and found seriously lacking if mention was not made of the good old time dinner-dance at The Barn, located inconveniently on the "edge of town". One must remember that Joxville is located on the prairies, not in Hogtown, more widely known as Toronto, or some other pseudo-sophisticated metropolis. The point of this distinction is the fact that the "western" flavor, meaning small town agrarian, is pervasive in Joxville ... now and likely for many more generations to come, if not forever. Small town agrarian is good. People are what they seem to be; not given to pretentious behavior which would be so very uncharacteristic of old timer hockey players.

Well anyhow, Saturday night was the "social highlight" of the week-end. The gals would get "dolled up" and the old guys would change into their best pair of jeans and, maybe a clean shirt. Off they would prance to shinny shindig, filled with vim and vigor and looking for a good fun time. At least that's the prevailing attitude ... until the old guys and gals enter the front door of The Barn, a place most commonly used by youth, those crazy kids who have deadened their hearing to the state of deafness. There they are met with a blast of recorded noise that causes hearing aids to squeal, faces to grimace in pain and guts to start wrenching. People shout at each other, even when they are nearly nose to nose. Anxiety and distress rocket up dramatically. Some folks wonder, out loud, about leaving even as they are arriving. Most soldier on into the vast expanse of the building which is reverberating with incomprehensibly loud noise blaring from amplifiers, tweeters, woofers and other wonders of the electronic age. But the human body, even of staid, stuck-in-their-ways, old guys and gals, shows its ability to adapt, just as Darwin said was necessary for human survival. In that holocaust of noise, folks don't talk very much to one another. Some use their lip-reading skills. Most regret not bringing ear plugs. Others head for the bar to buy a round or three or go back outside for relief to their nervous system.

Fortunately, the music torture subsided. There was the M.C. at the "mike", trying to turn it on and making a helluva racket ... especially because the noise magnifiers were still turned away, way up in the decibel range. After what seemed like an eternity in hell, some tech guy sauntered up to the stage, fiddled around with the mike and then wandered away, leaving the M.C. still shouting. Mr. "casual tech guy" ambled back to the massive bank of sound controls to turn down the volume. Seemed to the electronically-challenged old fellas that the young kid had the sequence wrong - like maybe he should have turned down the volume before getting the mike to work.

After some nice greetings and other blather by the M.C., the most important part of the evening was announced: "soups on!" Obediently, the famished folks follow the M.C.'s orders for attacking the food. Table by table, they march courteously toward the two long sets of serving tables, loaded with steaming hot bowls and platters of mushy potatoes, over-cooked veggies, very well done roast beef, day old salads and dried out buns along with an assortment of pickles, relishes, ketchup and mustard for flavor. But no old timer was complaining. Many had lived through the Great Depression and the dirty thirties. All have witnessed, personally or through the media, tragedies of poverty, hunger and starvation plaguing the world.

An hour or so later, after all but the "hogs" have been satiated, a band is assembling. On the stage with his band and their scawling faces are Tommy and the Tornadoes (TNT – they're dynamite) ... actually real live people with musical instruments ... that will not play at 78, 87 or 95 decibels ...

or well beyond the threshold of human pain. TNT are true friends, not foes, of old timer hockey players. In fact, two of the quartet are Old Boys and are very empathetic to their contemporaries. After a few more brews, some pleasant babble and one liners by Tommy, that the inattentive crowd did not hear, the band starts playing ... nice slow, almost quiet music. About the exchange of various looks, the old guys and their gals smile, say some warm words to each other, then get up out of their chairs and sashay off to the dance floor.

The pleasant evening endeth when fatigue is so great from dancing, eating, drinking and the physical drain of playing hockey that the weary bodies say their "good-byes", "adieus", "ciaos" or whatever and head out The Barn door into the chilly night, instantaneous sobriety, the quick trip into the arms of Amorphous and dreams of the free pancake breakfast in a few hours.

A few hours later, often too few, the old guys, their gals, any other family members or friends that might be around and have a pulse will get their bones out of bed, maybe have a shower, get dressed and head for the Ice Palace. There, in the back of the arena, beneath the climbing wall on which some rather fit and attractive bodies may be making like squirrels, monkeys or some other climbing animal, forty or fifty tables and about 20 times as many chairs are set up awaiting the onslaught of the hungry oldsters and their ravenous children and grandchildren. Yup, it's time "to tie on the old feed bag again", as they said back when, referring to the old days when horses used to be fed from feed bags.

But, Sunday morning breakfast was no ordinary feast, mainly because of the presence and persona of the chief chef - Big Mack - no relation to the Knife. Big Daddy (as he was fondly called by some) or Big Mack, like the truck, was obviously a large lad. And his personality was even larger. His never ending ebullience was legendary, at least wherever he had been for more than a few minutes. His exuberant voice, lingo and chatter brought joy to all who heard him. His roars of laughter could be heard for great distances. Big Mack was one larger-than-life fun guy. And he was one super cook, especially for that old western standby - flapjacks with the works.

Now Big Mack did not put on the Sunday morning pancake "extravaganza" by himself and he was the first to admit that. Several teams showed up to help. A few of the old geezers, who knew how to cook or at least assist usefully, headed for the kitchen, there to prepare the humungous quantities of juice, coffee, eggs, potatoes, sausages, pancakes and put out various "fixings" like cream or, more likely, some artificial "whitener" like dried paint, real sugar or artificial sweetener, syrups, ketchup and other sauces to augment the taste, of the "gourmet" breakfast forthcoming. The younger old fellows sauntered into the dining area where they congregated, shot the breeze for 15 or 20 minutes, awaited and then prepared for the onslaught of perpetually hungry hordes of men, women, children, grandchildren, relatives, friends, officials, refs who were really ravenous junior hockey players who came for Big Mack's "great big breakfast".

During the next couple of hours, scores of men, women and children of all ages enjoyed the vittles that had been prepared with tender loving care and considerable expertise for them and hundreds of others. "Shoot", shouted Big Mack, "there's enough food to feed the Army", to which some smart guy quipped, "Their stomachs aren't that tough." Sooner or later, somehow or other, the mountains of food disappeared - none of it wasted. With a huge sigh, Big Mack decided to close down the breakfast service. (Last Spring, the Lord shut down Big Mack's cooking for ever. He died of a cancer. For the Joxville Old Boys, there will never be another larger-than-life old guy like him. RIP, big guy. You sure are missed. The Sunday morning flapjacks with-the-works breakfasts will never be as good.)

And so it goes from Friday evening until some time on Sunday when the Joxville and other week-end tournament games are completed, the food is eaten, the booze is drunk and the old guys drag their weary bones, with flesh still attached, out of the arenas, hotels, motels, flop houses or wherever, get into their vehicles and head home with their gals and pals. Hopefully, most of them will be back next year, looking for their old "buds" to swap some new and old stories with, have a skate, drink some beer, eat some beans, beef or pancakes and just plain have fun. And why not? Life is so short and gets shorter with each passing year, month, week, day, minute.

XI. Very Special Times

For many old guys and gals, the words *"hockey"* or *"shinny"* trigger many, even streams of, memorable thoughts about playing, watching, "rooting", helping children put on their grungy equipment, especially in rather frigid conditions, coaching, officiating, managing or in various and sundry other ways. Most of the past experiences bring back pleasant memories ... of exceptionally enjoyable experiences and very special times. Among the ever-so-many, many experiences that old timers have had, some are more special than the typical ones. Many of Hank's special times related to the experiences he had with his Dad. His Mom never went to any games he played because she "did not want to see her son get hurt". For Hank to be with his Dad, playing, fishing, working and just simply being together were times of joy and happiness in their purest.

As most hockey players, young and old, female and male, will attest, moms and dads play key roles in the fun their kids have from playing games. In its most basic form, the fun is being with their parents and relishing the quality time, attention and affection, not to mention the hot dogs, of their folks. For Hank, like most oldsters, there are some Very Special Times related to the game of hockey over the years. They range from hours of laughs with "The King", meeting Mr. Hockey, an encounter with "Little Mark", dining with the greatest hockey player of all time to having breakfasts with a charming old coal-miner and caddying for Arnie.

Standing with Dad in the Leafs-Canadiens Passageway

Oh, I forgot to mention one the earliest, memorable fun times that Hank shared with his Dad. Away back at the far edges of his memory, old Hank recalled that when he was about five or maybe six years old, his Dad took him to an exhibition hockey game at the old Edmonton Gardens between the Montreal Canadiens and the Toronto Maple Leafs, two of the "original six". What a huge thrill for a small boy from a tiny town on the Prairies.

Sixty odd years later, Hank vividly remembered how hard he and his Dad laughed, along with the rest of the sell-out crowd, when Big Bill Durnan of Les Canadiens squealed, hollered and clambered up on top of his teetering nets after some prankster let a mouse onto the ice near the all-star goalie. For the cynic, that stunt was silly. For Hank, decades later, it brought back happy memories. And he could clearly remember how big the players were with all of the equipment and how fast they all skated, especially some guy by the name of "Rocket" Richard. But the real highlight and the soul-warming memory that burned brightly in Hank's mind was just simply standing beside his Dad in the players' passageway leading from their dressing rooms to the ice during one intermission of the game. Such a simple but enduring joy!

Back then, as a mere child, Henry was not sure why they were standing in the dimly lit hallway when the game was going to be played on the brightly lit ice surface. He was standing there because his Dad was and that was fine with the little boy.

A few minutes later, his boyish curiosity and doubt were satisfied as young Henry heard the thud, THud, THUD of skates, the banging of sticks and the escalating chatter of large men laughing, talking loudly and enthusiastically as they "thundered" toward them through the narrow passageway. As he looked up in wide-eyed amazement and disbelief, he saw the tallest (they had their skates on), largest (they had their hockey gear on) men that he had ever seen in his life, albeit of only a few years. He stood awestruck, frozen like an ice carving, by the sight of those larger-than-life, real hockey players – some of the best in the whole wide world. As they passed, some were talking in French, others in English, some in who knows what language - probably hockey talk, jargon or slang.

What was so amazing and memorable was how some of them looked down at him (from on high), said something to him, gave him a gapped-tooth smile and tousled his blonde hair. Young Hank was truly mesmerized; speechless until the thundering horde of National Hockey League players were out on the ice. Gobsmacked, he watched them disappear onto the ice as the gates closed. Little Henry felt all bubbly and excited inside. Then he looked up at his father and simply smiled with the pure joy of a little boy. Thanks Dad.

Recalling the thrill of watching the huge NHLers troop by and play that fun game reminded Hank of a story about the big amiable man from Floral.

Meeting the Big Man from Floral

For many years, even generations, Toronto was the hub of Canada and the home of the Maple Leafs. So, it was not entirely unlikely that Hank would be in that city one cold night in March of nineteen sixty something when the Leafs were playing the Red Wings from Detroit. He and a long time, home town buddy, Val, arranged to "have a cup of coffee" in the Royal York, then Toronto's fanciest and most historic hotel. So, at the agreed upon time, the-then two young men from a very small prairie town met in the magnificent lobby of the large hotel. After several minutes of reminiscing and kibitzing, Val asked Hank if he would like to meet Gordie Howe. Did birds fly? Did fish swim? Did night follow day? Hank's answer was equally as obvious.

The two long time athletic acquaintances ambled casually toward several over-stuffed chairs about several feet away, one of which was occupied by a man reading a newspaper. "Gordie", Val said, "I would like you to meet a buddy from my home town!" Immediately, yet rather slowly or deliberately, the paper was lowered and the pleasant face of the then-greatest hockey player in the world, outside of Quebec, appeared ... sort of like the sun rising over the horizon. Hank felt an instantaneous liking for this larger-than-life man. Effortlessly, he rose out of the depths of that overstuffed chair with the ease of an incredibly strong, well-conditioned athlete, rising to his full height and breadth. His mere standing created a presence that was impressive and not soon to be forgotten, like it is still remembered decades later.

"Gordie, this is Hank Hillhouse. Hank, meet Gordie Howe." That very simple introduction led to the two men gingerly shaking hands and exchanging nice warm smiles. "My Lord" thought Hank "my hand is like a child's in his ... and I thought I had a good-sized hand." Gordie Howe did have large hands, very large hands even by hockey player standards. Despite being six feet tall and over 180 pounds, Hank felt physically small in the presence of "Mr. Hockey".

"How do you do, Mr. Howe?" Hank asked respectfully. A huge smile came across the face of the big Red Wing right winger. Then he said with an edge, yet quite pleasantly, "It's Gordie ... not mister. Mister is for my father. O.K.!` Still smiling, he continued by saying "I'm fine, just fine .... nice to meet you. You must be from that small town .... what's it called ... *Wet...ass...agen*? "

"Hmmm", scoffed Hank, taking the bait and responding kind of impetuously but not completely uncomfortably in the presence of the big likeable man facing him. Ànd where are you from Gordie? Floral ... Sass-kat-chee-wan!

Still smiling but with a feigned frown, the big man expanded a little more hugely before saying softly and with an amused look, "Hmmm, smart guy, aren't you. Not many people know that I'm from Floral. Have you ever been there?"

The three men looked at each other, smiled, then slowly started to chuckle at the rhetorical question.

An Afternoon with the "King" (Clancy)

Following Hank's graduation with a degree in business administration, he flew to Toronto for job interviews with some steel company as well as Proctor and Gamble? While the sales job opportunities sounded neither challenging nor interesting, staying at that fancy Royal York Hotel was a real windfall benefit. Even more enjoyable was the prospect of getting together with his former team mate from their "days" of playing at Murray U. Johnny Mac was playing for the Maple Leafs of Toronto. Hank and his old buddy arranged to have dinner together following the Leafs' afternoon practice.

About 2 o'clock in the afternoon, Hank strolled into Maple Leaf Gardens, took some time to wander around the venerable arena, admiring the old photos, special newspaper clippings, impressive plaques and trophies in their stately cases, other memorabilia and even the beautiful wood that lined the hallowed walls of the famous "Gardens". Eventually, Hank found an entrance into the playing area of the arena. Gazing around like an awe-struck kid, he saw the familiar face of an older man sitting by himself among the many seats. That familiar face belonged to the incomparable, much-admired and respected, even revered, Francis Michael ("King") Clancy.

King was 60 years *young* at the time. During his illustrious career, he had played for the old Ottawa Senators from 1921 to 1930 and then joined the Maple Leafs, leading them to a Stanley Cup in 1932. He was reputed to be very tough, a gutsy player who played hockey "a lot bigger than his physical stature". His familiar face was one that looked much like a patchwork quilt with numerous stitch marks running every which way. Behind that face was a brilliant hockey mind and a great sense of humor. Following his playing days, King Clancy became a referee and official for the "Original Six" National Hockey League and then by years of being an executive with the Leafs.

Hank, not being bashful and seeing the King sitting by himself, wended his way over to the seats in which Mr. Clancy was situated. Hank introduced himself and a conversation began. King Clancy was a great conversationalist as well as an outstanding hockey man. That was part of the reason he was a member of the "Hot Stove League" that filled the air waves during the radio broadcasts of Hockey Night in Canada, prior to the advent of television. After a few minutes of chit-chat, King asked Hank to sit down. Whether he was a little lonely or just enjoyed gabbing with people, he certainly was a friendly, humorous gentleman. For the next couple of hours Hank enjoyed one of the most memorable afternoons of his life.

For most of the first hour King Clancy was sitting in the arena evaluating two minor hockey teams. The players` ages ranged from 12 to 14 years. Even in the early '60s the pros were searching for future NHLers and the King had a reputation and track record for spotting young hockey talents. While they sat there and watched the two teams play their game, King kept up a steady, humorous and incisive commentary about the young players. "See that big number 12?" he said. Before Hank could answer the renowned hockey man was expressing his evaluation of the kid's talents with comments like "see how he skates? .... he's strong on his skates .... hard to knock off his feet .... takes a check well but doesn't move laterally very well ... maybe he can be taught to maneuver better." `Probably still growing ...`, opined Hank. Pausing for a moment and taking a deep breath, King continued with his cryptic evaluations of the young players. "See that number 3 ... on defence? .... looks like Gus Mortsen when he was a kid ... strong ... not too good on his skates yet .... maybe they're too big for him ... but he handles himself well .... has some poise ..... confidence .... that's very good. Confidence is so important in playing hockey ... well in anything you do, I guess ... ." And so the up-beat and insightful commentary from the old hockey master went on until the end of the kids' game.

The second hour was less interesting and less entertaining than the previous hour. The focus changed from youngsters out having a good time playing a game to the professional Maple Leafs who were out practicing ... doing their job. That almost grim sense of purpose and mood made a big difference in their "play". While the energetic and enthusiastic kids were out having fun, yelling, cheering, passing erratically, missing passed pucks and many scoring opportunities, falling down and skating around somewhat randomly, the pros were almost totally opposite in their demeanor. Sure, there was the odd, short outburst of emotion and some scattered chatter among the players. But it lacked the spontaneity, levity and vitality of the kids' babble.

The pros were "taking care of business" ... almost like robots. Maybe it was the insecurity of their job in "the bigs". There were many other players who were +striving to play in the NHL. Maybe it was because the Maple Leafs had not played well recently. They had lost their last five games. Maybe it was the ominous presence of their coach, "Punch" Imlach, the no-nonsense, highly authoritarian, seemingly humorless man, much like the team`s sole, not soul, owner, Harold Ballard.

All the while, up in the stands, the gregarious, affable Mr. Clancy provided a most welcome contrast to the somber mood on the ice. Compared to his prattle about the kids` hockey, the King's steady stream of consciousness changed in its content but not in joviality. He was less analytical and more anecdotal in his on-going commentary. He seemed to have stories about every player on the ice and many tales about other players, coaches, refs, officials, owners and others related, however remotely, to the "great game of hockey". Unfortunately, those wonderful stories were not recorded either mechanically or mentally and are lost forever. But the memories of that wonderful hockey man, Francis Michael "King" Clancy live on ... and on ... and on.

An Encounter with "Little Mark" Messier

There is no question that hockey has had more than its fair share of unique characters; players, coaches, managers, scout and a raft of others who have unusual patterns of behavior that go along with how they think. Well, during Hank's many years in and around the good old game, one of the most unique and interesting guys was Doug Messier, father and hockey mentor of Mark Messier. Doug and Hank were on the same team in university. Even playing on the same team with Doug meant playing against him in practices and he was a big, strong, highly competitive, aggressive, mean, even vicious hockey player. Off the ice, he was another person all together; pleasant, gracious, jocular and enjoyable to be with. After their college playing days and while Doug was playing professional hockey with the Portland "Bucks" (Buckaroos), the two ex-team mates would get together and have a brew or two (or more) after a game. Occasionally, Hank would enjoy a family dinner at Pat and Doug's home. That was where Hank first met and played with "Little Mark", then about three or four years of age.

Fast forward this tale to the late 1980s at which time Little Mark had grown into a big, strong, highly competitive, aggressive, mean, even vicious, skilled hockey player. One night, following a game against the New York Rangers which the Edmonton Oilers lost, Hank and his good friend Ian were waiting to go for dinner with the Great One and his entourage. Well, Hank had had a few (too many) brew and was feeling quite happy when who should appear in the players' reception area but "Little Mark" Messier. Given the fact that Hank had not seen "Little Mark" for more than 20 years, the young man striding toward Hank was not so little. In fact, he was quite a fair size, brawny you might say. And he was still wearing his game face, complete with his scary scowl, dark glinting eyes, etc, etc, etc, on his menacing presence --- a ready reminder that they had lost to the Rangers.

That fact and a few other vital bits of intelligence and sensitivity were lost in Hank's murky mind. In his delight to see the young man he had known and played with when he was a child, Hank literally bounced out of his chair and walked toward the not-so-little Oiler player. Holding out his hand to shake Mark's hand, Hank said, without thinking very clearly, "Little Mark, how are you?" Well, you would think the not-so-little man had been speared in the nuts. He glowered at Hank with those deep-set, dark and angry eyes that intimidated other players for decades. That look got through Hank's murky mind very quickly and he even more quickly told the larger-than-life Mark what you just read above. During the nanoseconds it took Hank to tell Mark the relevant history of their relationship, Hank was not only watching the player's eyes but also holding on to his right hand, lest it get loose and clout him in the nose or other vulnerable parts of his aging body. Those few nanoseconds of hasty explanation were some of the scariest of Hank's encounters with hockey players, on or off of the ice.

Oh, yes, Not-So-Little Mark, did not get the humor in Hank's blunder or his hasty explanation, did not grin or smile but, most importantly, did not flatten Hank. Seems that Mark merely grunted, maybe like a moose, turned and walked away to join those who awaited him. A little shaken, Hank returned to his chair where he slowly recovered from the encounter with another life-preserving beer and some pleasant chatter with Ian and his wife.

Post-game dinner with #99, Wayne Gretzky

People of outstanding achievements typically are self-confident enough that they are genuine, not pretentious, even humble folks. As you will read later, the famous golfer, Arnold Palmer was one of those people. What you saw was what there was; a very pleasant, friendly man who liked his caddy to call him Arnie. Similarly, Nobel Peace Prize winner and Canadian Prime Minister Lester B. Pearson had many common man attributes and liked to be called Mike. Charles Schulz, the outstanding creator of Peanuts, probably the most famous cartoon strip in history, was generally affable, approachable (except when he was getting ready to play) and liked to be called Sparky. Present-day super star, Sidney Crosby from little Coal Harbour, Nova Scotia, also epitomizes such fine, down-to-earth, human beings. These and other people of fame and fortune are commonly just really decent people. Like Messrs. Palmer, Pearson, Schulz and Crosby, one of the most decent and intelligent hockey people that Hank ever met was Wayne Gretzky, then at the peak of his career and truly a "great one".

Hank's good friend Ian made the arrangements for Hank to have dinner with Wayne and his entourage of friends and family. Coincidentally, the evening with Wayne began just minutes after Hank had encountered "Little Mark" following the Oilers`loss to the Rangers. What a marked contrast in meeting the two hockey stars after the game: Messier came into the room like a bull (or moose), glowering and intimidating; Gretzky almost glided into the room with a pleasant demeanor, a ready smile and a welcoming persona. While Mark's handshake and personality were strong and slightly overwhelming, Wayne's were firm and comfortable. Comfortable was the way Hank felt from the moment he first met the Great One until they parted hours later.

Then as now, Wayne Gretzky was a "people person", much like Arnie, Mike and Sidney. Hank observed that attribute in the small group of people who accompanied Wayne to dinner that evening. There was his girl friend Vicki and her younger brother Joey. Wayne's brother and a friend from Brantford were there also. Two or three others that Wayne knew by name were part of the group along with Ian and Hank. By good luck or Ian's arrangement, Hank sat next to Wayne during the evening and had the opportunity to converse with him about various subjects ranging from the rights of minor hockey players to play where they chose to the decisions in the coin game he was playing with Ian.

Like his play on the ice, Wayne's vision and mind took in much, if not all of what was happening around the table. Like his passes, his conversation was multi-directional and he hit his targets gently and accurately, usually right on a key point at the right time. There was a vital, extraordinary intelligence in him that came out in his questions, his observations and his commentary. That evening with #99 and his friends was memorable for the experience of being in his presence as well as some of his valuable insights about hockey and various other topics of discussion.

And, mentioning presents, the Great One autographed two hockey sticks for Hank's son and daughter. What treasures from a really fine man, a great hockey player and a wonderful Canadian. His legacy grows ... and grows ... and grows.

The Spirit to Survive – George's Successful Fight to Live

One Sunday night in November of 1957, the Murray U. hockey team was scrimmaging toward the end of its practice. George, a talented, scrappy 20 year old forward, was back-checking a six foot, three inches, 210 pound defenceman from the opposing side. The rushing dman was hit low and flipped by a stocky, hard-hitting opposing defenceman. As the tall, long-legged player flipped through space, the back end of his old-style, open-ended, sharp-pointed skate blade struck feisty George on the left side of his head. Unlike today`s skates, it was *not* enclosed and did *not* have a cap or guard on the back end of the blade. The skate blade pierced George`s cranium and was stuck there while the skater tried mightily to jerk it free.

Hank was the closest player to his entangled teammates. Not being medically trained and trying to keep the skate blade from doing anymore damage, he carefully pulled the blade from George`s head. As Hank learned later, he took the skate blade out of the cranium ... too soon. Blood bubbled out of George's head. Hank nearly fainted. Teammates tried desperately to staunch the flow of blood – by holding towels over the wound. Fortunately, a former hockey player and medical intern was in the stands watching the Murray U team practice. The intern charged down the stairs of the arena, out onto the ice and was able to stop the bleeding. His fast and medically correct action kept George alive until medics, an ambulance arrived and the injured player was taken to a nearby hospital.

About 7 o`clock the following evening, while the team was having dinner as guests of a fraternity, their captain received a telephone call from the doctor in charge of George. The doctor told the team leader that George would not live through the night. A team of seven doctors, most of them highly trained specialists, including two or three neurosurgeons, had concluded there was nothing more that they could do to save George's life. Distraught, with tears streaming down his cheeks, the rugged captain agonizingly passed along the doctor's message to his teammates. Shortly afterwards, the team left their hosts and walked across the street to the university's chapel. Some of the players had never been to a church or a chapel before but, to a man, they felt compelled to pray that George's life be saved.

George lived through the night, the next day and many trying days to follow. The doctors were "stumped", pleased and guarded about how long he would live and, most importantly, in what condition he might live. During the first few weeks, the doctors' consensus was that "he would be a vegetable". For several months, their prognosis was correct. Day after day, George lay stone-like, unmoving in an incubator on life support, his breathing so slight that it was hardly discernible from a few feet away. His face was an ashen shade of grey. None of his extremities moved, not even his eye lashes, fingers or toes. He could have been a mummy. Yet, he lived.

The doctors continued to be at a loss to explain George's living. After several weeks of being comatose, the doctors suggested that there was a slim hope for the gritty guy's partial recovery. Guardedly, they suggested that some physical stimulation might possibly help to revive the gravely injured player. One doctor suggested using verbal stimulation such as yelling or hollering, even swearing, at

George. Since some of the team members were hellions who had backgrounds filled with mischief such behavior did not seem to be overly difficult, almost natural. Even those guys were reluctant to try such antics, especially in a hospital. But George's team mates wanted desperately to help keep him alive and the doctors were quite persuasive in their advice.

Reluctantly, softly and then increasing in volume, some of the team mates started to holler and yell, including vulgarities and swearing at the still body laying in the oxygen tent in a special room with the door and windows closed tightly. "C'mon George you lazy bastard .... wake up ... get up!", screamed one of George's buddies. "George, you (expletives deleted), get your fat ass out of that bed" was another challenge yelled by a team mate. Some of the worst vulgarity ever heard by Hank was a stream of trash talk that would have embarrassed the most foul-mouthed jock. For days, maybe weeks, team mates hollered verbal challenges and swore shamelessly at George. Then one afternoon, George's eye lashes fluttered. His eyes opened ever so slightly. A few days later, he moved his lips. Subsequently, his fingers and toes moved. George was recovering.

George's recovery from near death, albeit very slowly and limitedly, took years of tortuous therapy. It required gut-wrenching, pains-taking and incredibly courageous efforts by George just to move his limbs, take a few, halting steps, even with the assistance of caring people, medical specialists and equipment. But the feisty little guy persevered through the agonizing months of recovery, although not without some setbacks. His brain had been damaged so severely that he was partially paralyzed on the right side of his body. His speech was restored considerably although he never spoke clearly again. His long-time girl friend ended their relationship. Yet, George struggled on with his recovery. And what a recovery it was. From being very near, if not inside, death's door with a few hours to live to walking, talking, working and even instructing handicapped kids on how to ski in the Rocky Mountains, George came a long way back. The doctors concluded that it was not medical science but George's inner spirit that kept him alive.

Breakfasts with Mountain Man Mario

Among the anticipated but unpredictable joys of old timers' tournaments are the opportunities to have a good visit, chin wag or just shoot the breeze with hockey-playing buddies from days of yore. For many of the geezers, it was an occasion that they looked forward to with great and joyous anticipation. And so it was at the annual Ocean City tourneys that Hank looked forward to getting together with a fine, funny old octogenarian named Mario. And it came to pass, that one overcast, misty and dreary morning in March Hank joined Mario and his old crony Len for a leisurely and reasonably healthy breakfast of juice, muffins and coffee at the local Tim Horton's restaurant.

When Hank arrived, Mario and Len were already involved in an animated conversation. It seemed that Len, a lanky man of more than six feet in his socks, had not judged the height of the restaurant chair accurately. It was lower, by a few millimetres, than he was conditioned to or had expected. Consequently, he went that extra distance in a free fall. He plopped down quite heavily and awkwardly, spilling his latte as he landed. Lenny, having a very upbeat disposition, merely "shrugged off" his clumsiness and was laughing about it with Mario. Old Mario, having hockey foremost in his mind most of the time, was laughing as he talked about how low the benches were in the dressing rooms at "Sparky" Schulz's arena ... yes, like that of the late, great Charles Schulz whose tournament was chattered about previously.

Mario was telling about the first time he sat down on the Redwoods Arena dressing room bench, nearly falling over backwards as he lowered his bum down ... and down ... and down ... until he was off balance. And Mario was about five feet, eight inches tall. Chuckling as they spoke, Lenny and Hank recounted similar experiences. Mario guessed that the benches were only a foot or so high, depending on whose foot was used for measuring the height. The three old timers were laughing rather loudly, especially for old fellows in a public place, about some of the really large players, standing more than six feet tall, weighing 12 stones, more or less, and the difficulties they had while navigating their vertical descents to the bench. Those big old guys were far from being the most agile people around (round yes; agile, no!). When their mass was moving in one direction it was difficult to control and steer it, much like a huge, ocean-going freighter. Mind you, some of the more intelligent ones were smart enough to look before they sat down. Even so, a bench that is 10 or 12 inches high is about half the height of the typical chair, whether you're sober or not. So the three old timers were in the midst of a busy restaurant laughing like crazy about some of the guys who had stumbled, bumbled but not crumbled as they sat on those mini-midget benches at Sparky's ice emporium in Santa Rosa.

Len was going on and on about the foot high benches until Hank asked Mario about what he and his buddies sat on when they first started playing hockey. "A piece of snow or maybe a log", was Mario's response. "What did you big city boys sit on when you played outdoors?" Mario asked. (As a youth, Mario lived in an isolated mining hamlet at the base of the Rocky Mountains.) Like most, certified old timers, Len did not answer the question but started to yak about when he "started his *career* playing on a pond at a friend's farm, about three miles west of town". Hank chimed in about his first skating and hockey playing. "We used to play at Mallard's slough ... it usually froze first ... and it was only a short bike ride out there ... and they didn't mind us playing ... as long as we closed the gate so the cows didn't get out." "You guys had cows around", exclaimed Mario in his mischievous, interrogative way. "Shoot, we would more likely have had some bears wandering around where we played ... especially if we played at Small Fish Lake ... where the pike were two feet long but that's a story for another season." Len, looking quite incredulously at the "legend", said "Whoa, wait a minute, Mario! ... don't bears hibernate in the winter time?" Hesitantly, Mario replied,

"Ya, usually they do, but we got some pretty cold weather early in the fall ... like October ... before the bears went to bed for the winter." "Hmmm," mused Hank "... sounds like BS to me ... you know ... like bear smell."

Since part of the old timers' culture and lore is to stretch stories some, Lenny and Hank did not try to "nail Mario" down to precise details. Details and facts often destroy or diminish the humor of old timers' tales. Besides, fading memories and good senses of humor often cause story tellers to embellish their stories and make them more entertaining. Thus, it was about Mario's story of the bears prowling around while he and his buddies were playing shinny on the pond back in the late 1920s and early "dirty thirties".

Before many more minutes passed, the story-telling reverted back to the age old topic of the weather and how cold it was when they played outdoors. "In fact," said old Mario, "I never played indoors until I was 15 and we were in the playoffs in Red Deer. We always played outdoors ... and we would get a lot of snow out there in the 'sticks', meaning in the bush and foothills near Nordegg, about 110 miles west of "the Deer", through bogs, over trails and terrain that defied belief. We might get a foot of the white stuff in one dump, sometimes more, usually less. We would shovel snow for four or five hours just to uncover the ice ... then some more would fall or blow onto our rink ... and we would have to stop every now and then to clean the ice because we wouldn't know where the puck was ... and the cracks in the ice were wicked ... took some nasty falls ... one of our buddies broke a leg from catching his blade in a crack."

Do you know what was worse than the snow falling?", Mario asked with his eyes twinkling. Len and Hank looked at each momentarily with quizzical and amused looks on their faces. Before they could respond, Mario was already answering his own question. "Those damn railroad cinders", he said gruffly. "Every day or two the trains would bring in empty coal cars and take out full ones. Our rink was on the creek just below the tracks ... so when the trains passed they would shower us and the rink with cinders, soot and dirt ... they were old steam engines that huffed and puffed along the tracks ... making a terrible mess, especially on our rink ..... so we would have to get out the old scrapers and the shovels and anything else we could find ... like the goalie's brooms to clean off the ice ..... and cinders stick to the ice, especially if they were hot or had landed when they were hot ... they'd stick right into the ice, like ticks in a horse's hide. Len and Hank listened in rapt and smiling silence, not even drinking their coffee or munching on their muffins.

Being the consummate story teller, Mario continued with his vivid description of playing conditions on the outdoor rinks of times gone by. "We used to play in some wickedly cold weather ... 40, 50 below ... brutal. But we were young and didn't care ... or at least nobody griped too much about the cold. What were our alternatives? ...... sit at home in a one-bedroom shack with your family ... or somebody's else's family. Hell, we didn't even have a pool hall to hang out in." While Mario was catching his breath and having a sip of his cold coffee and Len was munching on his muffin, Hank took the opportunity to tell his favorite cold weather hockey story.

"We were playing at the University of North Dakota, back in late 1957 ... or maybe it was early in 1958 ..... playing in half of a big tin can ... you know something like a Quonset hut, only much larger. Anyhow, it was 56 below with wind chill ... 56 degrees below zero ... unbelievably cold!!! Well, one of our forwards bumped into the goal post and the ice was so brittle ... it was natural ice ... that a piece about three feet across broke right out ...... just shattered like a pane of glass. Believe it or not, we were back playing about 10 minutes later ..... the refs put the big pieces back in, added some water, made some slush and it froze back ... bingo... just like our hands and feet ... frozen." Mario, in his inimical, soft spoken way interjected, saying "the very coldest I ever played was about minus 60, give or take a few degrees." "Ya," said Len, "once the temperature gets below 20 or 30, it doesn't make much difference ... it's just bloody cold."

"We sure had long ... reaallly long hockey seasons, back then", mused Mario. "We might start playing before Thanksgiving, maybe about Labour Day. Out there in the trees ... and close to the mountains, winter could set in and you never knew when it would end ... it would go sometimes until Victoria Day ... around the end of May," Mario contended, as if his Canadian-born friends did not know when Victoria Day was, at least back then. "That was my parents' wedding anniversary", interjected Hank.

Len returned to the earlier chatter, insisting on knowing, in a teasing, jibing way what old Mario and his shinny-playing buddies sat on when they played outdoors. "Cripes, I told you already! What's the matter with you Lenny ... having a bout of *oldzheimers*? We sat on anything we could find ... stumps, logs, chunks of frozen snow or ice ... or on the ground ... just long enough to get our skates on, brush off our butts and get goin'", enthused Mario with a wry smile spread across his face and a far away, wistful look in his eyes.

Mario continued the reminiscing with a tale about his first pair of skates. A neighbor gave him an old pair of skates that were so broken down that they were split up the back seam. Mario could slip into them from the heel of the boot. Then he would have to wrap some electrician's tape or twine around his ankle and the boot so the skates would stay on his feet. "The sides of the boots were so soft that I skated on my ankles," lamented Mario. "Ya, me too" interjected Hank, "my first pair of skates had soft boots like that. I skated on my ankles and there was nothing I could do about. I remember my first goal in Bantam hockey was scored when I had a breakaway, shot, stumbled, fell down and slid into the goalie. I knocked him down and the puck went in the net ... but the referee called it a goal. I'm not sure what went in the net first ... the puck or me but it didn't make any difference. I got my second goal much the same way .... oh I was a pitiful skater. Not only were the boots soft but they were too big, too! Dad used to get them big ... so I would grow into them. Hell, they were sooo big I could nearly turn around inside of them", exaggerated Hank. "I never had a decent pair of skates until I went off to university and the coach felt so sorry for me, he sent me to the sports store to get a new pair .... the first new pair of skates that I ever had ... and they fit properly. I was eighteen years old then and had been playing organized hockey for 11 years ... 11 years without a decent pair of skates. By the time kids are that age today, they probably have had a dozen pairs of new skates ... if not more ... and fortunately, none of them are too large or have soft boots ... so they have to skate on their ankles."

Hank's monologue, rather impassioned by old timer standards, almost but not quite, exhausted the subject of the skates they wore in years gone by. As Hank and Lenny ate some of their breakfast, Mario continued the chatter about skates by telling a funny story about getting his old skates sharpened. "We would take our skates to be sharpened by the shoe maker, really a shoe repair man ... some called him a cobbler ... ever hear that word," asked Mario kind of slowly, as if he was thinking about something else and was distracted from what he wanted to say. But he continued, "This old man, I think he was about my age now ... then. He used to sharpen our skates across the blades with a hand file ..... what they called 'cross cut' sharpening ..... there was no equipment then to sharpen skates. Imagine, the skates would have teeth on the blades ...... like this," he said as he illustrated the effect by holding up a plastic knife that he had used to butter his muffin. "The skates had teeth on them ... like a saw. We had to run on our blades. We couldn't glide," adding "so help me God", when he saw the incredulous looks on the faces of his old buddies. "Honestly .... the blades had teeth on them," he repeated as he tried to convince his dubious friends. "Honestly ...."

The conversation turned to the topic of the other equipment that they used "away back when". Mario claimed that they made their own hockey sticks, mainly out of willow branches. "We had no money for hockey sticks or other equipment .... besides we had no place to buy it if we did have any money. Red Deer was over 100 miles away. There was no road and only the odd passenger car on the trains ... every now and then ... maybe once a month ... or so. We would hop a freight or a coal car every now and then ..... ride down the road a few miles and then walk back ..... just for something to do. We weren't supposed to do it. It was against the law. You could go to jail ... but we never did ... go to jail," Mario said as he completed his wandering thoughts sporadically but being sure to leave the impression that he was a good, law-abiding guy, even if he had not been in his younger years.

Lenny, having finally finished his less-than-robust breakfast, re-joined the chatter by telling about his original hockey gear. "When we first played road hockey, we used anything we could get our hands on. Goalies would use old brooms, some guys played with sticks like the sticks they use nowadays for ringette ... old broom sticks or mop handles. Some of the older guys would get broken sticks from the junior games ... take them home, splice the two pieces together with glue, shingle nail and wrap black tape around the splice. That was a first class stick back in those days."

Hank nodded in agreement, not sleepiness. "Same story with us ... when we were playing kids hockey. When I started playing, *Santa Claus*", chuckled Hank, "brought me a brand new hockey stick and a roll of hockey tape every Christmas. That was my new stick for the year. I played my first few games of league hockey before Dad even bought me a pair of shin pads ... Mom was opposed to me playing Bantam hockey. She didn't want me to play with those 'big, rough boys'. So Dad delayed the inevitable ... and I got hurt a lot ... but I kept on playing ... loved the game so much. Other guys would loan me some of their equipment ... when they weren't playing. I played my first season before he bought me a pair of used hockey gloves ... but I had good mitts ... they were okay for playing hockey ... on Mallard's slough or in the rink. Hell, I didn't care. All I wanted to do was play. The lack of equipment didn't keep me from it ... sure had a lot of bruises ... didn't get my first can until about the third season and then big Roger broke it with a shot in the first or second game ... it was made out of plastic. Dad bought me a metal one after that", Hank said with a contorted grin.

"Ya know, we were relatively well off with the little gear we had," said Lenny. "There were kids that had no equipment ... nothing. They would come out to play road hockey ... or on the slough in their boots with some kind of a 'stick', broom, whatever they could find ... or just be the goalie ... standing out there trying to stop the puck .... or the ball ... or the frozen horse turd.... or they would just run and try to play ... sort of like soccer players ... kicking the puck. Everybody who came out played ... sort of.... ."

Hank barged back into the conversation, saying "Remember how we picked the teams ... the two biggest guys ... or the best ones would be captains and then they would start picking ... they knew who were the best players and," adding reluctantly, "who were the worst. So we would go through this kind of cruel process of natural selection ... or so it seems now ... but didn't back then ... to pick teams ... so we could start playing ... quickly. And we would play by the hour. We would play on the road ... under the street light when it got dark ...... and it got dark before supper a lot of the time during winter. So we would go in for supper and then come back out ... usually in the same wet, dirty clothes that we went into the house with ..... and our good buddy Alf Schmidt used to freeze the back alley behind his house. We would play there on Saturday or Sunday afternoons ... kind of special .... like playing in Maple Leaf Gardens or the Forum. We even had a league of four teams that played road hockey. It got really competitive. Nobody wanted to lose to the guys in another neighborhood ... we had some real rivalries ... especially the kids from the north end of town .... against any of the other teams. There were a few bloody noses and some painful bruises from those games ... sure toughened us up."

"Well boys," Len said with a pensive look, "seems to me that there are some other folks here who could use this table. We've been here for more than an hour, shooting the breeze. Guess we better get goin' .... need to stretch the legs and do some things before we play our game this afternoon. Who are we playing?" he asked. Hank replied, "that Soupy River team ... I mean the Campbell River team. I think they're the Stealheads ... something fishy like that. So let's get going. We have to beat them if we want a chance to win our division ... and they usually have a pretty good team." "We should have breakfast again tomorrow," said dear old Mario. "This was really good. I enjoyed it." "Good idea, Mario," agreed Len. "Fine with me, too," added Hank.

The next morning, about nine o'clock, the three old timers strolled down the flowering tree-lined Gorge Road to Tim's where they re-convened their gab session over coffee, juice, fruit yogurt and "low cal" muffins. Hank was quite curious, even intrigued, about Mario's child hood and living out in the bush and mountain country. Hank had grown up in a small town a few hours away from where Mario lived. He and his Dad went fishing out in Nordegg country as it was called then. Those fishing trips with his Dad, once a year for several years, were very special times of his youth that Hank relished decades later.

So the second breakfast conversation started with "fishing stories". "Hey Mario, what's this BS about catching two foot trout in that Small Fish Lake of yours," queried Hank of his friend. "Hank, you're memory is slipping. I said two foot *pike* and by damn they were two feet ... some even longer", Mario shot back with a little more enthusiasm than normal. "I swear they were this long ... or longer," he said as he spread his hands apart by three feet or more. "Ya, ya, I've heard that story before ... two feet going on two yards .... the old fisherman's tale.... hmmm.... thought you were a honest guy, Mario," teased Len.

That comment sparked a spirited response from Mario. He went on a rant about the size of fish in the lakes and streams of the foothills country, about the damned trespassers who came from the cities, broke down the fences, let the cattle out, took too many fish and littered the countryside with cans, bottles, bags, etc, etc, before Lenny gently put his hand on Mario's scrawny arm and said "Mario, old friend, we are just pushing your buttons ... seems like we hit a hot one ... ha! ha!", the lanky defenceman said as he tried to calm down his buddy. "Ya, you're right. Hank, you're an agitator ... just like you are on the ice," Mario said with his wry grin returning to what had been a serious, even scowling face. Hank replied "Sorry, old fella ..... didn't mean to get you riled up so much .... we need to take care of our Legends."

Mario had become a "legend", at least at the Ocean View Tournament. He was playing in the Legends division (75 years plus). Factually speaking, the grand old guy was well into his eighties and still "lacing them up". As most perceptive people know, age is an human variable that can be misleading. Some people age faster than others. Mario was one of the "others". Despite being born in 1922, he was in "good shape" for an old timer or anyone else his age. He was not overweight like many old timers. He kept active and didn't eat or drink too much, despite being an Italian. "Wops like to eat, you know", he would say almost any time conversations would get around to the topics of food or eating. His eyes sparkled like polished gems and his mind was trice as bright. He was an inspiration to most of the younger old timers who know him. His life had not been an easy one; quite the contrary, he had lived a life that had more than its fair share of hardships.

Mario was born in Italy and immigrated with his parents and grandparents to Canada when he was two years old. That was in 1905. The men in the family came to western Alberta to "start a new life" .... as coal miners. They ended up in a desolate place named Nordegg. It was so small and so remote that it was not even known by most folks in the 17 year old Province of Alberta. It was not on any maps. Nordegg was at the end of the railway line because that was where the coal mine was located. There were no roads, other than the railroad. There was a narrow trail for horse-drawn wagons that wended throughout the bush-coverd area. It was a very isolated place. The nearest store was in the hamlet of Rocky Mountain House, 52 miles or five long days, in good weather, by horse and wagon to the east. Red Deer, an incorporated centre was another 50 miles east of that in central Alberta. Once or twice a month, a passenger car was added to the daily coal train to bring people to and from the place that Mario described as "so primitive .... but so beautiful in its natural splendor". Mario could make a sow's ear into a silk purse.

To most people, including Lenny and Hank, Mario's youth was perceived as harsh, if not brutal. His family of six lived in an one bedroom "house", more like a hut by today's standards. The four children slept in one medium-sized bed until the oldest were in their teens --- very cozy but not very spacious or hygienic. Considering how cold it was in the winter months, Mario, ever the optimist, thought it was a blessing that the kids slept together. "It kept us warmer, not necessarily warm but at least warmer." For people seeking a better life, times were tough. Mario's father and grandfather worked 10-12 hours a day, six days a week to support their wives and children. When Mario became 15 years old, he went to work in the mines, too ".... at $50 a week for 60 hours of work, very hard work," grimaced old Mario. "The mines were dirty ... unhealthy air .... dangerous. Equipment was crude ... mines were dug using picks, shovels, drills and dynamite. Lethal gases wafted through the tunnels ... and up the mine shafts. Working conditions were unsafe ... miners were often sick, many were injured and some died. The company didn't care a damn ... we were just wop workers and there were plenty more in Europe and elsewhere who were willing to come for work ... survive ... and die."

"In 1939, there was a major explosion in the mine and 29 miners were killed ... 29 dead husbands ... fathers ... brothers ... uncles. Another 20 or 30 were injured, some permanently. With deep emotion choking his voice and anger becoming apparent, Mario vividly recalled seeing

"13 miners laid out on the ground near the entrance to the deadly mine .... it was terrible .... and it did not have to happen. If the (expletives deleted) company had not been so careless and badly managed," Mario's words were now seething with anger. "Those greedy bastards were only interested in making as much money as they could. It was wartime and the demand for coal was 'sky high' .... so were the prices ... and those bastards didn't care about the workers ... just produce, produce, produce .... 'til you drop .... dead for some of them."

"That company was owned by some guys from Britain and France ... Canada was across the ocean from them ... it was a colony ... a place to exploit .... they didn't care about us .... until we got in the war and started to fight for them. Even then they didn't care about us ..... they only cared about making money for themselves .... those dirty rotten bastards," continued Mario with an intensity never before experienced by his two shocked, speechless hockey buddies. Such anger had never been evident with the usually amiable Mario, even when he was playing competitive hockey. "We could *not* join the army because the company said they needed us to produce coal. My brother and I both wanted to join up but the army said we couldn't because the coal had to be mined ... like we were the only guys who could dig coal ... you don't need to be too smart to do that .... and we wanted to go to war and kick the crap out of the Nazis ...!" Mario's voice trailed off as his mind drifted back into history and dwelt on his life as it was back then.

Hank and Len were getting concerned about Mario. They didn't want him to get too upset ... or God forbid, have a heart attack. So Lenny started talking about cars, a favorite topic of most men. Mario and Len were no exceptions. Having calmed down a bit, Mario started to tell about his father's brand new Chevrolet, back in 1937. "It cost 1,300 bucks. It was a real prestige car back in those days ... out there in the 'toolies'. We actually had something of a road then .... really more like a glorified cow path..." "You mean a bear path, don't you?", interjected Hank in a teasing voice. Ignoring Hank, Mario went on about prices "Gas was

30 cents a gallon ... insurance was only 50 cents a year ... less than a penny a day ..... can you imagine ... and for a whole year! ... and you only had to fill in a form with info like 'two legs, two arms' ... just kidding but the form was so simple ... and then all you had to do was send it back by mail to the government in Capital City."

Lenny, becoming enthused about the subject of cars, picked up on the topic. He started to tell about his cousin who used to steal cars then take then to other parts of the province and sell them for whatever he could get for them. "Back in those days, car registration was pretty 'loosey-goosey', just like gun registration is now," Len said sarcastically. Thinking about criminal behavior, Lenny referred to "his lovely cousin as a complete crook. Instead of buying regular gas or 'high test' from the pumps, he would go out to nearby farms late at night and steal 'purple gas' ... then he filtered it through ashes to take out the purple color .... and then add red or orange food coloring so it would look like high test or regular gas ... just in case the police checked his gas to see if he was using farmers' gas ... that they got without paying taxes on it," Len said finishing up his little "shpiel" about his crooked cousin ... with little apparent embarrassment but a lot of contempt for him.

While not a big enthusiast about cars, listening to Mario and Lenny talk about them reminded Hank about his father's first new car --- a 1947 Silver Streak Pontiac. "Boys, that was a beauty," Hank said enthusiastically as he started to describe his Dad's treasure. "Man, it was the most beautiful car I had ever seen ... it was so long ... a four door .... and it was a unique silver grey in color .... with two red and three chrome stripes on each side ... oh gosh, it was a beauty," enthused Hank. He continued. "I remember my first ride in it ... just Dad and me ... going down the highway ... so slowly ... like Dad was afraid the wheels would come off or something would happen to it. We must have been going about 20 miles an hour ..... or less ...... and that was on a paved road. Well, we went down the road about a mile or two and then Dad decided to turn around and go back to town ..... to show my Mom and sister. So we are heading back to town .... going so slowly ..... about the speed of a jogging horse. As we approached town, there was another, older car parked on the other side of the road ..... and an old guy started to walk .... actually stagger ... across the highway with his hand out ... reaching like he wanted to pat our car. Well, Dad honked the horn, hit the brakes and steered the car toward the right, swearing as we went ... well, that crazy guy keeps on walking, sort of stumbling toward the car with his hand out. We're heading for the ditch but Dad was able to drive past the guy ... and get the car back on the road and heading for home ... safely. Man, I will never ever forget that first ride ... beat the others we took in our old Ford. I used to get so 'car sick' in that old rattle trap. It was so drafty and dirty ..... we would be going somewhere and before long, up she would come ... in any direction... not very nice. Dad would get so mad at me. That bothered me more than getting sick."

Having a sensitive stomach, Len interrupted Hank by suggesting a change in the conversation. Hank apologized for "bringing up" the subject. Mario was happy to oblige. He started to talk eagerly about his family. In a mild burst of enthusiasm his eyes lit up. He began telling about getting married in 1943. "I was 21 then. We had to stay there and dig coal ... and there was this nice Italian girl ... Maria ... Maria and Mario ... sounds so good. She was a beauty ... 19 years old ... and we hit it off real well ... my older brother was kind of jealous ...... he liked her too. But for some reason," Mario said in his self-deprecating way, "she liked me ..... better. So we decided to get married. Her folks agreed. There was a priest out in that area ... kind of made the rounds ... he had stops here and there out in the bush. So he married us. Then ... listen to this you guys," Mario asserted gently, "we went 12 miles with a team of horses to spend a week in a tent beside a lake in the woods and do some fishing... . That was our honeymoon ... in a tent by a lake ... with a team of horses" he repeated for emphasis as he smiled mischievously, obviously recalling some of the joys of that time. And, Len and Hank were too gentlemanly to spoil his memories with crude questions about what Mario and Maria did when the newlyweds were not fishing.

Mario was starting to get "antsy". Even in his eighties, he did not like to sit still for very long. He must have been so hyperactive as a child; he still was fidgety as a senior adult. Besides he had a crucial Legends' game to play in a couple of hours and he wanted to "get ready". Hockey players, like other athletes and athletic pretenders develop routines and other idiosyncrasies that they perform, especially before games. And he had to "catch a ride" with another team mate who still drove his car. But then, according to Mario, he was just a "youngster. He's only 77 years young."

Visiting with Sammy

One of the highlights of Hank's visit to "the coast" was visiting with his friends on Salt Spring Island. Hank would leave Ocean City early in the morning, well, certainly by 9 am, and head out into the country with its verdant landscapes, rolling hills, lakes and ponds and the sheer majesty of nature spread out before him. He would drive 30 or 40 miles or metric equivalent to the ferry terminal, park his car, buy a two-way ferry ticket, then saunter onto the sleek craft for the passage through the beautiful islands to the dock at Salt Spring. There he would be met by his friend Sammy, the retired Dean, Professor and genial genius. They would walk through the hamlet up the hill to a house overlooking the inlet. Unless she was painting, at the library, walking the dog, shopping or doing one of a number of other activities, Sam's wife Bobbie would be waiting with a hug, warm smile, a fresh pot of coffee and some kind of goodies to savor. She was one fine cook.

Then, Hank and Sam, the aging academic, would launch into a pleasant day of chatting and discussing a wide range of topics --- always current political and business issues, investments and other financial matters, professional activities, memories and reminiscences and whatever other subjects came to their still active, fertile minds. Usually, they would go for a car ride, stopping here and there around the island --- at a bookshop, artist's gallery, gift store and always for a scrumptious lunch at the Eagle's Nest cafe. There, in the splendid, spacious log building with the glorious sunshine streaming warmly in through huge windows that overlooked a scenic cove, the three longtime friends would have a beer or two, eat too much chowder and talk for hours. What a wonderfully delightful, resuscitating way to spend some quality time. Later in the day, they would end up back at Sam and Bobbie's home, sitting on the deck, maybe sipping a brandy, watching the humming birds, eagles, countless other birds and the occasional boat in the inlet.

All too soon, the sun would start to fade behind the hills to the west and Hank would make some noises about having to leave. Sometime later, he and Sammy would walk down the hill, around the corner, along the "main" street to the ferry terminal. Since Sammy knew the schedule well, the wait was short. The chatter was always congenial, despite Hank's ability to "ruffle the feathers" of most people. Maybe it was because Sammy was such a laid-back, non-confrontational kind of guy. Whatever it was about Sammy, he sure was a pleasant and interesting man to visit. "Sure hoped he is around next year" Hank would muse to himself as he departed and sailed (actually ferried) back to Ocean City.

Caddying for Arnie

One of the windfall benefits of going to Murray U was the opportunity to earn some extra bucks caddying at the prestigious Mountainview Golf and Country Club. Not only was it a good place to earn some money while going to school but it was a great place to learn about golf; not only how to play the game better but also about the etiquette, the rules, regulations and what to do/not to do while playing the game. Caddying there for a couple of years was not only good training but it looked good on the caddy application form for the 1958 Canadian Open Golf Championship.

Hank had seen the advertisements and an article by the caddy master urging applications for caddies in the Edmonton Journal. He also had read about the great golfers that were expected to play in *the Open*. Top flight Canadian golfers like Al Balding, George Knudson and Moe Norman were scheduled to compete. Then there was a whole slew of American golfers entered; stars like Mike Souchak, Doug Ford, Tommy (Thunder) Bolt, Doug Saunders, Dow Finsterwald, Don January, the Hebert brothers and a rising *phenom* by the name of Arnold Palmer from Latrobe, Pennsylvania.

Back in those days, caddies were not professional. By today's standards, they were really quite non-professional. They did not travel around the pro circuit with the golfers. During tournaments, they did not walk around the course before each day's play, making calculations about distances, pin placements, sand trap, rough and grass conditions and umpteen other key elements vital to the success of the golfers. Caddies were usually young guys who liked the game, maybe knew something about playing it, wanted to earn some money and were willing to "pack" a bag containing a dozen or more clubs, dozens of balls, hundreds of tees, a sweater or two, jackets, rain gear, an umbrella or two, several pairs of gloves and maybe even mitts, various other garments, shoes, bottles of booze and Lord only knows what else in it. Caddies had to be in good shape as well as have horse hide on their shoulders to carry those bags. Be that as it was, let's get back to the main theme of this anecdote.

Hank decided to apply as a caddy for the Canadian Open. He had talked to Mr. Black, the caddy master and told him about his caddying experience at Mountainview plus the fact that Hank was managing a local golf course and was a pretty fair golfer himself. In response, Mr. Black urged young Hank, rather strongly, to apply and sent an application to him which Hank dutifully filled in and quickly returned to the old caddy master. A couple of weeks later, Mr. Black phoned Hank, thanked him for his application, told him that he was in the "A" (top) category of caddies and would be informed, within a week or two, about who he would be caddying for during the big tournament. Like most young guys who dream, Hank day-dreamed about caddying for the charismatic Arnold Palmer and then quickly put that idea out of his mind.

True to his word, Mr. Black phoned Hank about a week later and told him that he would be caddying for Arnold Palmer. Hank was stunned to silence and then incredulity. He did not believe the caller. He thought it was some sadist playing a prank on him. He asked the caller his name. "Mr. Black", came the rather curt, annoyed and assertive response. "Hank, you have been selected to caddy for Arnold Palmer." Pause. Silence. Hank did not know what to think, much less say. In fact, he went momentarily brain dead. "Hank?" asked the increasingly exasperated caddy master "...are you there?" "Yes sir", came the reticent response "and you just said that I will be caddying for Mr. Palmer? Are you sure ... are you kidding me", asked Hank as he came slowly to his senses after the initial shock of such good news. "Yes, no," came the caddy master's annoyed reply. "You sound uncertain about caddying for him. Do you want to caddy for someone else? Please hurry ... I have a lot to do ... and about a hundred other caddies to phone." "Yes sir, no sir" responded the confused young man. "Yes sir, no sir, what does that mean", growled the caddy master. By then, Hank's head had cleared enough to say clearly and distinctly (like his Grade Two teacher had taught him), "Yes sir, I want to caddy for Mr. Palmer!" Quickly and succinctly Mr. Black concluded, "Fine, then we'll see you here next Tuesday morning for his first practice round .... and, oh Hank, congratulations. I wanted to caddy for Arnold Palmer ..... you're a lucky guy." "Yes sir, I sure am", mumbled Hank as he lapsed back into his state of disbelief.

The next few days flew by. Young Hank tried to "come back down to earth", do his job at the golf course and be as normal as possible with his family and friends. Anybody who knew anything about pro golfers and Hank were not inclined to believe that Hank was caddying for Arnold Palmer. Hank was a "practical joker". And he was still dubious himself until the mail arrived on the Friday before the most important tournament in Canada. In the mail that day was an official envelope addressed to him which contained a form from the Royal Canadian Golf Association stating that he would be the caddy for Mr. Arnold Palmer at the Canadian Open. There it was in black and white.

Hank was quite busy over the week-end but when Monday came, he was getting nervous about his caddying assignment at the Canadian Open. He reminded himself that he had played plenty of pressure-packed golf and hockey games, especially at Murray U the past season when they won the NCAA hockey Championship ... and he had caddied for the "Sherman group" at Mountainview when they used to play for $1,000 a hole and some other very good golfers who "played for keeps". Despite his own reassurances and thoughtful words of support from his Dad, Hank did not sleep well Monday night-Tuesday morning. And he was awake and ready to go by 6 a.m. At seven o'clock in the morning, he was in his 1950 grey, four-door Chevrolet with the big sun visor and heading up Highway #2 to Capital City, a distance of just over 40 miles. It was a glorious summer day and Hank was filled with joy and enthusiasm, although some pangs of doubt popped into his head from time to time as he drove along listening to the radio, whistling and sometimes singing a song or, at least, parts of it.

Young Henry arrived at the Mayfair Golf and Country Club just after 8 a.m. Even at such an early hour, the place was a hive of activity, all in preparation for the big golf tournament; the first time it had ever been held in that city. He found the "caddy shack", actually a rather pleasant addition to the fancy club house and "reported for duty" with the caddy master. Mr. Gray looked pensively at the young man standing in front of him and then greeted him warmly. Then he quickly gave the eager young caddy another form to fill in, some tees, a golf hat and, most importantly, a Canadian Open tee shirt with the name PALMER on the back. "Seeing is believing" and looking at that shirt with the illustrious name on it finally made young Hank realize that he was indeed the caddy for the famous Arnold Palmer.

Looking at the caddy master Hank asked, "Is Mr. Palmer here?" "Not yet," replied Mr. Black. "Why don't you have a coffee and wait for him out there ... where the clubs are?" suggested the head caddy man. "OK", replied Hank happily. As he left the caddy shack, he picked up a couple of the club's score cards to study the distances and layouts of the holes. Then he walked around in the early morning sun, feeling like he was on top of the world.

After an hour or so, young Hank walked nervously back to the caddy shack and checked with Mr. Black to find out if Arnold Palmer had arrived at the golf course. "Did I miss him? ... is he not coming to the tournament?" asked the young lad anxiously. "Where is he, Mr. Black?"

Well, the caddy master had a lot of jobs to do, one of which was very urgent: find additional caddies for those who had phoned to say that they would not be available for the tournament. So, he was a little curt with Henry, saying "I don't know where he is! Why don't you phone the hotel ... they are staying at the Macdonald ... ."

Henry had enough good sense not to ask where there was a phone he could use. He had seen a pay phone outside. Off he went to phone Mr. Palmer. After finding the hotel's number from the phone book, he dropped in his dime and dialed the Macdonald. The receptionist put him through to Mr. Palmer's room. Ring, ring, ring ..... the phone must have rung a dozen times or more. Ring, ring, ring! Henry was getting ready to hang up the receiver, when he heard a very groggy voice slowly say, "Hello." Young Hank was so nervous and enthusiastic that he nearly dropped the receiver. As he grabbed the receiver in mid-air, he banged it into the telephone box. "Ouch", the voice said from the receiver. "Sorry, Mr. Palmer ... this is Henry Hillhouse ... your caddy ... phoning from the golf course ... the Mayfair Golf and Country Club ... where the Canadian Open is being played ... are you coming out to practice here today?" He talked so fast that it would have been difficult for a wide-awake person to understand the young caddy.

"Whoa! Slow down son" said Arnold softly. "We got here very late last night ... early this morning ... and I'm not really awake yet. What did you say your name was young man?" asked the famous golfer. "... and maybe you could talk a little softer, son."

"Oh, yes sir", the young man said in a much more modulated voice. "My name is Henry Hillhouse and I am your caddy for the tournament ... and I was wondering when you're coming out to the golf course. Are you coming out here today?"

Arnold Palmer replied hesitantly "Well, let's see what time it is? Hmmmm .... looks like about 9:30 or so ... by my watch. Does that sound about right Henry? ...... we flew in from St. Paul last night and I can't remember if I changed my watch ... or not. What time is it?," asked the golfer politely. Checking his wrist watch, Hank agreed that it was 9:30.

"Okay, young fella," Arnold said slowly awakening and gaining his senses. "I would think that we should be there in an hour or so ... so stay put and we will hit some balls and maybe play a round this afternoon ... oh, and I am sorry you had to phone. I used to be a caddy ... a few years ago," he said, suggesting that he knew what it was like when "the shoe was on the other foot". With those few words, Arnold Palmer showed young Henry that he was a very considerate, professional athlete.

As the details about the golfers' flight from St. Paul came out from the caddy master, other caddies, reporters and some of the golfers, apparently the tour pros had taken a charter flight to Edmonton. And that flight was loaded with booze which some of the golfers, including Mr. Palmer, had drunk to excess. In fact, one of the golfers drank so much that he did not even know that he was in Alberta ... in Canada. He was supposed to be down south in Louisiana ... with his pregnant wife who was due to give birth at any time. The hung-over golfer's plight was rather painful, yet funny for Hank when he happened to overhear part of hung over husband's emotional, convoluted and strained phone conversation with his wife ... thousands of miles away.

An hour or more passed before the pride of Latrobe appeared at the Mayfair. He looked a little haggard and moved a little slower and more gingerly than Hank had expected for a well-conditioned, tanned professional golfer. After brief introductions, Arnold said that he wanted to hit some balls out on the practice range. He asked Hank to pick up his clubs and his personal bags of Wilson Staff balls and meet him at the practice area.

Awhile later, Arnold Palmer strode out to the practice range. He seemed to be rejuvenated and much more vital. Some of his fellow pros were already hitting shots. All of them exchanged greetings and some teasing with the likable guy from the coal belt of Pennsylvania. "Hey Arnie, how's your head this morning?" asked one golfer. "Hey Arnie, do you know where you are? ... seems that Jay is not so sure", drawled another. And so it went ..... the jocular bantering and teasing of the pros ... just like Hank's team mates at Murray U.

From that somewhat tenuous start, Arnold Palmer and his caddy got to work --- fun work it was. There were so many highlights for young Henry that all of them are too numerous to describe. But three of Hank's more interesting experiences follow.

<u>"Just call me Arnie"</u> From the first time that Hank and Arnold Palmer spoke until mid-way through the first practice round of golf, the illustrious pro was addressed as Mr. Palmer by his young caddy. Hank had been brought up to respect his elders and not only was the golfer older but he was a man that was respected throughout the sports world, if not the entire universe. And so it went for hours until the eleventh hole of the first practice round when the larger-than-life, championship golfer slowly sauntered toward Hank and stopped about two feet in front of his nervous, young caddy. Then ever so softly he asked, "What do you like to be called? Immediately, the young caddy replied

"Hank is fine with me, Mr. Palmer." Then with a gentle smile and kind eyes, the famous professional golfer said "I like to be called Arnie."

<u>"Sonofabitch"</u> All competitive athletes are intense and emotional. How they control their emotions often is the difference between whether they are a champion or a chumpion level player. Arnold Palmer was a champion. He had a very stable and pleasant disposition. But like all other mere mortals, he did get annoyed from time to time, mainly due to his own errors. As the old saying goes, "To err is human … ." When Arnie was really annoyed, he would mutter so softly that anybody more than about five feet away could not hear what he would say. Usually what he muttered was "sonofabitch" ... and nothing more.

<u>Signing autographs for two pretty young fans</u> Anne and Sandy were two ardent golfers and attractive teenagers from Hank's home town. Every day of the tournament they followed and cheered for Arnold. On the final day, Sandy, the bolder of the two shy girls, asked Hank if they could get the famous golfer's autograph. As gracious as he was, Arnie was near the lead in the tournament and very focused on winning it. So, the pressure was on the golfer to make every shot as perfectly as humanly possible. Well, as it turned out Arnie came in fifth or sixth in the tournament. Just as he was dejectedly leaving the eighteenth green and with the young girls virtually dancing with anxious anticipation, Hank hesitantly asked Arnie if he would sign some autographs for "a couple of girls from his hometown?" With the famous smile and charm that made him world famous and even revered, he said "Sure … and what is your name, young lady?" His personal message and signature are still treasured by those two women …. half a century later.

Thus endeth a few of the many tales about the special times enjoyed over the years, about 60 of them, by Hank personally. There were others that could have been shared but "enough is enough" and hopefully not too much.

XII. The Bittersweet of Old Boys and Girls ... or the pleasures and pains of their hockey and living

Time out ... for a little reflection and philosophical expression

"Take time to smell the roses" is a trite but wise piece of metaphorical advice that most old folks have heard, assuming that their hearing aids and mental faculties are turned on. Such wisdom is more likely to be followed by oldsters than by busy youngsters and all the others in between. The vast majority of people are caught up and tied up in the rush and crush of every day "living" in North America and a few other "advanced" socio-economic places in this deteriorating old world, notably in the emotionally challenging and socially dysfunctional "big cities". Oh, the joys of traffic gridlock and the excessive numbers of cars, trucks, SUVs and other vehicles which cram the highways and byways of the world's cities and the roads leading into and out of them. Sense the tension, smell the exhaust, feel the eyes burning, watch the time tick by, sense the frustration, anxiety and distress of waiting impatiently in long lines of slow/no moving traffic.

Such vivid memories are of relatively prosperous situations and not of the deeply impoverished conditions that are found in every geo-political part of the world. One only has to watch the daily media reports to see, hear and otherwise sense the deplorable conditions in which many billions (that's with 000,000,000s) of innocent and powerless children and adults of all regions, races and ages struggle to survive the brutal ravages of warfare, terrorism, diseases, natural disasters and other forces over which they have no control and are forced to suffer with or die. Or one can experience poverty. Walk through the lowest socio-economic areas of almost any city or visit the vast impoverished rural areas of the world to get some sense of the desperate deprivation of too many human beings ... their deprivation of edible food, drinkable water, basic sewer systems, unpolluted air and the other basics of safe and healthy living. There is no joy in such widespread and despicable conditions, suffered by the vast majority of the world's human beings, especially while increasing numbers of wealthy people and corporations continue to exploit them, prosper obscenely and destroy the living systems around them.

What does such gloomy prose have to do with playing old timers' shinny? If nothing else, it provides perspective of global realities, stark contrasts and a grim realization of how very fortunate the gals and their old guys are to be playing the game they love in places and conditions that the great majority of the world's humanity would be happy just to live in .... much less play in. Against the backdrop of such relative global suffering, the seniors play their games of glorified shinny and enjoy them ... and well they should. Most have earned that privilege. They have worked their way through life, with its joys and sadness and have coped with many dire situations, some life-threatening ... and taking. One only has to remember going out to play one cool night in November and hearing about an Old Boy whose beautiful, talented 33 year old daughter had taken her own life for reasons that may never be known. The Old Boy and his wife were devastated, as most loving parents would be. Or we can share the deep sadness of another old guy whose step daughter was enduring a wretched breakdown in her young marriage, a vital part of which involved the well-being of her two small children. Or we think about the Old Boys and other senior hockey players who have suffered from heart attacks, debilitating injuries, from serious ailments and grim social situations which have adversely affected family, friends and loved ones. Or, ever more primally and pervasively, the miseries suffered by old guys and gals as they experience the physical and mental deterioration of ageing. As one Old Boy often laments: "These are *not* the golden years; these are the olden ones." Life for the Old Boys, like all others, has its pleasures but more and more they are tinged with pains and sorrows --- like those roses we are supposed to smell, with their beautiful, fragrant blooms and their sharp, hurtful thorns.

Note: This scribbler thought it was necessary to provide a little balance for our fun-biased view of life in the slow lane of old guys' shinny and related nonsense.

Back to the sunny side of the street (as the old Tommy Dorsey or was it the title of a Glen Miller tune?)

Some of the joys to follow, may be a bit of a "re-hash". But then, life has many repetitions, especially for old geezers. Just listen to their anecdotes and jokes. Chances are you have heard them before. But, as that guru of communications, Marshall McLuhan, claimed decades ago, "The medium is the message." Just watching most oldsters tell their stories is a source of laughter, joy and down-home simple fun. Most of them will likely embellish their repartee every time they tell a tale, joke, story or babble on about an humorous incident. Some, maybe even most, but not all of them, are worth repeating, not because of forgetfulness or *oldzheimers* but because they are worth sharing, even repetitiously.

So, "beat your feet to the sunny side of the street" and enjoy some more pleasures with the old guys and gals. As that delightful little three year old granddaughter says with her smiling face and bubbly personality: "Happy! happy! happy!"

Mentioning grandchildren, almost any old timer who has had children and their offspring become joyful, enthusiastic, even animated when they start thinking and talking about the fruit of their loins and wombs. Eyes light up, energy surges through the words that are uttered, muttered, mumbled or otherwise expressed. And the relatively animated body language, being mindful of the orator's ages, speaks volumes beyond the mere words. Old Boys are not much different than fathers and grandfathers around the globe. Naturally, they take great pride and joy in their offspring, whether or not their kids/grand kids play shinny of one form or other.

Oh sure, most youngsters, even the best of them, have perplexed Mom, Dad, Grandma or Grandpa, even aunts, uncles and other relations, during their challenging youth. Some old gaffers are able to remember their own young and foolish years and draw some wisdom or, at least a little guidance, from those "learning" experiences. How many geezers' stories include words like, "I remember when ......"?

All kids considered, they are plenteous sources of fun and joy for the aging guys and gals. They really enjoy showing photos as well as swapping stories about various generations of children. That's a vital part of the omnipresent camaraderie that they share with other old folks whether or not they have played with or agin' them for many years or just happen to meet another of their fossilizing contemporaries at a tournament, in a bar, or wherever.

Sharing the joys!!!

Supplementing the wonderful camaraderie, story-telling, celebrations, "beer-tasting", overindulging, various get-togethers and sundry other activities on and off of the ice, old fellows and their not-so-old ladies experience many other joys of playing organized shinny. Some old guys, like Mikey, Boom Boom and Charlie Hustle, simply have a joyful disposition. What fun they are and evoke. Their natural personas are perpetually pleasant and happy. Every now and then (whenever that is), that's the kind of guy you want to pop right in the old schnozola, especially if your back is aching painfully, other body parts are hurting and dysfunctional, family members are acting brattish and miserable or some investments have taken a beating through no fault of your astute decisions. Like Snoopy, acting as the Red Baron might exclaim, "Damn those over-paid, under-performing financial advisers"!

Then there are those strange people in the world who seem to be always happy. Hank clearly remembered one man that he passed many times on his way to work in Ottawa. He was older, maybe 60 years of age, a tall man about 6'4" in height, who ambled down the street with a long gait and an omnipresent, bigger-than-Mona Lisa smile on his face ... every one of the hundreds of days that he walked by Hank. The man's outward pleasant persona was a source of joy ... and curiosity to Hank.

One rather dreary, overcast, misty, cold and miserable morning in February, Hank's curiosity overcame him. He hailed the oncoming happy-faced man. Their conversation was something like ...

Hank: Good morning sir! My name is Hank ... really Henry Hillhouse. I work for DPW. (All bureaucrats talk in acronyms.) I don't believe that we know each other personally ... but we've walked by each other many times ... and you are always smiling. Would you mind telling me ... are you always happy ... or (with a little chuckle and a slight smile) is that a mask you're wearing?

Happy-faced man: Well, good morning to you Hank. My name is Shaun ... Shaun Cormican. I'm pleased to meet you. No, it's not a mask! I'm really a happy man. No doubt you are wondering why ... I've been asked many times so ... I will tell you why ... if you really want to know ...?

Hank: Yes ... please do ... Shaun!

Happy-faced Shaun: Well ... (he paused pensively) I'm reasonably healthy ... for a 64 year old coot who may retire in a year or so ...... at least from the federal government. Then I will probably take an extended vacation with my wonderful wife ...... maybe to Europe to visit some relatives ..... or to South America to see and enjoy that beautiful part of the world. We've not been there before but what we have seen and read sounds so interesting. And, as you may have figured out, I have a very wonderful wife ... she is such a pleasant ... effervescent, bubbly kind of gal. We've been married 40 wonderful years ... celebrated our anniversary last December ... just after Christmas ... . Well, my good man ... Hank. I don't really want to burden you with any more details ... but that's really the essence of my happiness ..... good health, a wonderful mate ... and a positive attitude. It's really quite simple ... quite basic. Well, Henry ... I have an uncle named Henry ... he's a fine fellow. I like that name. Please excuse me but I must be getting along. I have an important meeting in a few minutes ... mustn't be late. So cheerio ... and have a good day ... a bientot ... .

Hank: Ah, merci beaucoup, mon ami ... et tu avez un bon jour, aussi ... a bientot.

To this day, more than 20 years later, Hank vividly remembers the pleasant-faced man and their brief but very meaningful conversation on Wellington Street that miserable morning in the nation's capital. For reasons which are difficult to explain, the lingering memory lifts Hank's spirits and has a very pleasant, uplifting sense of encouragement, maybe even some inspiration.

Some of the old timers who Hank has played hockey with were really happy, pleasant men like Shaun. Some goalies come readily to his mind. There was roly-poly Joey, the clowning goal tender from nearby Cowtown who always seemed to be laughing, chuckling, smiling and causing others to do likewise. Almost always, he was telling a funny story, cracking a joke (not a yolk) and doing silly stunts like making others' coins disappear or taking a playing card out of some guy's collar, shirt pocket or other parts of their clothing. Then there was that zany goalie, Andy the performer, on the Old Boys' team. He was the old guy who sang, chanted or otherwise jocularly expressed "Happy

Birthday" wishes to or "puttin' on the dog" routine for his team mates. Still thinking about kooky goalies, Willie was another jocular and pleasant fellow. He usually had a funny story to tell about himself or others in seniors' shinny, sports or business. Some of them were factual; some of them were fictional; and most were probably a mix. Who cared whether the humor was factual, fictional or contradictional? ... so long as it was funny ... and no one was defamed, slandered or otherwise denigrated.

As Hank's mind meandered through the different positions on shinny teams, he started to think about any happy d'men who he had played with over the years. He started chuckling just at the thought of Mikey. That big, ebullient salesman was one of the most naturally funny guys you would ever meet. Mikey reminded Hank of Buddy Hackett or Jackie Gleason and sometimes of that moon-faced guy in the Three Stooges. Just the public persona of those guys reeked of humor which was always better than reeking of garlic which Mikey did from time to time, especially after one of his voluminous burps.

Then there was Koko, the very large Cowtown policeman who played Santa Claus for all kinds of kids at Christmas and "clowned" at other times during the year. Koko, the Kop had a big belly-shaking laugh that amused kids of all ages. Just watching him laugh was entertaining .... and he had some funny stories, jokes and lines of witty babble that brought joy to young and old alike, at Christmas and throughout the year.

A third "star" for being un bon homme was Gabby. Gabriel Michael Teasan, a.k.a. Tease since he was a very young boy. (No Old Boy could imagine why this incorrigible guy was named after two angels. His momma and his poppa must have had lofty aspirations for their bambino.) Gabby or Tease, call him what you wanted because not much ever seemed to bother him, was another guy who would walk or waddle into a room with a huge smile on his big face and the whole room would light up. And the teasing, chiding, banter and related hijinks would virtually erupt around the room. Guys, who normally would be quite quiet or soft-spoken at their loudest, would give Gabby their "best shots" immediately because they knew that once the "big wop" (as he referred to himself) got going, he would dominate the verbiage and other behavior of the inner sanctum. And so it went ... joyously with those big old guys.

Hank could go and on about pleasant, funny old hockey guys' who brought joy into the lives of others, whether or not they intended to do so. There was Boom Boom, his roly-poly presence and smiling face or Charley Hustle with his boundless, endless energy and enthusiasm. Or even Sam with his sad-faced appearance which for reasons unknown brought smiles n' chuckles (but not chocolates) to his team mates. Or maybe it was his "dry as chips" sense of humor which brought gut-wrenching belly laughs and humorous reactions from the Old Boys. Who knows? Who cares? What is important is the fact that these old geezers and others like them brought joy not only to the Old Boys but countless others ... all of whom probably needed and really enjoyed a good laugh ... at any time.

Internal wellsprings

While others brought fun to the Old Boys, most of them had their own inner sources of happiness, at least some of the time ... like on their "best days". For most athletic types of all ages, it was the simple joys, like being accepted by your team mates, coaches, managers, stick boys and referees. Just being involved in a game that they enjoyed so much .... especially before and after the actual contest, provided many sources and forms of enjoyment. The fun flowing from simple team camaraderie cannot be overstated. And just being "above the ground" and more or less able, physically and mentally, to put on that stinky old gear and play the game in a respectable way, was a source of joy. Old guys enjoyed the basics, like home-cooked meat and potatoes, liked feeling the cool breeze on their face as they skated around the rink; warming up, stretching their muscles and being thankful that they were there. Seems kind of simple minded but then so is smelling the roses.

While most old timers find fun in down-to-earth, simple ways there is no denying that extraordinary experiences, like scoring a goal or two or three are always sources of considerable joy. Some old guys, notably the ones who did not score very often, like Sal, Sam and most d'men, had difficulty controlling their emotions when they got a goal ... or maybe even an assist. Sal would raise both hands and give out the occasional yell after he scored one of his very infrequent goals. Sam would just smile modestly, a broad-faced grin that warmed the rink. Even Big Gerry, Larry and James would get rather excited after they scored. Occasionally and unpredictably, Guy would pump his fist and ride around on his hockey stick like a kid riding a stick horse and pretending he was the Lone Ranger. Max would let out a yelp or some such noise and then a series of vulgarities which defied any reason or political correctness but then who cared about such conventional norms when an old guy has just scored one of his infrequent goals?

Other rare goal scorers, like Boom Boom, Jean Pierre and Hank, who only rarely experienced the joy of scoring the odd goal each season, tried to be nonchalant and "cool". But inside those somber-looking guys were happy feelings that really bubbled up inside them like a freshly opened bottle of *champanski* (as they refer to it in Russia). Then there were the snipers, the Old Boys like Doc, Dirk and Charley Hustle who scored regularly on the ice (and probably elsewhere), who just took their goal scoring prowess in stride, like "what's the big deal"? They were supposed to score. That's "what they were paid the big bucks to do" ... ha! ha! ha! Their big concern was the fact that the association had a three goal limit on their scoring during each game. Otherwise they were penalized, like sitting in the "sin bin", as well as being obligated to buying a round for their teammates ... for scoring goals! How ironical is that? But then old timers' hockey is filled with ironies, oxymorons and just plain old morons.

Then there are the special fun-times for goalies; a shutout, very much like a no-hitter in baseball or a hole-in-one playing golf --- very, very RARE. Even playing a game in which they leak less than five goals, especially if their old team mates scored more than that, might be a source of satisfaction if not great joy to old timers' who defend the nets against enemy snipers. (Sounds like war, doesn't it?) By the very nature of their position as the last line of defence against goals being scored, guardians of the goals have the most pressure of any player on a hockey team, even a team of old guys. Most of the goalies, really "have a thing" about letting pucks into the nets for which they are charged with protecting against such trespasses. Stopping a puck from going into their net is satisfying. Making a difficult or an extraordinary save brings instantaneous feelings of great joy and jubilation. Hank vividly remembered playing goal when he was in Juvenile hockey ... and getting a shutout even though that feat required stopping one puck unintentionally with his mouth. (It was during the era before masks and helmets.) Many years later he remembered that shutout with great satisfaction and tried to forget the loosen teeth, swollen purple lips and the pain that he felt in and around his mouth for several days after the game.

Winning the game is the most basic source of fun for any hockey team or player, even if they are fifty, sixty years of age or as old as Methuselah. Whoever said that losing was okay was likely the same esoteric spectator that said, "it was not whether you win or lose but how you play the game." And playing a tie game has been likened to kissing one's sister which is not an experience most players would relish unless maybe they have incestuous tendencies. Winning a game enabled the snipers and the goalies to forget the *&%#?)^(* goals that they missed. It allowed them to "laugh off" the ones they should have had --- shoulda, woulda, coulda!!! Winning provides great balm for the wounds of letting the opposing players skate around the defenceman or a goalie not blocking or catching pucks that "ordinarily" (whatever that means) they would have had, IF only .... !

The Pains of the Contest ... and Afterwards

Transgressions, penalties and other "no-nos"

The Old Boys, like most old timer hockey players, are not angels. As stated in several ways and passages of the Good Book (as Hank's Dad used to refer to the Bible), we are all sinners, although it could be added that some have transgressed far worse than others. The odd one has even spent some time in the "house", like a jail or like accommodation. Others have broken or bent some laws and may or may not have been penalized accordingly. Most have gone around or beyond the bounds of the Ten Commandments, moral codes and other generally accepted norms of society. Some of the "no-no" behavior is merely trash talk or dark, ugly humor. By most social standards it is rather innocuous except with the most straight-laced, up-tight masochists or those hypocrites who have a compulsive obsession for being politically correct.

On the other hand, like classical economists and indecisive decision makers are inclined to say, some acts are against the 8th century English Marquess of Queensberry rules of shinny and may even be injurious, physically. Most of the penalties in old timers' hockey are for being overly eager or aggressive on the ice, for example, slap-shooting, crashing into the goal tender or from charging into opponents and team mates, all of which might cause grievous harm to the victim. More moderate infractions include cheating acts such as hooking, holding, tripping or sticking one's wayward knee or elbow into an opponent, especially his unprotected areas, thus causing some discomfort and distraction, loss of concentration and making mistakes which often lead to goals being scored against a team. Very rarely are penalties imposed for vicious, malicious and intentionally injurious acts such as fighting, slashing, spearing or butt-ending, head-butting, cross-checking, especially into the boards, and high-sticking, forearm shivers and "clothes-lining" (nasty uses of one's arms that are carry-overs from playing football).

So the old guys' penalties that are described hereafter and theretofore are relatively minor misdeeds quite unlike the mugging and serious injury that was wrought upon Steve Moore of the Colorado Avalanche by then #44 of the Vancouver Canucks a few years ago, or what Wild Bill Ezinicki did to Cal Gardner with his stick decades ago or what Chico Maki did to Teddy Green. Basically, the old fellows are laid back and mellow. Most of the infractions tend to be accidental, although there are always some "bad apples" in the barrel. Probably, they should be put over the barrel or on the rack (an old, historic form of inhumane punishment, idly rumored to have been used more recently in Iraq by the USA and its "coalition of the willing".)

In old guys' shinny, penalties are rare --- very rare, maybe about as rare as a hat trick of goals or assists. Some of the Old Boys have played their entire old timers' "careers" without a penalty. A penalty to them would be like them beating their wife or kicking their dog (man's best friend, or so the old saying goes). Entire games are played without any harmful misdeeds or infractions apparent to the referees. Some of that depends on the refs and their ability or inability to see, think, make decisions and blow their whistle. That's a lot of multi-tasking, especially for some refs. For the most part, the absence of penalties is due to the fact that old timers play by the conventional rules of organized shinny ... that they know or can remember, as well as the Golden Rule and civil society's rules against injuring others on the ice, including their own players as well as the refs and those on opposing teams. So, most of the players become acculturated by the ethics of old timers and play "clean hockey", except in some tournaments when obstreperous outsiders invade joyful Joxville and bring their own rules, aggressive play and other behavior contrary to the olde Marquis of Queensberry's morals, principles and creed.

Boom Boom's hat trick (of penalties)

Just to give some sense of the seriousness of three penalties in an old timers' game, think about a tsunami, earthquake or an eclipse of the sun. That's how unusual a three-peat of penalties is for Old Boys. So, what were Boom Boom's "sins" during that infamous game against the Blue Bloozers? Well, the first one was given to him for a head-on collision he had with some guy who wasn't looking where he was going and ran smack-dab into the rotund Old Boy who is limited in his capacity to move, much less get out of the way of another robust player who was skating his way with his head down.

Unfortunately (or fortunately depending on how you think about weight), the Bloozer weighed about 50 pounds less than Boomer. Down he went -- *thud* -- onto the ice ... with old Boom Boom still standing and virtually unmoved physically (no doubt he was greatly affected, emotionally). Tweet! tweet! went the whistle of Abbott or was it Costello, neither one of whom has had a distinguished career in refereeing. One of the refs gave big Boomer a penalty for who knows what. Now, in an impartial court of law, a judge would likely rule that there was a lack of due diligence and contributory negligence on the part of the Bloozer and find Boomer not guilty. Be that as it may, old timers' hockey is not part of a well-developed legal system. It has a justice system of its own, complete with warts and whatever other shortcomings, including not infrequent dubious decisions made by the refs.

In the Joxville league, the culprit goes to his players' or the penalty box for a "rest". The aggrieved player used to get a penalty shot at the goalie of the "offending" player's team. Oftentimes, in the true spirit of sportingliness (if there is such a word but you must know what is meant), the player who was taking the penalty shot would intentionally shot wide of the goal, at the pads of the goalie or otherwise did not take advantage of a questionable or unjust call by the refs. Most old timers abide by an unwritten code of "fair play". It is a gratifying, intangible attribute of playing such organized shinny. But, as fate would have it, the zealous, "rookie" Bloozer scored. As is often said in sports' jargon, that was the "turning point" in the game. It was the Bloozers' first goal and tied the score. Stated nicely, the Old

Boys were "pissed off" (but then Confucius reportedly said, "Tis better to be pissed off than pissed on".) They didn't believe that Boomer deserved the penalty. To add insult to injury, the "hot shot" Bloozer scored instead of abiding by the unwritten rule of missing an undeserved penalty shot. (More recently, after heated protest and a near revolt by the goalies who alleged blatant discrimination, the Old Boys' Association changed the penalty merely to send the offending player off the ice for three minutes and allow both teams to play at "full strength". Really, it was fairer and less stressful for the guys wearing the idiot gear).

Well, the game went on at a fairly fast, furious and frenzied pace (by Old Boys' standards). The Bloozers were younger, faster and more aggressive than their more aged opponents. Most of the play was in the Old Boys' end of the rink. Being "bogged down" in one's own defensive zone gets kind of hectic and tiresome, especially for the Old Boys' goalie and "dmen". "Where the hell are those &*%$#@><*& forwards", yelled Mikey out of futility and frustration. "Who knows?" came Big Gerry's reply "... can't see them .... maybe they're having a beer." The Bloozers were swarming all around the Old Boys' nets. Andy was yelling and swearing at who knows whom but, quite probably, his own team mates as well as the opposition. Other guys were hollering. Some were grunting and groaning as old bodies strained, twisted, turned, fell, got up and tried to get control of the puck so they can do what they want with it, like get the puck "to hell out" of their defensive zone ... or ideally, score on the other team.

Well, that little black disk was skittering around, between and among the skates of Boomer and a Bloozer. Both tried to get possession of it. Other players joined the action and were poking at it. The Bloozer turned away in partial control of the puck. Believe it or not, Boom Boom grabbed his jersey with his gloved hand and then gave him a gentle, yet firm, tug. The knock-kneed, weak skating, bleary-eyed Bloozer fell down on his butt – kerplunk. "Tweet! tweet! went the whistle of Abbott or Costello or Moe of the Three Stooges? Boom Boom was penalized. Old Boys cried foul

.... "that Bloozer should get a penalty for diving. Where's the justice? Ref, you suck" hollered one of Boomer's team mates. None of that verbiage had a positive effect on the refs. The Bloozer took his penalty shot. The Old Boys waited with "bated breath". But Andy "stoned" him. The Old Boys rejoiced. Boom Boom started breathing again ... in the sin bin. And the game went on.

One reason that Ronny or Boom Boom was sometimes referred to as "Rover" was because he meandered all around the ice surface, not paying too much attention to the position he was supposed to be playing. His more astute play mates recognized such innate tendencies and adjusted to them. To his credit, Rover was a good player. He handled the puck well and scored more than his share of goals and assists which made playing with him a lot more satisfying, if no less frustrating. The main "weapon" in his "arsenal" was a "snap shot" that he used quite frequently and fairly effectively ever since he started playing with the Old Boys a decade or so ago. So there he was just inside the Blue Bloozers' blue line and let go a snap shot like he had done countless times before in old timers' hockey. The game was tied with less than five minutes to play. "Tweet! tweet! goes that damnable whistle of you know who --- one of those blind, brain-challenged refs.

Well, you can imagine the "rest of the story" (like that famous and forgotten radio commentator, Paul Harvey, used to say). The "hot shot" Bloozer took the shot. He scored. The wrong team won and the wronged team lost by one goal (sounds like double jeopardy). The Old Boys were really annoyed, not at Boom Boom or Andy, but at the stupidity of the refs. Seems that they were smitten with an infectious disease called "officialitis". The only "saving grace" was that the Old Boys shamed, coerced and otherwise convinced Boomer that he should buy a round of beer because he got a "hat trick". Being the nice guy that he was and still is, he bought a round for his team. They toasted him ... for his "hat trick ... and basically for being a good guy.

Dirk's dastardly deeds

In the short annals of Old Boy hockey history, Boom Boom was not alone in achieving his hat trick of misdeeds, due in large part to the faulty senses, misperceptions and challenged judgments of the referees. Heck, every body dislikes the refs so why not join the chorus of derision? (That's a throwaway question that does not merit a response, just like some others uttered in this narrative, previously and subsequently.) Back to the line of thought ... Boom Boom was not alone in his ignominy. Dirk was similarly found guilty of three infractions (two of them for holding his opponents' sticks and the third for inadvertently tripping a clumsy oaf). What made Dirk's dastardly deeds (effective alliteration even if it does overstate the transgressions) worthy of mention was his reactions to the penalties. For a man in his fifties and many years of playing organized and disorganized shinny, his reaction to each of the three penalties called against him was in a word: petulant.... like a kid during puberty. Probably something or other was bothering him about his store, his kids, his bad back or Lord knows what. But mature men are not expected to complain, whine, pout and sulk after they have been penalized. End of the sermon. Amen!!! ... again.

Jocko's temper tantrum

Occasionally, an old timer "loses it" like the time Jocko, nicknamed after his father Gentleman Jack or Jock, received a well-deserved penalty one night late in January of 02. Maybe it was a full moon, family or business problems, a little pre-game imbibing or some other extraneous factor but Jocko was really "acting up" during the game that night. He was giving not-so-subtle hooks and pokes with his stick and holds on opposing players, especially a former team mate by the name of Alfie. Well, old Hans was refereeing and was getting tired of giving Jocko knowing and increasingly disapproving looks. Consequently, the next time that Jocko pulled one of his little stunts, like tripping Alfie, both the refs "called" a penalty on Jocko. For reasons unknown to this day, Jocko skated off of the ice, muttering obscenities, slamming the players' box door so hard that it was nearly knocked off its hinges and, as the last act of petulance, he threw a water bottle onto the playing surface. Such misconduct could have been "written up" by the refs and sent to the Association's disciplinary committee. Well, the refs mulled over that prospect, other options and then decided, in part because they were too lazy, that Jocko was a good guy and usually well-behaved, that they wouldn't report him to the committee. Ever since, Jocko has been an exemplary player. Guess he just had a "bad night" but then don't we all have some of those bad nights, days, weeks or other periods of time???

Apple's "charge of the not-so-light brigade"

Rarely, very, very rarely, do Old Boys do something that might intentionally injure another player. That's why the following incident is so nasty, nefarious and noteworthy. But, first a little background to the incident might provide a bit of useful perspective. Over the years, the Old Boys and Les Rouges have had some spirited contests or, in other words, some damned bitter games. For anybody who has played competitive sports, business or politics, they know that such contests can get rather mean and nasty, if not downright cruel and hurtful. And so it was one night in frigid February when the two teams were locked in mortal combat (not really ... but it sounds dramatic).

Rick, a big old guy who no longer plays old timer hockey, was causing some problems for the Old Boys. What the oaf lacked in skill he made up for with determination, guile, brutish bulk and strength. Notable in his bag of tricks was the tendency to harass the opponents' goalies, like whacking their sticks, giving their skates a little push, standing in front screening the goal tender's vision, backing into the over-padded puck stoppers, trash-talking and various other annoying stunts. Goalies, unless they have the patience of Job, the wisdom of Solomon and the virtue of the Lord, do not take kindly to such blankety-blank nonsense and often react by yelling, swearing, pushing and occasionally spearing Rick, the old buffoon.

So, during the game in question, Willie was yapping at Ricky in a not-so-very hushed scream and pushing him out of his crease. For some reason or other, still unknown, Rick took exception to the goalie claiming his rightful domain and pushed him hard and back, like on his butt side, into the nets. Well, as anybody knows who has played hockey or any form of shinny, *you just don't mess with the goalie.* He's a sacred cow or, more usually, a sacred bull. And you know what happens when you mess with the bull .... you get the horn.

Apples, the nickname for a bulky Old Guy who subsequently passed on from cancer, saw what was happening in front of the goal and came roaring in from the blue line to "nail" tricky Ricky ... to the back boards, in the upper deck of the arena or anywhere else he could. Apples was no midget or even anemic and underweight. He was about five feet, ten inches tall and weighed about 240 without his gear on that sturdy frame. He was a full-time farmer who worked every day, except on the Sabbath, tending to his herd of Angus cattle, his section of fertile farmland (that's 640 acres or metric equivalent for city folk), all the farm equipment, buildings, other chores and his family of five. Usually, Apples was a placid, easy-going guy who minded his own business and played hockey like a normal human being. For Apples to be "taking a run" at Ricky was an extraordinary example of deviant behavior.

Anyhow, there were Rick and Willie pushing and shoving beside the goal with big Apples bearing down on the transgressor at a speed that was reckless at best and insane at worst. Just before Apples was going to flatten Ricky was when the latter's devious guile came into play. He leaned off to his right side as the oncoming mass of man hurtled toward him ... but he left his left leg behind. (The lefts and rights get a little confusing ... right?) Oh, mon dieu! what a collision Apples had ... with the boards after he fell over tricky Ricky's limp left leg. He drooped to the ice, moaning in agony. Then he just sort of collapsed into a heap before slowly unbending and laying down, coughing and sputtering ... stunned.

Apples recovered from his collision with the boards without any apparent, serious injuries, although he did not play any more hockey that season or ever. Tragically, cancer took care of that. Neither did Rick play old timers' shinny again. Whether he felt guilty for the nasty incident or thought that he somehow contributed to Apples' demise is not known. But they both just packed it up and called it quits after that game. Such a shame, given how much fun and recreational the *game* can be.

Battle of the "banties"

In the history of Joxville Old Boys' hockey, fortunately there have been few other incidents as nasty as the one involving Apples, Rick and Willy. (Willie spelled his nickname two ways, that is, with a "y" when he was busy or lazy and an "ie" when he was in a leisurely, laid back state. Besides, goalies are so damned idiosyncratic and spelling one's nickname two ways is merely a scintilla of evidence reflecting such peculiarities). Be that as it may and that is relatively irrelevant, few other incidents have been observed that were as nasty as the one just described. However, one incident could have been as nasty if it had not been for the fact that the combatants were two little banty roosters, each about five feet six inches tall in their skates and weighing about 150 or 160 pounds with their gear on. (The stats are understated to protect the innocent.)

As with many of hockey's "dust ups", this one took place along the boards where Hal, for Harold, and Angie, for Angelo, were trying to gain possession of the puck. Needless to say, they played on opposing teams and were really competing intensely toward the end of a close game. As often happens, one of the players (Angie's) elbows got a little high ... like in Hal's face (good reason to wear a full mask). Up came Hal's gloved hands, elbows and stick into Angie's face. That definitely was not a nice, gentlemanly gesture by Hal. Well, what those two little guys lacked in size, strength and skill they made up with feistiness. They started yapping and pushing at each other. Angie, in an act of retaliation, pushed Hal back in the face with a stronger effort than had been received from his antagonist. That was the point of no return ...... "tipping point" seems to be the popular buzz phrase. Both of them started sort of swinging or slapping at each other ... like two roosters in the barnyard ... arms flapping, mouths yapping and causing a whole lot of commotion.

Since neither one of them were built for fighting nor normally inclined to do so, several tweets on the referees' whistles was all it took for the two well-aged, unfit, usually calm and responsible old buggers to stop their pushing, shoving and pawing at each other with their gloved fists. Note: keeping their hockey gloves on was just one clue that these oldsters were not experienced fighters. Another clue was the way they flailed or flapped at each other. After the refs banished the two players from the game, they met in the hallway leading to their dressing rooms, apologized to each other, shook hands and went to Hal's dressing room for a beer and a renewal of acquaintances which, according to reliable reports, did not involve any acrimony of any form.

Challenges (or Life is a bowl of cherries and sometimes you end up with just the pits)

Everyone, young, old and in between, has their momentary, hourly, daily, weekly, monthly or perpetual ups and downs in life. Some have physical or mental handicaps from birth; others suffer such disabilities or diseases along the way through life, often for reasons that escape the afflicted as well as medical science. Hiding behind many of the "hale fellow well met" faces and *macho masks* of old timers are many and various problems of life. Some have encountered employment or financial difficulties; others have suffered from health problems. Most, if not all, have faced challenges of one kind or other with their wives, children, other family members, friends or other *homo sapiens*. We all are challenged at various times in numerous ways. Some, maybe even a representative sample, have been experienced by the Old Boys and other players involved in old timers' hockey. Most of the tales to follow are "good news" stories. Some are not.

Obesity - a common condition of the geriatric guys and gals

With few exceptions, most old geezers are OVERweight and high up on the Body Mass Index (BMI), some to the extent of serious flabbiness and health challenges. Many weigh well over 200 pounds (or metric equivalent). A few "tip the scales" at 300 or more on the imperial standard. One is rumored to be close to 400; yes four hundred pounds. No wonder these guys suffer from health problems, especially bad backs and heart attacks. Bellies hang out, movement is impeded (like putting on or, worse still, taking off their skates), vitality is sapped and the oldsters' state of wellness suffers. Two views seem to pervade old guys' mindsets: "what the hell, we're going to die anyhow so why not really enjoy ourselves while we're alive?"; and "I've tried to lose weight but it just doesn't seem to come off the old *bod* like it should. Guess it is part of getting older." (*Aging* is an unspoken word, like it is a curse.) A third, albeit a tiny minority, view is that "I have to lose weight and I will do it." This third mindset usually follows some kind of "wake up call" or serious situation ... think diabetes and/or heart attack. Only a rare old bugger "bites the bullet" and changes his diet, exercises more frequently (like more than playing shinny once or twice a week), loses some weight and gets in "shape". Such a transformation usually occurs only after some "felt experience" really scares them. Max's near-fatal heart attack motivated him to change his eating habits drastically (like no fried eggs every morning and start "eating like a rabbit"), join AA, quit boozing, lose 30 ugly pounds (without cutting off his head) ... and he was only 5' 8' (or the metric equivalent). Similarly for Feisty, Harry, Lenny and the other heart attack victims ... who survived. Thank the Lord for such blessings!!!

Being overweight is not some mysterious condition or deep dark secret. Just look around an old timers' dressing room and it is blatantly obvious, even bloody ugly. And it's not that the old timers are some kind of hermits, cave dwellers or ignoramuses. Most of them can read; whether they do or not is another matter. They watch tv and see the medical reports about obesity – about it being the next tobacco-like curse on personal health and medical care systems. For many old fellas, being overweight is largely a matter of attitude. Most of the old guys like to eat ... and eat ... and eat some more, especially high fat foods, like greasy fries, chicken wings, big burgers and pizza pies or any other kind of pie, cake, candy, cookies or any other sweets for that matter, as well as calorie-laden drinks, like beer, rum, whiskey and soda pop. Fruits and veggies, in solid or liquid forms, are quite conspicuous by their absence. Maybe these geezers aren't so smart after all!

So much for the non-scientific observations, personal biases and rants. Let's look at some cold, hard facts. For example, early in 2003, Canada's "national newspaper", with its predominant Hogtown orientation, carried a front page article about obesity cutting life spans dramatically. The *Globe and Mail* duly reported on research published in the highly credible *Journal of the American Medical Association* showing the consequences of obesity included conditions such as diabetes, cardio-vascular disease, other "chronic conditions" ... and a *shortening of life* (that's really scary for most people, including old guys who thought they were invincible and would live forever. Strange, how when you get into your '60s, the end of the road of life becomes so much clearer and apparent ... and it's not a pleasant prospect.)

Another study found that being overweight reduces life expectancy more than smoking does. To assist the readers in determining their weight, The *Globe and Mail* described how a person could calculate their BMI, a measure that indicates one's approximate body fat. (It is estimated by multiplying a person's weight by 703 and dividing it by their height in inches squared.)

With some trepidation, Hank calculated his BMI. (He would have preferred a BMW, like in fancy automobile.) At the time, Hank weighed 210 pounds and was 6 feet tall. By doing the calculations, Hank found that he had an index of 28.48 which put him "well" into the overweight range of 25 - 29.9. To get into the Normal category with an 18.5 to 24.9 range, Hank figured he would have to grow another 4 or 5 inches (not likely at his age) or lose 26 pounds (12.4 percent of his total weight) so that he would weigh 184 pounds for an index of 24.88. On January 3rd, he started his efforts to lose weight. By one week later, he had lost only two pounds. At the end of the next week, he had shed another one. (One year later, his weight was 200 pounds, his BMI was 27.12. Despite his conscientious efforts, Hank was still in the "Overweight" range although a little closer to the "Normal" category.) Although Hank was going in the right direction with his weight, he did not know how much effort and time he would take to achieve his short term goal of 190 pounds. It was a "work in progress". He knew it would be difficult to do ... and it was, even though he cut back on his ice cream and cookie consumption, the size of his meals, eliminated evening snacks, walked more and played his shinny games more vigorously. His beer consumption remained constant.

His efforts were supported by Heidi who decided she needed to lose some weight, also. She changed her cooking practices, by using more calorie-conscious recipes, substituting margarine for butter in baking, eliminating deserts and serving smaller portions of the meals.

"Oh, the joys of getting older", muttered Hank as he stepped off the newly purchased weighing scales ... with the indicator hovering around 206.

"Well, if it's any consolation, honey, you have lots of company ... but at least you are trying to do something about it," she replied empathetically. "Besides, I need to lose some of this flab too ... so we can do it together."

"I'd rather being doing something else together," Hank retorted with a mischievous look.

"We can do that too, big guy! It will help us lose weight ... enjoyably", Heidi said with a jolly little giggle.

"Hmmmm, sounds good to me, baby ......," mused her horny husband.

Hank's concern or, at least, interest in being overweight did not stop with himself. Before the game the following night he offhandedly threw out the question: "Did any of you guys see that article about obesity in the paper?"

Mike: "No, I can't read ... what did it say?"

Max: "Who the 'f' has time to read the paper ... I'm workin' for a living."

Boom Boom: "Why are you looking at me, you guys?"

Hank (trying to be a little diplomatic): "Well ... maybe if the shoe fits ... wear it!"

Mike (not known for his diplomacy): "Hell, that would be about the only part of his clothing that fits ... Boomer can't even see if his shoes are on."

James (the most slender and fit of the Old Boys): "What did it say, Hank?"

Hank started to recite some of the vital information in the article and then, knowing that the Old Boys had a short attention span for the fatso subject, switched to telling about the way to calculate their BMIs. About the time he was talking about multiplying his weight times 703, Mikey rudely interjected some comment to the effect that a quadratic equation would be needed to figure out Boomer's weight. Guy piped up and told him to "fermez le bouche ... shut up you dumb Anglo, so I can hear what Hank is saying." But that did not stop or even deter Mikey from blathering on about quadratic equations, derivatives and some other irrelevant mathematical-sounding mumbo-jumbo.

Injuries

Anybody who says that playing hockey is all fun has not played the game, is an idiot, lying, on drugs or all of the above. Even playing old guys' and gals' shinny has a lot of hurts in it. Oftentimes, old timers bump into one another, awkwardly, usually unintentionally, fuelled by keen competition and a robust enthusiasm for the game. Added to the competitive enthusiasm is the fact that old geezers, with age and compounded by obesity, lose some (more or all) of their coordination, agility and balance, if they ever had it, and plow into another player, often on their own team.

One of the most dangerous Old Boys was Big Barry, a powerful construction worker cum owner, often referred to as The Bull, like in a china shop. Too often he would be roaring around, out of control, commonly with his head down and apparently unaware of others on the ice. In recent years he has had numerous near misses and some bone-jarring, although apparently unintentional, injurious collisions with other players, on his own team as well as with opponents. One of the more serious collisions he had with a team mate was the night he barged into James, about 50 or 60 pounds lighter, knocking poor Jimmy into "la la land". Jamie boy suffered damages to his spine, neck, head and probably his brain. He had an aching back, a stiff neck and headaches for weeks afterwards. Needless to say, but it will be said anyhow, Jamie and other Old Boys really keep their heads up and their senses on full alert when their good buddy Barry is on the ice.

Big Barry was not alone in his unintended infliction of injury, severe pain and suffering on other players. Even little Max could do that. Actually "little" Max was built somewhat like a "brick outhouse" or a hog. He was short, stocky and had a low center of gravity. Even at his advanced years, he continued to labor for the city which may seem like an oxymoron but the tough little guy was strong and in relatively good shape --- all factors considered. Hank experienced that inconvenient truth (with apologies to Al Gore) in a most undesirable and injurious way.

And so it came to pass during a game against the Blue Bloozers that little old Max, with his head down, barged, like a tug boat, into Hank in their own end of the rink. Believe it or not but Max who was usually located around center ice was back-checking, a rare and unfamiliar act for him. He must have been disoriented or somehow discombobulated. Hank sure did not expect him to come roaring back into his own end of the rink and plow smack dab into him. Those hits hurt the most because they are just not expected or prepared for, especially but your own "mates". Usually Max was somewhere between the red line and the other team's blue line, waiting for a pass. (Because of his advanced aged and decrepitude, Max received special dispensation from the Old Boys and was not expected or required to be in his own team's end of the pond.) Ironically, the much taller and larger but unprepared Hank was hit in the ribs, knocked down and winded by his team mate. For months after the "run-in", the d'man told Max quite candidly and very emphatically not to back-check, at least not on his side of the rink.

Then there are other times when some "jerk", for whatever reason (if there is any reasoning involved) "blindsides", charges or hits another player and hurts him, sometimes seriously ... like the time James was flattened from behind by a bereft Blue Bloozer. For weeks following, Jamie Boy suffered painfully from headaches and other symptoms of a concussion - very scary. Penalties are usually called for such transgressions before any retribution is sought and inflicted. But penalties are small consolation to the poor bloke suffering from headaches and other aches and pains weeks or months later.

Most old geezers get hit with wayward body parts, sticks or pucks. Some of the old timers can still shoot that frozen biscuit with some considerable, even crippling, velocity. Then there are the big guys with the "heavy shots". Most sane and reasonably mobile oldsters get out of the way of those heavy shots, if they are able to do so. Some dumb defencemen are either too conditioned to blocking shots, too immobile or too macho to get out of the way of such shots ... and suffer the logical consequences from getting in the way of such missiles, unfortunately. Large purplish–black welts on a young player's body used to be considered a badge of courage. But such injuries to an old guy is clear evidence of bloody stupidity, maybe a cause for some empathy in the dressing room and sympathy in the bedroom. But they still are painful ... sometimes for weeks. OUCH!

Most non-masochistic old shinny players typically try, very consciously and diligently, to avoid being injured. By the time they are old enough to play seniors' hockey they usually are experienced enough, if not smart enough, to know some, if not all, of the consequences of having their bodies, minds and souls damaged. Typically, they avoid injuries like they would have assumedly avoided the Great Plague of the 17th century. As may have been expressed previously, old timers are well aware that their fellow players have to get up the next morning, go to work, wash their car(s), shovel some snow or cut the grass, have coffee with their "buds", go shopping with their gal and take care of various and sundry other tasks, duties and responsibilities. Moreover, the old guys know all too well about getting older (remember *aging* is a naughty word) and the awful aches, pains, non-erectile stiffness and other physical deterioration of their bodies. So, the combination of natural deterioration and the normal bumps and bruises of playing the game logically leads to injuries, some that were often inflicted away back when the old guys were youngsters playing shinny or minor hockey. Many of those earlier injuries accumulate and contribute to chronic conditions such as head aches, arthritis and rheumatism ... miseries masked by smiles or stoicism.

Injuries and health challenges of old timers, like the rest of society, are not limited to physical conditions. Oldsters have endured numerous and various social-psychological hurts, also. Over the years, several of the Old Boys had suffered through divorces, problem children, financial difficulties, alcoholism, mental health and other adverse situations. They bear (and, at times, bare) the scars of their minds, hearts and souls as well as on the external surface of their bodies. One of the inherent benefits of playing old timers' hockey is knowing that others have suffered and need empathy and support. Misery likes company, especially between and among understanding, empathetic buddies. Whatever the causes, the injuries give the Old Boys no end of pain and suffering. What follows is more or less a random sample of hurts to the aging bodies of some Old Boys.

Ever-sufferin' goal tenders

Even goalies, with their all-encompassing over-padding, suffer from some of the heavy shooters. And we're not talking about the shots of booze that are quaffed down by macho types, both male and female. For example, during the exhibition game against the Tailgaters, Big Bad Bobby Brown let go with one of his "howitzers" that Willie stopped high on his goalie pad. He felt it right through to the fibula and expressed his pain in very descriptive, vulgar terms, like "Oh damn" and many, many more naughty words and guttural sounds. After the game and for weeks later, a pretty purplish bruise was evident and Willy was not being very pleasant about the source of his pain.

Andy the hypochondriac

"Well, look who the hell is here" hollered Max as Andy more or less staggered into the dressing room, looking like death warmed over. "What is your f'g name old timer? We don't recognize you ... are you lost?" "Shut up, Max you blithering old fool", shot back the sad, decrepit-looking puck stopper. I've been injured ... bloody back is killing me ... couple of discs are shot ... and a vertebrate is out of sync ... hurts like a bastard", grumbled Andy. The not unusual and unpleasant sounding conversation continued.

Max: "Andy, you're a f'g wuss ... you've got more injuries than all the goalies in the NHL put together", said the guy who had had a very serious, life-threatening heart attack a few years earlier ... and was still playing ... sort of ... mostly between the blue lines.

Andy: "What's bothering you, you old bastard?"

Max: "Cripes, you always seem to have something f'g wrong with you ..... a pulled f'g ligament ... probably the one between your f'g legs .... buggered up shoulder, bad back, whatever .... who knows what your f'g problems are ... medical science probably couldn't f'g figure them all out, you f'g hypochondriac ... ."

Andy: "Shut up, you old fart ... your f'g breath smells bad". (Vulgarity can be contagious ... a social disease.)

And so Andy was "welcomed" back to the Old Boys following his back injury which virtually immobilized the old goalie. Old guys rarely recover fully from their injuries, if for no other reason that there tends to be some weakness in their muscles, ligaments, tendons, joints or all of the above as well as some arthritis, rheumatism or both remaining in their bones. Be that as it may, Andy was warmly welcomed back by the Old Boys ..... in their own inimical ways. The gregarious goalie had been genuinely missed by his team mates. Several of them were anxious to know the status of his health. "How're you feeling, Andy old boy", Dirk inquired in a serious-sounding voice. "Okay", replied Andy with the universal word of concurrence. And so the chatter went on until, like most old timers' conversations, attention dwindled and boredom or diminishing marginal utility set in.

But who cares about marginal utility in an old timers' dressing room? What mattered was that Andy was back and ready to play. Like Willie, Andy was a good goaltender, a great guy and fun to have on the team. Like them all, he was coming to the end of his "playing days". Andy was in his '60s, how far in was not known for certain. As Mikey was heard to say, "he was kind of anal about his age". What was known for sure was that he was slowing down, especially after an increasing number and growing severity of injuries. While slowing down in old timer hockey is as natural as breathing, slowing down as a goalie is the "kiss of death" for them, especially when the shots don't slow down at the same rate and go in the net more frequently. Still and away (whatever that phrase means), Andy was well liked. Being liked was more important than being good. The Old Boys were happy to have him back, even if they knew they would have to play harder and keep the puck out of their own end. For Andy, that's the least they could (and likely would) do.

Willie's woes

More recently, Willie was injured when his worn out, really olde leather and horse hair leg pads failed to protect his tender skin and bones from Big Bad Bobby Brown's bullet or, as the late, great hockey announcer, Danny Gallivan might say, "cannonading" shot. Then to compound the problem, a couple of weeks later the ancient goalie made a save by "butterflying". No, he wasn't flitting out in the fields chasing butterflies with a net. For those who are in the know about goal tending, "butterflying" is a relatively recent, like 20 odd years old, technique to keeping pucks out of the net by their minders. It is best used by young goalies who have limber (not lumber) tendons, muscles, bones, joints and other youthful physical conditions. For sure, Willie did not qualify ... physically.

Well, the goofy goalie went down to stop the puck with his knees together and his skates kicked out toward each goal post. "Oh damn" or words to that effect indicated he was hurting, in or around the knee, that most complex of male bodily joints (if you ignore the penis and its many psycho-physiological complexities --- whatever that means). After a few minutes of respite and consoling by his team mates, Willie continued to play, like the "good trooper" hockey players, young and old, are expected to be. That noble effort, quite likely exacerbated the injury, pain and suffering because the last time Hank talked to him, Willie was still recovering from the painful damage to his aged medial collateral ligament (MCL, for those who have difficulty saying such unfamiliar, multi-syllabic words). He was getting some physiotherapy on the damaged joints and their connectors, putting on some kind of sensuous salve or ointment, applying ice and heat, doing a little exercise so his leg would not atrophy but otherwise "taking it easy" ... unhappily.

About the best Hank could do as he listened to Willie's tale of woe was to try to empathize with the old goalie and suggest that he come out to coach the Old Boys.

Hank: "Willie, we need all the help we can get. Why don't you come out and coach us?"

Willie: "You guys are beyond coaching. You know that old saying ... about not being able to teach old dogs new tricks!"

Hank: (with a tone of teasing tinged with a little sarcasm) "Well, that may be true but we could sure use your moral support and motivational skills ... you didn't get to the top on your good looks, Willie Boy."

Willy (same guy): (chuckling good-naturedly) "That might not be a bad idea ... not saying it's good ... but it's not bad ... that phony flattery."

Hank: (interrupts) "What the hell are you saying ... maybe this ... maybe that ... you sound like a bloody economist ... on one hand this .... on the other hand that. ... just come on out on Tuesday night and have some laughs ... get you out of Mitzy's hair ... or wherever ... and have a beer with the boys."

Willie: (with some enthusiasm) "Ya, that sounds like a good idea. I miss the Old Boys .... they're a good bunch .... have a couple of beers ..... give you some crap. You deserve that, eh! Okay, we'll see you on Tuesday night.

I have to go to Speedy Creek on Wednesday so I can't be led astray by you guys ... hmmm, guess I should be okay."

Hank: (with more teasing sarcasm) "Why don't you bring your nurse maid to ensure that you will be okay and that the big bad Old Boys don't lead you astray ... fat chance of you going any further astray than you have already been ... the guy from East Montreal."

Willy: "You never know ... might be kind of fun to do some straying ... got to go now. See you Tuesday!"

Hank reflected briefly on his conversation with Willie. The old puck stopper sounded kind of down "in his cups", as the Brits might say. Those damned injuries seem to hurt more and take so much longer to heal when you get older, Hank mused to himself. That gets to a guy, especially when he does not have a job or other consuming interest. Willie had been retired with his not-so-"golden handshake" last November after 24+ years with that Prairie Gold Corporation ... just before Christmas and about six month short of 25 years when he would have received a much more rewarding pension. Being gypped like that as well as losing his job really hurt - his ego, his self worth, his confidence, his income and security.

And the question or, more importantly, the challenge facing Willie and others who are cut adrift by those exploitive corps (like corpse) is: what to do with all of the extra time that has to be taken up, preferably with some kind of useful, meaningful activities. But then, corporations have never been known for their sensitivity to people ... just profits, profits and more profits, thought Hank as he felt his annoyance rising rapidly. So, "it will be good for the old bugger to get out of the house and into the rink with the boys", said Hank half-aloud to himself. He had a habit of such musings to himself, supposedly a first sign of being kind of goofy. "Oh well, what the hell, I'm not hurting anybody ... so long as I'm kept in this padded room", smiling slightly at his warped "sense of humor".

Andy's sorry situation

One cold night in January, the Old Boys gathered to do battle with one of their many arch-rivals, the Rogues Rouge team. As usual, Andy was in the dressing room early, probably the earliest. He took quite a while to get his gear on, in part because he liked to sort out his equipment (and probably himself) as well as blather endlessly with his team mates. That night he was kind of subdued ... for Andy, who was normally upbeat and ebullient. And he would be even more subdued, even submerged, during the game that was to be played.

On the RR's first goal, Andy was a way out of position. Normally, he would have stopped the second goal ... but he "whiffed" when he tried to clear the puck from in front of the goal. On the third goal against, he anticipated a pass but the shooter put the puck high into the net on the short side. That was the first goal that Hank was on the ice for and, to put it mildly, the big d'man was rather "pissed off". He muttered a string of vulgarities and then reminded Andy about "taking the shooter and leave the pass to us". Andy replied with some rather choice vulgarities of his own. From then on, his goal-tending went from bad to bloody awful. The Old Boys were soundly trounced by a score of 8 or 9 to 3. "Would have needed a touchdown to win", said Mikey as the team tromped dejectedly back to its dreary dressing room.

After the game and before they had started to drink their beer, the Old Boys were dispirited, maybe even sullen; not a whole lot of joy in their dressing room ... like the day the mighty Babe struck out in Mudville. A little later, Hank was in the shower room with Andy, Big Gerry and Max. There was some banter but for the most part, the wet, steamy room symbolized the mood of the players. Like a bolt out of the blue,

Andy exclaimed: "I've had a bitch of a week. A few days ago, my best friend committed suicide ..... for no reason ... apparently. Our trio played at his birthday a few weeks ago ... and at his son's wedding last summer ... we were the best of buddies .... and he up and does himself in ..... son of a bitch."

Taken aback, the others in the showers muttered some appropriate, sincere words of sympathy. Silence! Nothing was heard but the sound of the steamy showers beating down on the bodies and the splashing of them washing and rinsing themselves. A few minutes later, Andy continued his tale of woe.

Andy (blurt out): "Then my #^&xz*^#+x sister-in-law moves in with us and she is out of her head ... really whacko. Our house is a crazy place to live .... she's really a f'g nutcake!"

Big Gerry (in his insensitive, sarcastic way): "I bet she fits right in, eh!"

Andy: (angrily): "Screw you, fatso."

Mixed responses flowed from the other Old Boys. Andy looked stunned, then annoyed. Hank tried to keep a straight face and be empathetic. Big Gerry and Max burst out laughing. Hank tried to change the subject but quickly finished his showering and left the room filled with rancorous noises.

When Andy reappeared in the dressing room, Charley, James, Mikey and others took turns trying to lift the goalie's sunken spirits.

Charley: "Hey Andy, let's go to Barney's for some wings with the boys ...?"

Andy (reflecting on the suggestion): "Naw, i don't think so .... not tonight... maybe another time .... ya .... another time! Thanks!"

James: "Come on, Andy! Do yourself a favor and come drink beer with the boys. You can buy a round ... make us feel good ... and you, too."

Andy (guffawing): "You must be kidding! Buy you guys a round! Hell, I don't have that much money. Your rounds are endless .. like a circle."

Max (coming back into the dressing room from the showers): "F'k man, if I had your f''g money I would throw mine away."

James (to Andy): "You can use your credit card ... it must have a high limit ... you're a big shot ... "

Mikey: "A big what ...?"

James: "Shot, man .... shot!"

Hank (striding across the room toward Andy stops to get a beer out of the bag): "Hey flake, lighten ... brighten up. You'll be okay. Come have a beer ... that will pick you up."

Max: "Would take a huge f''g crane to pick that fat f''r up."

Andy (sounding dejected): "No thanks. I better go home and be with Marg. She has been with her sister most of the day ... she needs some help."

None of the Old Boys' efforts seemed to "buck up" Andy. He was really blue. Shortly afterwards, Andy had his gear packed and headed out the door, an unusually early departure for him. Andy had not had a good night but like the good old guy that he was, he would be back with his banter, stories, trivia and a better game in goal. Like most old folks, he was resilient.

Sam's sore shoulders

Sam was a tough old geezer. He had been a career policeman until, at the age of 65, he was retired ... by the force's policy. He had seen, done and otherwise experienced a lot in his lifetime. Whether by dint of his genetics, personality, upbringing or police training, Sad Sam was very quiet, almost withdrawn ... much of the time. If you didn't look for him, you might not know he was in the dressing room, on the ice or anywhere else. Sam sure seemed like the ideal guy for surveillance, criminal investigation, espionage or whatever other low profile activities that sleuths or spies perform. Most of that is irrelevant to the story following.

Another cold night in February and Sam was in the process of scoring a goal when he was "dumped" (tripped) by an opposing and obviously disgruntled Rogues' defenceman. Down Sam went ... thud, right on his left shoulder. A series of rather unpleasant, even snarly, utterances followed spontaneously ..... probably some sayings that he learned from a police manual or, maybe, on the beat and need not be repeated here or anywhere. What he said was irrelevant and immaterial, as Perry Mason used to say. Sam was hurt. He was sadder and more silent than usual, especially after just scoring a goal (given that he was not the most prolific sniper on the team ... sort of down the list with Barry a.k.a. Cement for his hands, Hank and the goal tenders).

That fall ended the sad man's season. His left shoulder was dislocated. It took many months to heal. Even then, his shoulder was so painful that he had difficulty lifting his left arm to drink his beer. That is the "acid test" for all injured old guys. Fortunately, he was predominantly right-handed so he did not suffer unduly from thirst. He could slake his parched throat with the best of them. He proved that capability repeatedly because Sam liked "being with the boys", especially since his wife was a miserable old broad. He had some empathetic guys to talk to about his sore shoulder and assorted other injuries from the past. Although he was a quiet, introverted type, Sad Sam enjoyed the camaraderie, an integral part of which was having a beer or six, shooting the breeze and having some laughs, although the sad man really did not laugh ... overtly. When he was happy, he had an exaggerated Mona Lisa kind of smile on his mug. Nevertheless, being with the boys provided some balm for his wounded shoulder, other body parts and spirits.

More serious situations

Attacks on the old tickers

Heart attacks are the most common, serious health problems encountered by old guys playing organized shinny. In a recent year, at least five of the 150 active Old Boys had heart attacks. How that 3.3% compares to senior men in the general populous is beyond the scope of this raconteur's tales and his knowledge. Be that as it may, even a single heart attack by an Old Boy is too many for the rest of them. However, given the realities of the *North Americanus's* life cycle, aging, physical deterioration and all of the other lovely consequences of being old buggers, the Old Boys are well aware of heart attacks and their symptoms, if not what to do when one occurs or being willing and able to prevent them. (By golly, that sure was a long, convoluted, difficult-to-understand sentence.)

That awareness is created and/or heightened by various media programs, articles, reports and documentaries. Following are selected parts of a script from *Health Matters*, a Newsworld television program, shown a few years ago on the Canadian Broadcasting Corporation (CBC).

Commentator: "Tom Buffett doesn't like being on the sidelines. But that's the closest he gets to the games these days ... since he had a heart attack... on the ice."

Buffett: "... went to play at 6 o'clock, my usual hockey team. Was on about half an hour and started to develop some pains in my chest ... and funny numb feelings in my hands.

Doctor (later, talking to Buffett in his office): "... it's somewhat surprising that someone with your risk factors actually had a heart attack."

Commentator: "Buffett was 39. A non-smoker. Long time hockey buff. He'd been treated for high blood pressure. But he had no idea he was heading for trouble."

Buffett: "I felt great when I went on the ice. I felt good the last few years. No health problems.

Commentator: "Exactly the kind of case that piqued the interest of cardiologist Paul MacDonald. He was seeing an unusual number of apparently healthy men having heart attacks, after a night of hockey."

MacDonald (in office): And so we wondered if there was something different about the people who played hockey or was it potentially the activity itself putting them at higher risk."

Commentator: "MacDonald decided to take a closer look at recreational hockey. He attached heart monitors to more than 100 men. Average age: 42. The result: All of them were pushing their heart rates into dangerous territory. And in many cases, hearts were beating too fast, for far too long."

MacDonald (at game): When the heart rates increase, the blood pressure will increase significantly. That's a lot of extra strain or work on the heart. Working the heart is part of the goal, with any kind of exercise. But every heart has its limits. At extremes ... very rigorous exercise ... high heart rates can cause heart attacks and this has been proven particularly so in people who don't exercise regularly. So that's our concern. People exercising too hard and too vigorously and they're not in shape to do so."

MacDonald (later at the hockey game): "What is it about this rec hockey that strains the heart? Unlike the pros, most of these players aren't in top shape. This is often the only exercise they get. And despite that, they tend to play hard ..."

Buffett: "We push it every game. You know, you're 40 years old and you go on the ice and you think you're Bobby Orr. And with gentlemen's (?) hockey, there often aren't enough players ... players spend most of the game on the ice. With little time to rest."

MacDonald (at game): "We haven't studied or proven this but our feeling after looking at these very high heart rates for a sustained period of time is that you need to play with enough substitution so that you can get a break and your body gets a chance to recover during hockey. There can also be hidden problems. Conditions that may even be undiagnosed ... but could make a strenuous game of hockey even riskier.

Testing after his heart attack revealed Tom Buffett had several clogged arteries. There was no sign of that, before his heart attack.

Jack Porter (another medical expert, during game): "It's important to get the right age group and skill level to play with too because if they're too young, the tendency is to chase them and you're really going to get into trouble."

Porter (after the game): "... characteristic of the male species, we have a tendency to think we're 24 when we're 44 (or 64) ... and we just have to monitor your heart rates, with the charts we've developed, so we're wiser ... when we're playing hockey and we can play much longer in our lives and enjoy an active lifestyle, which is critical."

MacDonald (in office): "... initially I think there was a bit of reluctance from hockey players. They were concerned that we were suggesting they shouldn't play hockey ... that it wasn't the right thing to do. And that's not our message at all. We're quite anxious for them to continue playing hockey. We just want them to exercise more regularly, besides playing hockey so that they'll be in good shape when they do play."

Commentator (showing Buffett opening door to go out for his walk): "Tom Buffett isn't pushing his heart rate these days. He's waiting for a triple bypass. His only exercise is a daily walk."

Given that script with its medical expertise and research base, one has good reason to ponder the heart attacks suffered by Max, Feisty and Harry that follow as well as some others suffered by old guys playing hockey in Joxville.

Max's heart attack

Over the years, Hank had "first hand" experience with several serious injuries, including death, both on and off of the ice. "Death ain't fun", he muttered rather inanely while talking to Charley Hustle, Mikey and Boom Boom about Max's heart attack back in '98.

Hank (slowly, solemnly): "So Max was lucky that night when he collapsed in the dressing room. He was lucky that Ryan and Stan were playing that night. They were off-duty firemen and had paramedic training ... or at least CPR training ... what a blessing that was because as soon as they were told about Max collapsing they came rushing off the ice... into the dressing room and just took over. They saved Max's life ... no doubt about it. They pounded on the little bugger's chest ... we were worried that they would break his bones ... and they breathed into his mouth .... ya, they were holding his nose too ... . Well, little Max started to breathe again ... he had stopped breathing for a few seconds ... he had some pulse but he didn't jump up and say "let's go" ... he laid on that floor very still ... he was a pasty color. He looked like a dead man for a few minutes ... then he started to move a little bit ... but not much for such a hyperactive ... and mouthy guy."

"A few minutes later the regular firemen, you know, the on-duty guys came bursting into the room ... obviously some one had phoned them. Well, talk about 'pros' ... they cleared everybody back, set down their bags, machines ... seems like they had a portable oxygen tank and some other equipment ... and then went to work on Max in such a proficient manner ... it was awesome .... very impressive and, best of all, successful. Within minutes they had assessed his condition, gave him an injection of something or other, half-lifted, half-rolled him on to a stretcher and hauled him away to the ambulance. I was right behind them with Max's clothes. Just seconds after they got him into the ambulance, they yelled something about him ... Max ... 'quitting'. So they grabbed that 'paddle' and slapped it on his chest, turned on a machine and gave Max a jolt that lifted him right off the stretcher. I was awe struck ... never seen anything like that before ... then they said something like 'hit him again' and they gave him another jolt ... lifted him right off the stretcher again .... Max wasn't a big guy but he must have weighed 170 pounds or so ... and there he was being shocked right off the stretcher ... unbelievable ... scary".

"Well, those firemen got that ambulance out of the parking lot and to the hospital in minutes.... boy, they knew what they were doing and they did it well because they saved Max's life. Those firemen deserve the credit and respect of the community ... not to mention Max and the rest of the Old Boys ... ."

An actual tragedy

Telling the tale about Max's close call with death reminded Hank of a tragic accident that occurred while he was playing college hockey. Slowly, and thoughtfully he recounted the terrible accident to Mikey, Boom Boom and Charley Hustle.

"We were having a Sunday night practice at Murray U ... back in November 1959", he said hesitantly like he didn't really want to talk about the situation but somehow felt compelled to do so. Guess that's ambivalence. Hank sure showed the conflicting feelings in his words and facial expressions.

Reluctantly, he continued with his account of the fateful practice

> "We were in our end and their attacking defenceman blasted a slap shot toward our goal. It was Con Jordan ... had a hard, heavy shot ... he was about five ten and weighted 210 ... powerful guy. Well, that damned puck hit a forward's thigh guard and deflected right up onto the side of Mark's head ... he was my defence partner. Mark went down as if he had been pole-axed ... and he was a big man ... 6 foot, 3 inches, 225 pounds ... and in good shape. Initially, he was knocked out, I guess ... hell, I'm no medical doctor. But he laid on the ice ... very still ... ominously still and his face lost its natural color. My God, he looked so bloody pale, a sickly white. We kept him calm while someone phoned for an ambulance and a doctor ... or some medical people. Well, those medical people got there pretty quickly, attended to Mark right there on the ice ... put him on a stretcher and took him off to the hospital. That would have been about 8 o'clock. Well, that ugly incident pretty well killed the practice ... sorry about the choice of words. We scrimmaged for a little while, skated some laps, did some wind sprints and then the coach called it a night. Our dressing room was gloomy .... really gloomy ... like a morgue ... as the guys took off their gear, showered and went their way, mostly back to the dorms. Wasn't too much chatter that night. Strange feeling ... really eerie ... for such normally boisterous guys to be so quiet, so pensive, so worried ... but that's they way they were. It was really eerie."

"Early next morning, I don't know ... maybe 6 or 7 am, our coach got a phone call from the doctors. A while later, he phoned us with the bad news. Big Mark was dead ... . My God, what a shock ... even after George's near fatal accident the previous year. Well, apparently Mark was in the hospital being treated ... I don't know all the details ... and I don't want to ... I just know that the coach was told that he went into convulsions and died instantaneously ... of a brain tumor or something like that. He had just graduated, been married for a few months and then that happened ... just doesn't seem right or fair but then whoever said that life was right or fair?"

Feisty's heart failure

About 16 years ago, William, a.k.a. Wild Bill, Willy (not to be confused with Willy or Willie the goal tender) and, since his heart attack, re-named Feisty, keeled over all by himself in the corner of the arena. He had just "rushed" (relatively speaking, real old timers don't seem to rush anywhere) up the ice with the puck and then the ticker gave out. According to first hand reports, old Feisty just laid on the ice as peacefully as a baby sleeping in its crib. But his stillness bothered Stan, the off-duty fireman, who was playing against Feisty that night. Like the trained pro that he was, Stan checked the vital signs of the prone old timer, laid him flat on his back and then started the CPR process. Well, the details are a little vague after that but two facts are for sure: a few days later, Feisty had open heart surgery (the scar down the front of his chest remains) and the miserable old bugger is still very much alive, fortunately.

Although some time passed before he made his "comeback", Feisty played for several more years. He was slower, more cautious and tentative for a while but he slowly changed back to a moderately aggressive style. His red hair must have been a clue to his temperament. Well, after he retired from "active" playing, Feisty refereed for years. He had his own unique style of refereeing; kind of laid back and very courteous. When he was ready to drop the puck for a face-off, he would always say "Gentlemen, are you ready?", or just plain "Gentlemen"! Such courteous words said so politely seemed really incongruent with Feisty and hockey players, at least while they were playing.

Even when Feisty resigned from the Association a couple of years ago, he was a courteous gentleman, despite being "steamed" at a perceived slight to him by that august body and its executive. In his true tempestuous way, Feisty resigned abruptly near the end of the Spring general meeting of the Association. He stood up and presented a sound case to the Executive and the membership at large, that he deserved to be recognized as one of the original founders. According to several members, including the recognized founders, the current Prez and members of the executive, Feisty was not really "an original" ... close but not quite ... which is kind of splitting hairs.

So, as a matter of his "honor", he resigned, complete with a well-prepared statement for the local media (which, by all accounts, was never printed or broadcasted), a formal letter of resignation, an address, albeit brief, to the members and executive, the return of a citation and other memorabilia from old timers' hockey. What a shame that such a nice guy had to end his 25 year association with one of the best hockey organizations that most of us have had the pleasure of experiencing during our eons of playing, coaching, refing, spectatoring (if there is such a word) and otherwise being involved in the best athletic game played in the whole wide wonderful world.

Harry's coronary malfunctions in Mexico

Heart problems seem to be an annual "event" for members of the Old Boys' league. While Max and Feisty were playing when they had their seizures, Harry was strolling on the Mayan Riviera beach in Mexico with his wife when he was "attacked" by his heart. They were on a vacation, in part celebrating their 25th wedding anniversary and his 50th birthday. According to Harry, "we (he and Marilyn) were walking along the beach on a warm, sunny morning ... it was Saturday .... our second last day there ... chatting and enjoying the sun, sights and sounds of a mariachi band. Couldn't get much better than that ... ordinarily." But, then Harry "started to have difficulty breathing." Although he was seriously over weight, he was in fairly good condition, usually playing a couple of hockey games a week; as well as a few tournaments each season. And, he played the whole year round ... even during the summertime."

Harry's continued with his tale of woe.

"the shortage of breath scared him a little and concerned 'Lynnie' a lot. So, right then and there, they sat down on the beach to rest and let him 'catch his breath.' He caught enough of it that he decided to go back to their room for a rest. But, before he arrived at the room, 'all hell broke loose'. He was in the lobby of the hotel when he felt very hot and really nauseated. So he headed for the nearest men's room. There he started to 'sweat buckets' and felt so weak he had to sit down 'on the can' ... a good place, especially if 'you're going to puke'. Minutes later, he felt good enough to continue his 'trek' back to the room. Then came the pains in his chest which 'took my breath away', followed by 'shots of pain across my back' ... like stopping Big Gerry's slap shot with your chest. Oh, I was hurting ... even laying on the bed. Those pains were really intense."

"Fortunately, Lynnie came back ... wondering how I was. Boy, it didn't take her long to phone for a doctor. There was one at the hotel next to ours ... he came to the room pretty quickly, especially by Mexican standards ... maybe 15-20 minutes. Well, the doctor kind of looked me over, took my pulse, checked my heart with his stethoscope and said I was fine. I sure as hell didn't feel fine. I had real difficulty breathing deeply, still felt nauseated and had some pain in my chest and back. So I laid around for a while ... didn't feel like eating ... or even having a drink ... except some water ... which is unusual for me, very unusual ... especially when we're on vacation and it is an all inclusive deal. So, I really wasn't well."

Harry paused for a few seconds of reflection and stress relief before he continued his account of the heart attack.

"Marilyn was getting more upset than I was. I was trying to stay calm. That afternoon she phoned the doctor again and he came to our room. He did another visual inspection, gave me some Aspirin and said 'You will be fine ... just take it easy ... get some rest.' Hell, all I was doing was just layin' around, taking some Aspirin, having the odd drink of water and peeing ... that's about as easy goin' as it gets ... right!?"

"Fortunately, Lynnie didn't leave the room except for a few minutes ... to go to the restaurant and order something to eat ... for herself ... not me. I had no appetite ... which is very unusual. She probably needed a change of scenery ... some fresh air ... a chance to sort of unwind. And the bugger of it was that we had planned to have our 'last night celebration' that night ..... bugger ..... what a celebration. Guess maybe it was a celebration of living and I didn't realize it, eh!. Anyhow, Lynnie was back soon ... very soon. She did the packing and 'took care of business' which was fine with me. By then, I just wanted to get back home ... being three or four thousand miles away ... from home when you feel like hell gives you a very uncomfortable feeling."

"The worst of it ... or so it seemed at the time ... was that my misery screwed up our last night there. We had planned a real romantic evening ... you know ... a nice dinner ... some wine ... some lovin' ... the whole nine yards! Those plans went out the window. About all we did that was romantic that night was chat and look out the window ... at the palms, the beach, ocean, waves and the sunset ... that was pretty damned nice ... even if we were just laying on the bed ... just chatting, looking out the window. Bugger!!!"

"I didn't sleep worth a damn that night ... maybe a couple of hours ... couldn't get comfortable ... tossed and turned ... woke Lynnie up ... several times ... poor kid ... she had a lousy sleep too. But she was bright enough to phone the doctor again the next morning ... Sunday morning ... kind of surprised that he was there ... on duty ... but he was. So he came over and took another look at me ... honest to God, that's all he did was look at me ... my eyes, my tongue ... didn't even bring his stethoscope ... just looked at me. But he did give me some sleeping pills to take before I got on the plane .... so I would sleep during the flight ... and some nitroglycerine pills in case I had 'another attack' ... or couldn't breath. Then he left ...... seems like all he was really interested in was the 80 bucks he collected for his visits ... 240 dollars in total ... U.S. dollars, at that..."

"I slept all the way home. As soon as we arrived in Cowtown, Lynnie took me to the hospital ... the nearest one to the airport ... the Rocky View or whatever it's called ... makes no difference. As soon as we arrived there, the admitting lady took one look at me and sent me to emergency. The nurse there took one look at me and directed me to a bed, told me to get undressed, put on a gown and lay down ... she'd be right back ... and she was... with instructions ... lay down ... take off your gown ... take these pills. She was in charge. She put some suction cups with wires attached on my chest ... took some blood out of my finger ... put me on IV ... and then I kind of faded away ... went to sleep."

"It turns out that they gave me some routine tests for a suspected heart attack. One test had to do with enzymes in your blood. The standard enzyme rating is supposed to be .03 ... mine was 3.60 ...

12 times more than the safe level is supposed to be ... can you believe it? ... incredible! (Please note: the arithmetic is wrong but that was what Harry said.) According to the nurse, that was the second highest level the doc had ever seen for a heart attack survivor. Man, I'm lucky to be alive. They did some more tests and found that the main artery to my heart was 90 percent clogged and the others were clogged ... also. I was an emergency case."

"Guess the doctor had some discussions with Lynnie and they decided to fix me up ... right then and there. So they did some angioplasties on me. I stayed in the hospital for a few days ... was kind of dopey from all of the drugs they put into me ... and then it was back home. Now, seven months later, I feel great ... back at work ... walk every day, do some aerobic exercises twice a week .... on Tuesdays and Thursdays ... the same day you guys play hockey ...... have lost 30 pounds or so ... sure have changed what I eat ... that's okay. I'm lucky to be alive ... and want to stay that way. But, you know what gripes me most ... that damned doctor telling us three times that I was fine ... and the doctors here telling me I had had a very severe ... not just a severe heart attack ... *a very severe heart attack.* Guess I should have gone to their hospital ... there was a naval hospital just a couple of blocks away ... could've taken a taxi for a few pesos ... might have been better off .... 'woulda, coulda, shoulda.' But I'm feeling great now ... hope to start skating in a couple of weeks ... maybe do some 'refing' ... maybe back playing next season ... hopefully."

And the Old Boys were looking forward to the affable Harry's return to the rink and hopefully playing again.

In addition to hoping for Harry's return, some of the Old Boys became quite concerned about the growing number of heart attacks being suffered by their team mates; at least five in one year. So Jock decided to do something about it. He started by photocopying and distributing, to the Association's members and executive, a very compelling article, entitled "*Dying with their skates on*" that appeared in *The Globe and Mail*, early in December, 2005. He aggressively "lobbied" the Board for a greater awareness of the threat and an action plan of prevention and life-saving practices. Further, Jock inquired into the presence of defibrillators at the Joxville arenas (as well as the training in their use and cardiopulmonary resuscitation [CPR] of the arena personnel) and sent out the following suggestions to the membership:

Heart-healthy hockey

* Appoint one or two members of your team to learn and be competent in the life-saving techniques of cardiopulmonary resuscitation (CPR) and/or the use of an automatic external defibrillator.

* Be sure to warm up before playing.

* Don't sit down between shifts. Although it may sound like hockey heresy, experts advise players to stand and keep the legs moving between shifts. Avoid creating peaks and valleys in the heart rate. Sitting between shifts can produce abrupt drops in heart rate. By standing or walking, the removal of lactic acid is enhanced and the player will have a fresher shift the next time he is on the ice.

* Expand the team rosters to ensure that more that 8 or ten skaters play. Avoid too many back-to-back shifts and too much time with players' hearts pounding above the safe target range.

* Warm down after playing. Players should bring down their heart rate gradually to a resting rate. Cut the last period short and skate off the accumulated lactic acid.

* Stop being overly macho and expending all the testosterone trying to impress other men. Re-define old timers' hockey. Consider a co-ed game. 10

While Hank was not so naive as to believe that most of the six suggestions outlined above would be accepted by the Old Boys, he hoped that some of them would be and the awareness of the members would be increased. He knew that some players, especially the older ones, were more conscious of heart attack threats and would be receptive to trying to safeguard against such a deadly prospect. Hank was certainly conscious of such a prospect. His father died of a massive heart attack, at age 68, years younger than Hank was presently. And his father had smoked for 50 years or more, had emphysema, allergies, had a very stressful job and was out of shape from the lack of exercise. Notwithstanding the differences in health, Hank was concerned about heart attacks. They were the #1 killer of men.

XIII. Traded

Rumors, rumors, ridiculous rumors!?!?

One very cold but very sunny day in late December, replete with a brilliant blue sky and sparkling white snow, Hank and Boom Boom were having one of their "spirited", occasional lunches at Ray's Eatery in beautiful downtown Joxville. Decades ago, they had grown up in a small prairie town and were long time friends. On that wonderful day to be alive, they were reminiscing, joking and having a good time talking about all kinds of pleasant subjects ... especially about going south to do some golfing. During the course of that jocular, entertaining conversation, Ronald (his given name at birth but not widely used by the Old Boys) kind of quipped that Hank had been traded ... again. Hank, quickly remembered the previous summer when Boomer had left a mischievous message on his telephone recorder saying that Hank had been traded to a new team. Clearly, he remembered how bothered he was by the prospect of changing teams. Heck, even Wayne Gretzky cried when he was traded to the L.A. Kings by the Edmonton Oilers and he was a vital, confident young man.

Boom Boom (with a look of pseudo solemnity): "Yup, some of the teams are getting shaken up .... some of the guys are getting moved?"

Hank (looking annoyed): "Ah baloney, mulroney! ..... you're so full of B.S.!

Boomer (brow furrowed): "I'm not kiddin'!"

Hank (smirking): "For sure ..... you're too old to be that...."

Boom (sternly): "I'm serious ... read my lips!"

Hank (sarcastically): "Thanks George Bush ... you're about as credible!"

After their brief, relatively animated and rapid fire exchange, the two Old Boys returned momentarily to their lunch. Very carefully, Hank studied Boomer's face and especially his eyes. He sensed that his buddy was telling the truth. With some discomfort, Hank picked up on the trade conversation.

Hank (dubiously): "You seem serious about this trade nonsense. Why would they (the Board) want to shift players at this time of the year? Cripes, it's half way through the season. It doesn't make a whole lot of sense. I don't like it?"

Boom Boom (pensively): "Well, that's what the majority of the guys wanted at the general meeting last week ... they voted on the issue ... strong support for making some changes in the teams .... where were you? How come you weren't there? You missed the free beer...."

Hank (somewhat chagrined, muttered): "Had something else to do. I'm not a great fan of meetings .... too much talk .... too little done ... waste of time ... even if there is free beer... besides nothing is free ... even the beer at old timers' meetings."

Boomer (interjecting with considerable levity in his voice): "They got somethin' done this time .... you and a bunch of others got traded .... ha! ha! ha! big guy".

Hank (still dubious and quite miffed with his buddy's blather, fired off several questions quite quickly):"Who did I get traded to? Did you get traded? Who else was traded? What's all this nonsense about trading players? Doesn't the executive know that most of the old timers play hockey for the camaraderie that comes from knowing each other ... really well ... and developing trust and some meaningful relations? Why would they trade players at this time in the season?

Boom Boom: "The guys seemed to want it .... really a consensus .. to break up some cliques on the teams ...... and break up some of the rivalries that were forming ... and causing some problems .... you know like Les Rouges and the Mid Knights .... those two teams have had some serious dust ups .... even the Old Boys had some scuffles with the Bloozers .... that guy Herman belted you from behind last year .... remember, he blindsided you ....!"

Hank (reacting angrily): "How could I forget? That dirty sonofabitch nearly knocked me out .... I had headaches and a sore neck for a month ... six weeks it was. Ya, I still owe him one ... wished he was 20 years older ... better still, I wished I was 20 years younger ... I'd kick the crap out of that sneaky bastard!"

Boom Boom "Whoa ... calm down ... you'll have a hernia! Remember ... Big Gerry crunched Herm for you ... that same game ... so let it go ... it's history ... besides you're going to the Bloozers ... so you'll be able to player with your buddy ... Herm ... that should be fun!"

Hank: "You've got to be kiddin'! I've got to play with that ugly s.o.b. ... that doesn't sounds like fun. Who else is on that team ... anybody I know?"

Boom Boom: "Probably ... you've been around the league for nearly 20 years or more ... haven't you? You must know some of their other guys ..... like Gordie and Wicks ..... you know Wikstrom .... and Henri .... what's his name? ... Desjardins. He's good ... a real hustler ... skates like the wind .... like Guy. Don't know what it is about those peasoupers but they sure can skate. Must be genetic ... a superior race ... of skaters ... pardon the pun ... wonder if Hitler ever thought about that ... doubt it. Oh ya, I nearly forgot ... James was traded to the Bloozers ... too. He can hold your hand until you meet some of new guys ... and make some new friends ... get some new play mates ... little boy"

Hank: (kind of preoccupied): "Screw you Boomer! Answer my damned question. Who else is on that team?"

Boom Boom (getting annoyed): "Hank, for cripes sake pay attention. I just answered your damned question ... Henri, Gordie, Wicker ... for three ... probably some more that you know ... I'm not sure ... I saw the team lists on the internet ... check it out when you get home ... you know our website .... www.... whatever the hell it is!"

Hank (sarcastically): "Hey Boomer, you're on the Board and you can't even remember our website. How do you expect me to remember it??? You're a lot of help, you are ..... guess I better get back to work (as Hank stood up, he started to put his winter jacket on and move away from the table) .... let's go, big guy ... if you can get your big gut out from under the table ... need a hand? ... a winch? ... a crane? Did you see where some incredible percentage of Canadians ... kids especially and old guys included ... were classed as *obese* ... like over 20 percent ... one in five ... and another 30 - 40 odd percent were overweight ... it's becoming a national *crisis* ..... even worse than smoking for old guys ..... *worse than smoking*! You better smarten up ..... or start smoking ... just kidding!!!!

Boom Boom (looking a little embarrassed, probably because of his more than "ample girth"): "No ... didn't see it ... it's probably propaganda ... against us jolly fellows!"

Hank (feigning some guilt, continued sarcastically) "Ya right! ..... but I'm sorry about that ..... didn't mean to hurt your feelings ...... as if you could feel through all that insulation"

Boomer (in a louder than usual voice and just a little miffed at his buddy): "What are you trying to say ..... slim? Do you think I am obese just because I'm about 50 pounds overweight? .... and I do have feelings ... and you're hurting them ... so stop it you big bully before I punch you out ... right here and now!!!"

Hank (somewhat chagrined): "Calm down, Boomer ..... you're causing a bit of a scene. This is a public place ... not the dressing room. Anyhow, thanks for lunch. I'll buy next time ... you can have watercress and melba toast."

Hank (continuing, with a slight smile on his face): Do you remember that gorgeous girl in high school ... her name was Melba .... but she was not flat like toast!!! She was from Wheaton ... oooo la la ... do you remember the big boobs she had ... like melons .... and she was still maturing. Wonder where she is ... if she is married .... oh boy, she sure was built ... much better than the proverbial outhouse. Anyhow, see you, big guy ... hopefully on the same team ..... sometime. I'm used to carrying you ... how many years have we played together ... 5? 6? 7? ... seems like a long time .... maybe that's because I've had to play your position, too!"

Boom Boom (still with a pleasant smile on his face and levity in his voice): "... or maybe it's because you're getting so damned old ... and slow. It just seemed like you have an extra load. Don't be such a whiner."

Hank (feigning hurt feelings): "Ouch! You're cruel ... and everybody thinks you're such a nice guy. Oh well, you know what that old circus guy Barnum said about fooling people ... still it's not very nice ... ."

After doing up their overcoats and putting on their gloves, the two Old Boys left the warm, cozy restaurant and went out into the chilling breezes and temperatures of winter on the Prairies.

Hank: Brrrr! ... bloody cold!.

Boom Boom: "You're right about that Hanker ... but remember where we are ... and what month it is .... got to be goin' now. See you soon. Take care..."

Hank (hurrying away and hollering over his shoulder): "Chao!!!" and was going to add that he was not talking about eating some more but, given the wind and the growing distance, he decided to keep quiet and head for his car .... as fast as he could slip and slide along. "Traded ... crap ... I really enjoyed playing with the Old Boys," he muttered to himself as he trundled down the street and into his car. "Phooey ... hope Boomer is wrong!"

The "news"

One dark miserable Saturday night in early January, between the second and third periods of Hockey Night in Canada, an old timer hockey player by the name of Ken phoned Hank. They had some frivolous chitter-chatter about the lousy weather and the game between Les Canadiens and the Canucks on tv. While Hank listened to the "small talk", he felt an uncomfortable sense of discomfort, even dread, spreading throughout his mind and body. Eventually, Ken got around to telling Hank why he had phoned. He was the team rep for the Bloozers and wanted Hank to know that he had been traded and was most welcome to their team. Ken sure seemed like a decent chap, thought Hank to himself. The Bloozer rep went on to express some nice-sounding words about their team needing a good, solid, stay-at-home defenceman. Hank's cynical, albeit silent, thoughts were not very nice. "Quit patronizing me. You're just trying to make me feel better about not being a very good rusher and scorer", he mused cynically to himself while Ken continued his schpiel. He told Hank that their first game in January was the following Tuesday "... at 8 o'clock ... in the Anderson arena."

Hank asked Ken about who else was on the Bloozers, particularly the other dmen and the goalies. Ken quickly rattled off some names of their players, a few of whom were familiar to Hank ...... like Gordie, Henri, Wicker, Bobby and Bruce. But the ex-Old Boy listened with some sadness and not a lot of interest or enthusiasm. He really liked the Old Boys. They were a super bunch of guys. He would miss playing with them and sharing the laughs and kibitzing in the dressing room before and after the game. Hank even gave some thought to whether or not he wanted to play the rest of the season. At that moment, he was ambivalent. Maybe he should talk about it with Heidi. She was a good "sounding board" (and broad) and usually had some worthwhile comments to make. At times like this, she could even be a good listener.

After a few more minutes of idle-minded conversation and saying "adieu" to Ken, Hank hung up the phone, sat down rather sadly and called to his wife.

Hank: "Hey Heidi! .... what cha' doin'?"

Heidi: "Reading ... big guy! Why ... what do you want?", came the reply "... and don't get your hopes up ... or anything else for that matter!" she added with a light-hearted giggle. "I've got a headache."

Hank: "Ah, don't flatter yourself there, baby," her husband responded, biting his tongue so he would not say something that he might regret later ... and for a long time ... to come. "Women have the most incredible memories for minutia and throw away comments," he mused aloud. Then he said, "I was wondering if we could have a cup of coffee and a chat. Are you available for that?"

Heidi: "Sure," she said happily. "I would be delighted to have a chat with you." She really was a social animal and liked to be with others, talk (lots of talk) and otherwise interact with people. And she was such a pleasant person, with a very positive attitude who was very rarely critical or disparaging. She bounced down the stairs into the tv room, asking, "Well, where's the coffee ... I brought the chatter."

Hank (started to smile and then laughed at his beautiful bride of 22 years): "You are so cute ... no wonder I love you."

Heidi (playfully): "Don't try to seduce me, you big hunk. Where's the coffee?"

Hank: "You must be horny ... you keep mentioning sex ... and no so subtly."

Heidi (feigning annoyance): "Where's the java, big guy?"

Hank: "It's still in the conceptual stage ... that's the place to start ... you can take it from there .... can't you?"

Heidi (grinning): "What a guy .... all talk! You know how to make coffee. I've seen you do it ... so get with the program ... make us some java!"

Hank (smiling warmly and holding out his open arms): "Hey, what are you getting paid for? .... other than your good looks ...? Come here and I'll give you a big hug!"

Heidi (who was a chronic cuddler, snuggled into her husband's strong arms and warm body, pounding her little fist gently onto Hank's chest and then said sweetly, "Is that enough ... for now?"

Hank: "Sure it is ... you big sweetie."

And so the banter went, somewhat like in the Old Boys dressing room. Heidi was a good sport and usually she could give as good as she got from Hank, as long as he did not get too intense ... mean or sarcastic with his quips ... "throwaway comments" as he referred to many of his verbal jibes. And she could be a good listener when she had to be and she sensed something was bothering her husband.

Heidi: "What's bothering you, Hank?", she asked as she took the coffee jar out of the fridge while Hank started to pour some water into the percolator.

Hank: "Well," he said rather hesitantly, not sure that he wanted to talk about being traded ... just yet.

An awkward silence crept into the kitchen. They looked at each other. Heidi was trying to be empathetic. Hank was feeling uncertain and uncomfortable.

Heidi: "What's the matter, honey," she asked gently. "Something's bothering you, isn't it?" she suggested softly.

More silence from Hank as he seemed to struggle with what he wanted to say or do. Finally, he said "How's the coffee coming?" Then, hearing the "perc" bubbling, he realized the mindlessness of the question.

Hank (hesitantly and misty-eyed): "Well, ... I don't know if I want to play old timers hockey anymore."

Heidi was thunderstruck. She would not have been more stunned than if she had been hit by a bolt of lightning. Here was her husband who loved to play hockey. He had been playing organized hockey since he was seven years old ... and years of road hockey, shinny on the ponds, sloughs and outdoor rinks for more years than she had even lived. He had played minor hockey for ten or eleven years at least. He had gone to university out of high school and earned a four year hockey scholarship at Murray U. While he was a prof at Pacific U., he and his good neighbor Jamie hooted and hollered as they drank beer and watched Hockey Night in Canada on television. Religiously, he went to the college games ... read books about hockey ... even had some thoughts about writing one about hockey .... talked hockey .... probably breathed the damned game ...

would eat it if he could ... and he's talking about quitting. Is he out of his mind? Has he gone mad? thought Heidi to herself. Then softly she asked, "Why Hank? ... why would you quit playing old timers?"

Pause. Ominous silence. Hank raised his head slowly from staring at the floor and looked at Heidi with misty eyes. Vividly, he remembered the sight of Wayne Gretzky crying when the Great One met the media people after being traded from the Oilers to the Kings. "I've been traded," Hank said slowly and choking back his emotions. "I've been traded. After all my years of playing hockey, I've never ever been traded before. I really love playing with the Old Boys. They're such good guys. We have so much fun together ... such great camaraderie. I don't want to play for another team!"

"You've been traded. What does that mean?" Heidi inquired quickly but very gently and sincerely. She could sense, beyond seeing, that Hank was upset, even hurt.

"That means that I have been put on another team ...... I have to play with another team .... I can't play with the Old Boys anymore ... at least for this season ... unless I protest or appeal to the Association ...... and that would make me look like a spoiled kid ... like a complainer ... some kind of whuss ... and that sucks," replied Hank with a mixture of sadness and sarcasm in his voice.

Trying to control her impulse to say "so what" or "what's the big deal", Heidi responded positively saying, "You know what Hank, you will probably meet some really nice new guys. You like most of the old timers ... ."

Hank (sadly but with some strong emotion): "Ya, they're a good bunch of guys ... but the Old Boys were so special. There's no other guys like Boom Boom, Mikey, Guy, Charley Hustle ... Doc and Max ... and J.P. and Big Gerry, Andy, Willie, Larry, Sammy ... and the others" as he rattled off his teammates' names almost as fast as he could count from 1 to 12. "Those guys really mean something to me ... and I mean something to them. I was with Maxie when he had his heart attack ... from his laying on the dressing room floor ... to the EMS ambulance when they hit him with those paddles ... to the intensive care ... and well into the night ... morning ... with his two daughters ... and then to the hospital in Cowtown. Taking a deep breath, Hank went on "Those guys ... like Charlie and Boomer ... and Maxie and Willie ... they encouraged me to keep playing old timers ... not to quit because I thought maybe I wasn't playing well enough ... that I was getting too old ... that I might be hurting the team! They seemed to care ... we all cared about each other .... about Max after he had his heart attack .... and after Mike lost his job a couple of years ago .... and the same when Guy lost his job at the power company ... and on and on and on. Phooey," Hank muttered as he caught himself before uttering a vulgar word. "Fuddle duddle ...... as Pierre Elliott Trudeau apparently said in public once upon a time."

Heidi (trying to console his unhappy husband): "Well Hank, you have to give it a try. You can't just quit. You're no quitter. You would really regret that ... not playing hockey. Besides, you would be perceived as a spoiled kid ... petulant. You don't want the other guys to think that about you ... do you?"

Hank (with a mix of anger and sarcasm creeping back into his words): "Sweetie, I don't give a rat's ass about what anybody else thinks. I'm really pissed off. Why can't that damned executive leave well enough alone? You know, if it ain't broken, then don't break it or something like that. I don't know what to think ... sure would have been nice if those hot shot board guys had asked me ... given me a choice rather than just tell me ... that's not the way the old timers should operate" as he shuffled dejectedly across the room to get a couple of cups for the coffee. Would you like a cuppa?, he asked Heidi.

Heidi: "Sure,"... how about some of those chocolate chip cookies, I made yesterday?"

She knew that chocolate chip cookies were one of Hank's real weaknesses. By his own admission he was a "cookieholic."

Hank: "Ya, sounds good ... I can always eat cookies .... even if I can't play with the Old Boys ... there's a trade off ... eating cookies instead of playing hockey. Doesn't that sound like a recipe for obesity ... and an early grave."

Heidi (responded sharply): "Oh, hush Hank!" "I don't like that kind of talk ... it's so silly to react so strongly ... so buck up ... quit sounding like the spoiled kid that you don't want to sound like."

Hank (with his ire rising and his eyes narrowing with intensity): "Don't you lecture me, Heidi! I really don't appreciate it" as he took his coffee, cookies and walked out of the room and into his den, closing the door rather loudly behind himself. Hank was really upset ... with himself, with Heidi, with the Association. Why couldn't they leave well enough alone? I was having so much fun. Now they have buggered it all up. "Son of a bitch", he muttered to himself and wiped some dew from his eyes. "If the Great One could cry when he was traded, why can't I", he wondered to himself.

The following Tuesday evening, laden with ambivalence and melancholy, Hank went to the storage room in the basement and packed up his hockey gear. Part of his thoughts were, "Ah, what the hell, I may as well stay home and read a good book or watch the Flames – Oilers ... the "Battle of Alberta" game on tv ... maybe play Scrabble with Heidi ... no, that's not likely," he thought as he recalled that she had been grading students' essays and had some preparation to do for her classes tomorrow. Feeling a surge of anger at himself, he said half-aloud, "I've never been a quitter before. Why start now? Get your act together ... asshole. Go play! (uttering the words on a poster in his den) Give it a shot. Have some fun! What the hell ... nothing to lose ... I've already paid my dues for the season."

As Hank walked toward the door with his hockey bag slung over his shoulder, Heidi appeared from her office and exclaimed, "I hope you have a really good time, Hankie". Hank, was spontaneously angered. He really did not like to be called Hankie because it reminded him of "snot rags". Kids in grade school used to tease him with that name --- amazing how some experiences stick in one's mind, even after several decades. Ah yes, long term memory is strong in older people, like old timers' hockey players. Remembering who had just called him that bothersome name, Hank cooled off.

Hank: "Thanks sweetie", Hank replied, appreciating his wife's support and encouragement.

Heidi: "Play smart", she added with a smile that made the sun seem dim.

Hank: "Oh ... you beautiful doll .... you great big beautiful doll," he crooned as his petite wife approached him for their good bye kisses.

Heidi: "What time will you be back?" she inquired.

Hank: "Oh, about 10:30 ... depending on how many beers I have ... and how interesting the conversation is ... maybe sooner".

Heidi: "Well, I'll try to wait up for you ... might be snoozin' on the couch ... or might be in bed but I'll be dreaming about you ... play safe ... I love you so much ... be careful."

Hank: "Thanks Heidi. Sweet dreams!!!!"

Adapting to the New Team

With his big bulky bag slung over his shoulder Hank ambled down the stairs to the front door and pulled his hockey jacket from the closet. While putting it on, he thought about the typical garb of the old pucksters. Most old guys wore a team hockey jacket, well worn blue jeans, baggy shirt, grungy boots, shoes or sneakers and a soiled or sweat-stained ball cap, even in the "dead of winter" when the temperatures dropped to minus 30 and beyond. They were truly symbolic of their culture. "You would think that they're a bunch of hobos or a flock of sheep", Hank muttered to himself with a chuckle. "Oh well", he mused, "that's what makes old timers be old timers. What you see is what you get. Turning his wandering thoughts to the Blue Bloozers, he wondered who he was going to get for new team mates? Kind of a selfish way of looking at the situation. Look what they're getting ..... and I'm no Bobby Orr, Raymond Bourque or Larry Robinson," he thought with a slight smile on his face and some of his dark humor creeping through his mind.

While he drove to the arena, Hank wondered some more, about his new team mates and about himself. He had played against the Bloozers several times each season and they seemed like a decent bunch of guys ... just a couple "hot shots" ... but then every team had some of those jerks. Hank pondered why he was so bothered about being traded? That was the one question that really preoccupied his idle thoughts. He mentally divided the reasons into two simple categories --- one, the joys of playing with the Old Boys and the prospect of not enjoying the rest of the season as much as the first half --- or maybe it was the feeling of being rejected or disliked. "No! no!" he said half aloud. "Apparently, several other players are being moved to different teams. So it is nothing personal, dumbkopf," he said to himself. He thought some more about the trade and in a positive vein concluded that maybe it was because the Directors really wanted to do as Boom Boom had said ... break up some of the cliques, dilute some of the rivalries, balance out some of the teams ... but why me? I really enjoyed the Old Boys team!

Hmmmm, Hank mused, "I wonder who ... or what the Old Boys are getting for me? Hope it's more than a couple of old broken sticks! Maybe a six pack!" He chuckled to himself as he thought about the "greats" who had been traded in the NHL --- the "Greatest" had been traded twice, Bobby Orr, Bobby Hull, Raymond Bourque, even the great Babe Ruth ... an endless list of really superstar players had been traded. Was Gordie Howe traded or did he just jump to the WHA so he could play with his sons? Hank wondered to himself. Wonder how those pros felt when they were traded ... even if they were being paid big bucks and had many fans and the media eating out of their hands? "Oh well," Hank mused out loud, "the sun will still rise in the 'morrow and life goes on ... nothing serious like a heart attack ... or losing Heidi."

Twenty minutes or so later, Hank reluctantly entered the Bloozers' dressing room. He was early. Only five other players were there, in various stages of undressing or putting on their hockey gear. Hank headed for the far corner of the room. He always had liked being in a corner of a dressing room, as far back as he could remember playing hockey, football, basketball or any other sport that used dressing rooms. Somewhat noisily, he dropped his bag on the floor and then started walking around the room to introduce himself. He had done this many times playing for tournament teams and so it was sort of natural, nothing new, yet he felt uncomfortable.

"Hi, I'm Hank!" he said to the first Bloozer who just happened to be Ken, the team rep.

Ken (smiling pleasantly): "Welcome aboard, Hank ... glad to meet you. Didn't we play on the same team a couple of years ago ... in our tournament here?"

Hank replied, "Ya, maybe so ... on that Old Goats team ... ya, that was a good bunch of guys ... we were good hosts ... lost all of our games ... didn't we?"

Ken (looking pensive said): "Seems to me that we won one of those games ... maybe against the Fading Stars ... from Vernon. Anyhow, it was a good bunch of guys. Hope you enjoy playing with the Bloozers ... we're a good bunch of guys .... even if I say so myself. Guess you probably need a sweater ....,. and some socks", Ken said as he started bending over a big blue bag sitting in the middle of the room. "Not much of a selection .... obviously .... hope you're not superstitious .... and want a special number ... like Bobby Orr's number four or Big Bird's (referring to Larry Robinson of Canadien's fame) ... whatever number it was ...... 19, I think."

Hank (answering Ken's question): "No, I'm not very superstitious ... any low number will do", realizing that he was, in fact, being at least partially superstitious.

"How about number six?" asked Ken. "Sure, wasn't that Potvin's number? That's fine," replied Hank. "I'm quite familiar with that number ... that was the number my defence partner wore on the Old Boys .... I saw so much of his back side ... I used to call him by number ... didn't have to remember his name ... hey number six, get back here and help, I used to yell at Boomer. Do you remember playing with him ... or against him?" asked Hank, with a twinge of melancholy as he thought about all of the good times he had had with Ronny and the other Old Boys in the past.

Having had a pleasant introductory conversation with Ken and needing to get dressed for the game, Hank started to move away from the team rep. "Hey Hank, you forgot your socks. Here's a pair that seem to match ... no holes either." Hank stifled the urge to ask how he was supposed to get them on as Ken was saying "Let me introduce you to big Bruce."

Yes, thought Hank, Bruce is big, even more humungous than I remember him being. Holy smoke, he's a big guy .... should call him Brute, thought Hank to himself. "Hi Hank", thundered a voice from somewhere in the guts of the huge body in front of him. "How are you? You look good .. like you might be in shape. Glad to meet you? Welcome to the Bloozers ... we're big drinkers. Hope you are too," the big guy said and then reflectively added "... guess it doesn't make a whole lot of difference if you are or not ... our beer fund is pretty flush already .... but your timing is good .... we're going to have an after-Christmas party pretty soon ... we've got too much money in the kitty .... big drinkers .... some dirty players .... the old beer fund grows pretty quickly when you have guys like that on your team. Did Ken tell you the rules about penalty fines? ... two bucks in the kitty for each penalty ..... and beer is three for five bucks ... let's see what else? .... hmmm, if you get a hat trick ... that's a round of beers for the team..." "Ha!" exclaimed Hank, almost choking on his tongue, "I won't have to worry about any hat trick ... haven't had one of those since bantam ... oh, maybe the odd defenceman's hat trick but none of those three goal efforts ..... that's up to the snipers. I just try to help them get their hat tricks," chuckled the stay-at–home d-man "... hat tricks ... ha! ... not with these cement hands. Three goals ... that's a good season's output for me!"

About that time, a familiar face, attached to a roly-poly body, entered the room. "Hey, Pie", enthused Hank as he recognized a former team mate from the Old Boys. "Geez, it's been years since I've seen you. Thought you were dead ... or in jail ... or Lord knows where. Where've you been? How are the hell are you? Good to see ya!!!" Donald Wilson, commonly known as Donny, Pie and sometimes Moon, for one obvious reason --- he was really round ... and really happy and very funny. "He's a good guy to play with", thought Hank. Pie was a salesman; a naturally amiable, likeable man who everybody liked to be with. He was so upbeat, always seemed to have a "good word" to say or so it seemed.

Donny, a.k.a. Pie: "How are you, Hanker?"

Hank: "Better now that I know you're on the team. How are you doing? Still selling more cars than anybody else in town?"

Pie: "Don't I wish!!! exclaimed Pie, with his usual enthusiasm. "How's that old beater of yours?" he asked.

Hank (feigning annoyance replied): "Don't talk about Heidi that way!!! They both laughed. Donny picked up the conversation instantaneously

Pie: "Hank, you look great ... for an old bugger ... how's it hangin'?"

Hank (chuckling): "I haven't heard that quip since college days .... Pie, you need some new material ... you must be as old as I am ... or damned close to it!"

Donny (responded, with enthusiasm): "Don't kid yourself, Hanker. Nobody is as old as you are!"

Hank (interjected saying): "Nice talk ... I said 'or damned close to it' ... didn't I? Pie, you're no spring chicken ... or maybe you are ... but suffering from that bird flu!" Someone in the room added: " ... chicken pot pie", "That's Donny, chicken pot pie."

And so, Hank was back "in sync" with the old timers ... well, with some of them at least.

Hank: "We'll talk some more later, Donny. I have to get dressed ... and meet a few of the other guys."

Pie: "Great ... good to see you again ... hope you enjoy playing with us ... pretty good bunch of guys ... all things considered."

Sitting nearby was a new guy to Hank. He was sitting, quietly putting on his gear which was rather rare for old guys. As Hank approached, the quiet old fellow smiled pleasantly and stood up. "Hi!" I'm Hank," said the new

Bloozer. "Hi! my name is Hiro", responded the small smiling man, about six inches shorter than Hank, even with his skates on. "Hmmmm", thought Hank to himself, "... maybe another Larry as Hank recalled the resemblance between Hiro and his former Old Boys' team mate. That would be great ... Larry had been such a good hockey player even if he was so short ... really fast, quick and so smart ... and so pleasant ... seems like a common trait of Japanese people, mused Hank as he remembered all of the Japanese he had met while doing his doctoral research on cultural values and patterns of consumption for three generations of Japanese living in Seattle. When Hank mentioned his doctoral research, Hiro seemed to be quite attentive and interested. He said he was born in Canada ... a second generation Canadian. "Sansei", Hank said aloud. "Yes", said Hiro with a little broader smile on his face. He was so courteous and soft spoken. "What position do you play?" asked Hank. Hiro replied shyly with his Japanese-English diction, "Oh, I am frexible ... mostly pray center ... sometimes pray wing, but never pray goal .... that's for crazy men .... rike Charles ... that's our goalie ... most of the time."

Because of his interest in playing defence and the guys who were supposed to keep the puck out of the nets, Hank wondered "Who is Charles?" He looked around the room and spotted the guy with the biggest hockey bag and the big pads setting beside it. Excusing himself to Hiro, Hank walked toward the goal tender. "Charles!!!" he said to the apparent goalie, "I'm Hank!" "Charles, my ass ... call me Charlie ... or Chuck," growled the large, half-dressed hairy-chested man bending over, tying his skates.

This guy was different from Andy or Willie, Hank thought to himself. Most goalies are kind of different from others ... from real people, mused Hank before he responded to the player who was straightening up in front of the new team mate. "Pleased to meet you Charlie", said Hank, while extending his hand. The men shook hands, eying each other as they did. "So, you're the new 'stay at home' defenceman, aren't you," queried the net minder in a somewhat hostile, challenging way. "That's me," replied Hank with a sharp edge to his voice, adding sarcastically, "Always like to stick around goalies ... they're such interesting guys." "Ya, B.S.!" growled the goalie, missing the pun, "...but it will be nice to have another guy around when the other team is in our end of the rink. Most of our guys say 'good bye' to me at the start of the game .... and don't renew acquaintances until we shake hands ... at the end of the game." "Well, you will have company with me out there," said Hank "I don't skate very far ... or very fast. That's my way of keeping up with the young guys ... by staying in position ... whatever. Good to meet you Charlie ... guess I better get my gear on."

The room was filling up with players, most of them happily talking, chiding and joking with others. Hank walked around the room, introducing himself to the guys he had not met. There was an Al, a Gus, a Paul, a Michel, and some others that he met --- too many names to remember from a hurried, first introduction. And he renewed acquaintances with Henri, Wicker and Bruce. Apparently, Gordie was out of town with his son's hockey team and Bobby was working on a night shift at the city water plant. As he exchanged intros around the room, there was another "familiar face". James seemed to be as pleased to see Hank as Hank was to see him. "Good to see you Hank! How was Christmas? How's that gal Heidi? asked James rapidly with a wide, toothy smile. "Fine, fine, fine!" replied Hank. "How are you?" While James was responding, Hank thought that it was rather unusual for a team rep to be traded during the season. Ya, it was not a job that required any special training or huge obligations but Hank had never heard of a rep being traded during the season. Wonder why James was traded, pondered Hank.

Hank tuned back into James banter and picked up on the question about Heidi. "Oh Heidi's fine ... same as ever ... busy... happy ... a joy to be with," enthused Hank. "How's Krista", Hank asked. With that question, James launched into another long-winded response. Hmmmmm, Hank mused ...... don't remember Jimmy Boy being so talkative before. Maybe he misses the Old Boys as much as I do... if that is possible!

There certainly was no Max or Mikey, Boom Boom or Charlie Hustle, Guy or Sam, Andy or Willie --- "dommage", Hank mumbled to himself. "What did you say?" asked James. "Nothing important", shrugged Hank. James, who was bilingual, heard the comment and was a pretty perceptive guy, saw the look of melancholy in Hank's eyes and nodded knowingly and said softly, "Ya, i miss them too." It's amazing how old timers or anybody who works or plays together for a while get to know one another intuitively. "Guess that's what is known as bonding," thought Hank, his misty eyes staring at James but his mind somewhere else in space - actually thinking about the "dressing room" of years gone by when the Old Boys were together. "It'll never be the same", thought Hank. Then adjusting his mind and eyes back to James again, he said "Now I have some understanding of how vets feel after they come home from the wars or serving in the military ... you miss your buddies ... the stunts, the jokes, the laughs ... the camaraderie."

Then James and Hank turned to the "task at hand" - opening their bags and getting ready to put on their equipment. As most players get older, putting on the gear becomes a task, especially "strappin'" on the blades. (*Strappin' on the blades* probably originated back in the times when skate blades were actually attached by straps to the footwear, usually boots, of the skater.)

A subtle smile came over Hank's face as he thought about some of the old timers' putting on their gear in years gone by. Poor old "Coach", he thought, recalling how much difficulty Gentleman Jack had bending over, just getting his skates on ... and off his feet. Jock would grumble about how stiff he was and the difficulty of bending over; about his arms getting shorter or maybe his legs getting longer. Other Old Boys would howl with laughter, responding with comments about how much Jock was growing ..... all of 5 foot, 8 inches of him ... with his skates on ... or how the growth was mostly horizontal, not vertical. Factually speaking, the old Scot was in darn good shape for a guy on the long side of 70 years. He was just having to cope with the realities of life - aging and its insidious effects.

And so it went for Hank, James and probably all of the other old guys who had been "traded" to other teams, in years gone by. Certainly it was not a smooth, unemotional transition from the good Old Boys to the Blue Bloozers. "But little social or personal change is", mused Hank silently. Like that guy Charles Darwin said, people just have to be adaptable ... whether they are old or young. "Besides", thought Hank, "I'm still playing shinny and that's what counts most ... almost as much as playing road hockey under the street lights years ago ... when we were kids." As he reflected on the many guys, hundreds of them, that he had played with and against during the past 60 odd years ... only a few jerks came to mind ... and some of them were dead. Hmmm, wonder if there is any correlation? So few bozos among so many good guys. "Wow!!" he said half aloud ... that's a pretty good percentage of good guys. No doubt the Blue Bloozers will be "the same breed of cat," he thought. And I better not be a bozo. So "shape up Hank" he told himself as he walked out of the dressing room and headed for the ice ... to play another game of the sport he loved.

Bibliography

1. Peter Shostak, *Hockey .... under winter skies*, Victoria, British Columbia: Yalenka Enterprises, Inc., 2000, p.8.
2. Ibid
3. Bill Burke, Gloucester 98s Hockey Team, *The Hockey Post,* Fall 2002, p. 5.
4. Ken Dryden and Roy MacGregor, *Home game: hockey and life in Canada,* Toronto: McClelland & Stewart Inc, 1989, p. 13
5. *Ibid*, p. 38
6. *Ibid,* p. 15.
7. Colette Derworiz, "What's living in your hockey bag?', *Calgary Herald,* January 18, 2003, A3
8. *Ibid*.
9. Bruce Culp, "A hockey bag contains a childhood", *The Globe and Mail,* February 17, 2004, A16.
10. Tom Price, "The Happy Birthday Song", Lethbridge, Alberta, October 25, 2005
11. Based on James Christie, "Dying with their skates on", *The Globe and Mail,* December 3, 2005, p. F8.

Printed in the United States
124331LV00001B/175-276/P

9 781438 908663